DATE DUE FEB − − 2007

DEMCO 38-296

AMERICAN GUESTWORKERS

AMERICAN
GUESTWORKERS

JAMAICANS

AND

MEXICANS

IN THE

U.S. LABOR MARKET

DAVID GRIFFITH

THE PENNSYLVANIA STATE UNIVERSITY PRESS
UNIVERSITY PARK, PENNSYLVANIA

LIBRARY OF CONGRESS CATALOGING-IN-PUBLICATION DATA

Griffith, David Craig, 1951–
American guestworkers : Jamaicans and Mexicans in the U.S. labor market /
by David Griffith.
p.   cm.—(Rural studies series)
Includes bibliographical references and index.
ISBN 0-271-02949-8 (cloth : alk. paper)
1. Alien labor, Mexican—United States—History.
2. Alien labor, Jamaican—United States—History.
3. Mexican Americans—Employment—History.
4. Jamaican Americans—Employment—History.
5. Temporary employment—United States—History.
I. Title.

HD8081.M6G75 2006
331.6′272073—dc22
2006017756

For Nancy, Emily, and Brook,
WITHOUT WHOM I WOULD NOT LOVE MY WORK

CONTENTS

PREFACE

In 1978 my wife, Nancy, and I moved with our two-year-old daughter, Emily, from Iowa City to Gainesville during one of the hottest Julys in Florida history. Theodore Bundy's trial was under way in Gainesville and young girls were driving from as far away as Pensacola to glimpse the handsome serial killer live in the courtroom. His self-prepared defense consumed the first minutes of nightly newscasts, though he never had much of a chance. In the years before his trial, Florida had executed more individuals than any other state in the union. Once he was captured for the murders of two students in the Chi Omega sorority house in Tallahassee and twelve-year-old Kimberly Leach of Lake City, north of Gainesville, his death sentence was assured. There were witnesses. There was physical evidence. There was his history. He was no more careful with killing than tourists are careful with rental houses and motel rooms.

We watched his case unfold from our eighteen-dollar motel room after spending the day boring through our meager savings to pay for phone calls and gas, seeking an apartment and jobs. I had a low-paying teaching assistantship at the University of Florida lined up for the fall, and we were on the waiting list for married-student housing, but we needed income and a roof over our heads until September. Thus our first experiences as Yankees in the South—beyond the dialect and Spanish moss—were of the housing and job markets. Any apartment we found, and any job, would be temporary, so where we looked for housing and jobs were the same places drifters and transients looked. In Florida, as in many parts of the South, these were not particularly inviting places. That adjective, *temporary*, colors the character of all kinds of experiences.

Florida's economy rests heavily on drifters, tourists, transients, and temporary residents of all kinds. Unfortunately, many temporary residents— college students, for example, or immigrant workers—occupy the same spaces as more unsavory drifters and transients, at work, in city and county service centers, and in neighborhoods. This sometimes results in a kind of guilt by association developing toward people who have come to Florida to study or work. Most students and most labor migrants never rob or murder anyone. Even if they are lucky enough not to occupy the same neighborhoods as the unsavory, they often find themselves in institutional housing and occupational settings that have been thoroughly planned, constructed, and sometimes patrolled and controlled, such as dormitories or labor camps.

After a year in graduate school, I took a temporary job teaching in Florida's prison system. In prison I began wondering whether some relationship might exist between Florida's economy and its high levels of crime and capital punishment. Might Bundy's move to the state and other criminal immigration be linked to its tourism, its amusement parks, its corporate agriculture, and its overwhelming economic dependence on immigrants of all kinds, evil and good alike? One of my pupils, a severe young white man whose name I won't reveal, visited Florida one winter, driving south from Ohio, and robbed a convenience store soon after crossing the state line. High on the feeling of reaching his destination, he stopped for beer, corn chips, smoked sausages, armed robbery, and gas.

He was from out of town. He didn't know anybody. There wasn't a single high school classmate, neighbor, mail carrier, or minister who might recognize his car, something about the way he walked or combed his hair, the sound of his voice. Free of this social enclosure, he held a gun on a stranger, demanded what wasn't his, and fled. He was a stranger to the store clerk, a new immigrant to the state, a criminal before the law. Like a refugee he fled, a fugitive, but was caught, incarcerated, and offered courses in literature and anthropology. He was returned to a social context, one highly structured, patrolled, controlled, and resembling the social contexts that most of us know hardly at all, but a social context nevertheless.

This book begins in Florida, but it begins in the sense of departure, for the temporary foreign workers who began coming to Florida long before Nancy and Emily and I, long before Theodore Bundy or my armed robber student, helped to found and shape a guestworker program that expanded beyond Florida to entangle lives, communities, industries, and economies throughout the Americas and has, even now, begun reaching into Laos, eastern Europe, mainland China, and other poor, distant corners of the world. It is called the H-2 program, and its abuses have been the subject of award-winning films and popular books and congressional investigations as well as academic texts like this. The people who enter the United

States, more than a hundred thousand of them every year, to perform low-wage, temporary seasonal work make up a small and perhaps arcane component of the millions of immigrants who arrive in North America every year, but the guestworker program they represent is in many ways a harbinger of labor processes that are already creeping into the personnel strategies of Wal-Mart and General Motors and nearly every major university across the United States and Canada.

I have deep attachments to Florida. My second daughter, Brook, was born there. And it was from the University of Florida that I began, twenty-five years ago, shortly after Brook was born, studying the subject of this book: the longest-running guestworker program in the history of North America. No one can study a phenomenon for a quarter-century without amassing a mountain of professional and personal debt. While most of my debts are acknowledged in the following section, my deepest gratitude is to the hundreds of H-2 workers I have had the pleasure of meeting and talking with in Jamaica, Mexico, and several locations around the United States. These conversations took place in half-finished concrete houses on mountain slopes, in apple groves, beneath breadfruit trees, beside chicken coops and outdoor ovens where elderly village women baked small, spiral-shaped, unleavened, slightly sweetened bread, and in the crowded dormitories and ramshackle rural houses where workers lived, usually without their families, for months on end. Even in the workers' housing, these conversations were nearly always accompanied by gracious invitations to share meals, accept drinks, or take part in the daily affirmations of the importance of family and friends. I cannot adequately express the pleasure I have taken in the grace and charm of so many of these people. I cannot express the utter dignity with which so many of these people held up under the difficult conditions of some of the nation's most trying occupations and most abusive, at times even sadistic, employers. It is the lives of these individuals and their families—along with their experiences at work, in communities abroad, and at home—that I hope I represent accurately in this book. They have helped me immeasurably. They have made me smile and laugh, frown and cry, and have stirred me to be ashamed of, and angry with, my country. They have nourished my sense of justice. They have taught me lessons about human rights that no one, in the twenty-first century, should have to learn.

ACKNOWLEDGMENTS

Beyond the many workers and employers who worked with me to gather the information for this book, several individuals, professional associations, and funding agencies contributed to the work in various ways. Professors Terry McCoy and Charles Wood, at the University of Florida, first got me interested in the H-2 program and shaped my early views of the how sugar workers were incorporated into south Florida's economy. Lawyers for Florida Rural Legal Services Greg Schell and Rob Williams gave me access to files they had tediously assembled while putting together their case on behalf of the sugar workers. Perhaps most important, however, was my association with Monica Heppel and Luis Torres, formerly of the Commission on Agricultural Workers and the Inter-American Institute on Migration and Labor. I worked closely with the two of them on two projects dealing with H-2A and H-2B labor, the first funded by the U.S. Department of Labor through the West Virginia Employment Security Commission and the second funded by the Ford Foundation. Robert Lee Maril, currently chair of East Carolina University's Sociology Department, also worked on these projects.

Elżbieta Goździak and Rogelio Sanchez provided feedback on an earlier draft of this manuscript. From the Institute for the Study of International Migration at Georgetown University, Elżbieta, along with Micah Bump, have been very supportive of my work on immigrants and immigration in the United States. Labor historians Cindy Hahamovich, Gunther Peck, and Mae Ngai shared their views of contract-labor programs with me at a conference in Washington, D.C. I am grateful to Bruce Goldstein, of the Farmworker Justice Fund, for organizing the conference in conjunction with the AFL-CIO, National Council of La Raza, Service Employees International Union, and the Southern Poverty Law Center. In Canada, Rudy Robinson, of the North-South Institute, was able to assemble a group of researchers that examined Canada's guestworker program with Mexico, which gave me the pleasure of working with Kerry Preibisch, Gustavo Verduzco, Roy Russell, Veena Verma, Anthony Downes, C. Odell-Worrell, and Ann Weston. They introduced me to additional work by Tanya Basok, Leigh Binford, and Josephine Smart on Canada's program. A second working group, organized by Ed Kissam, Mark Miller, Bruce Goldstein, and Aguirre International, has enabled me to consider the policy dimensions of guestworker proposals, and in this group I am indebted in particular to Cornelia Flora, Marta María Maldonado, Phil Martin, Rick Mines, and Susan Gabbard. My long-term working relationship with Ed Kissam of Aguirre continues to be among the most fruitful and productive of my life. Vernon Kelley, Anna García, Jeronimo Campseco, Larry McSwain, Brent Stoffle, and Carly Fox provided research assistance at various times. Tim Dunn and Joe Heyman gave me important feedback on a paper on labor contracting that I presented at the annual meeting of the Society for Applied Anthropology.

Several organizations and agencies funded various components of this work. I have already mentioned the Ford Foundation and the U.S. Department of Labor, but additional funds came from two projects funded by the National Science Foundation. During the first, Interethnic Relations in South Florida (DBS-9211620), working with Alex Stepick, Karen Richman, Guillermo Grenier, Jeronimo Camposeco, and Ed Kissam, I was able to collect and assemble a great deal of historical and contemporary data about Florida and its populations of African Americans, Cubans, Guatemalans, Haitians, and Mexicans—this information shaped much of the introduction and conclusion to this book. The second, Multiple Livelihoods and Human, Social, and Cultural Capital (SBR-9706637), funded comparative work on the experiences of African American crab and hotel workers, Mexican H-2B crab workers, and Jamaican H-2B hotel workers; this research shaped this book. The National Institutes of Occupational Safety and Health, through the Southeastern Agromedicine Center, provided funds for additional work on the farm labor market in the context of a study of occupational risk among youth on farms. I thank the center's previous director, Susan Gustke, and its current director, John Sabella, for their support of my work. Current work funded by the U.S. Department of Agriculture's Fund for Rural America also allowed additional work on immigrants in rural communities in the United States—work that was particularly important to understanding relationships between H-2 workers and immigrant populations settling in North Carolina and Georgia. Two projects funded by the UNC Sea Grant College Program, one on coastal development and a second on new immigration into coastal communities, were similarly helpful. The Inter-American Foundation, Wenner-Gren Foundation for Anthropological Research, the Fulbright-Hayes Program, and the University of Florida's Department of Anthropology funded the early research on Jamaican H-2 workers in Jamaica and the eastern United States.

Finally, as always, I am grateful to many of my friends and colleagues at East Carolina University's Institute for Coastal and Marine Resources and Department of Anthropology, who continue to support my research efforts year after year. My longtime friend and partner in much research, Jeff Johnson, has been a reliable and entertaining colleague for more than twenty years. Bill Queen's support and wisdom have guided my professional career in both subtle and obvious ways for which I cannot express sufficient thanks. Institute pillars Cindy Harper and Kay Evans enliven my entire life with their quick wit and seemingly bottomless kindness. In the Anthropology Department, John Bort, Holly Mathews, Christine Avenarius, Bob Bunger, and Jamie Leibowitz have been steadfast fellow cultural anthropologists from whom I have learned a good deal; John accompanied me into the field on more than one occasion, and I was impressed with his skill at fieldwork. Linda Wolfe, the department chair these past several years, has endured my absence from departmental meetings and any problems my light teaching load has created for the department without, I believe, grumbling too awfully much. Finally, East Carolina University has given me a solid base for research, teaching, and scholarship, enabling both the independence and the intellectual curiosity that I seem to require in order to wake up every morning to my writing.

PART I

OUT OF FLORIDA

INTRODUCTION:
IN THE STATE WITH THE PRETTIEST NAME

The state with the prettiest name,
the state that floats in brackish water,
held together by mangrove roots
that bear while living oysters in clusters,
and when dead strew white swamps with skeletons

—ELIZABETH BISHOP, from "Florida" (1946)

Florida's historians agree that Henry Flagler, John D. Rockefeller's partner in Standard Oil, pioneered economic development all along the state's east coast. His late nineteenth- and early twentieth-century construction projects and investments in agriculture converted swampy, tangled jungles of palmetto and cabbage palm into first inhabitable and later highly desirable places to visit and live. His hotels in St. Augustine and Palm Beach were among the finest and most expensive in the world, and his railroad, feeder roads, and canals first linked Jacksonville to Key West, stimulating settlements further inland and up and down the coast. Flagler's men platted and built cities, drained wetlands, planted fruit trees, cleared land for farming, laid hundreds of miles of rail, and erected massive hotels of wood and a mixture of concrete and coquina shells.

Less well documented are the circumstances of the men who worked for Flagler, even though the construction and land development projects of the kind Flagler financed required thousands of skilled and unskilled workers. Among Flagler's most daunting tasks were the recruitment and retention of labor—the construction, in short, of an adequate labor force. This was especially difficult because Florida's forbidding landscape did not attract large numbers of people willing to work in jobs like digging canals and laying railroad ties. With the exceptions of Key West and Tampa, which together had around seventeen thousand inhabitants, most Floridians lived in the northern region bordering Georgia and along the Panhandle. Inhabiting the state's interior and east coast were primarily Seminole, plume hunters, Bahamian and other West Indian fishing families, and various explorers, fugitives, and Civil War deserters. One of the first permanent dwellings was built on Palm Beach by a Civil War draft dodger named Charles Lang, and a second by a fugitive from Chicago, Charles Moore. In the early 1890s, when Flagler began quietly acquiring land on Palm Beach, fewer than a dozen families lived on the island, and neither West Palm Beach nor the town of Lake Worth existed. Labor, therefore, would have to be enticed, brought in, provisioned, and housed.

The African Americans, West Indians, Irish, Italians, and other immigrants who built Flagler's Royal Poinciana Hotel arrived in Florida by different paths. Some were recruited through labor-contracting firms in Philadelphia and New York. Some came by sea as fishermen, and others filtered into south Florida from communities in the Deep South where opportunities for sharecropping or working the lumber mills or turpentine stills had dwindled.

However they arrived, by May 1893, when the first work on the Royal Poinciana began, many of the African American and Caribbean workers had begun building their own small settlement north of the hotel construction site. Named after the mythological river that led to hell, the settlement came to be known as the Styx. Surviving photographs of the Styx show it to be a long, cleared avenue of wooden houses and fences built from a mix of good lumber, flotsam, and scrap. It looks to have been an active, outdoorsy kind of place, lively and busy, small groups gathering on the street or sitting together on porches. A few cabbage palms and live oaks heavy with Spanish moss provided mattress stuffing, mistletoe, and shade. Descriptions of the Styx portray a neighborhood of juke joints, rum shops, and other small businesses, scattered gardens and livestock, and enduring ties to the sea. After construction on the Royal Poinciana was finished, some residents returned to fishing, salvaging shipwrecks, and hunting, while others continued working for Flagler's hotels.

Founded in 1893, the Styx was not part of Henry Flagler's plan. A lively black neighborhood this close to his exclusive resorts was out of step with the structured luxuries enjoyed by the John J. Ashtons and Vanderbilts and out of his direct control—a kind of frontier settlement of alternative cultural backgrounds that undermined his own Disneyesque world. Consequently, shortly after he began construction on the Royal Poinciana, he began building West Palm Beach specifically as a town for his workers. His engineers, in typically methodical fashion, laid it out in a grid pattern and named the streets alphabetically after local flowers and plants. Many Styx residents, at his bidding, moved to West Palm, but others preferred the cool island breezes and the proximity to the resorts, and the Styx remained a viable and vibrant community—the first and last black presence on the island of Palm Beach—for a dozen years.

November 5, 1905, the last day of the Styx's existence, was Guy Fawkes Day, the day commemorating the foiling of Guy Fawkes's attempt to blow up the English king and Parliament for what Fawkes perceived as their growing repression of Roman Catholics. Because many of the West Indians were part of the British Empire, Guy Fawkes Day had been an annual celebration and festive event every year since 1893. And because November 5, 1905, was the tercentennial anniversary of the failed assassination attempt, the day promised to be especially festive. Having witnessed how heartily his workers celebrated the holiday, Flagler marked the occasion himself by sponsoring a circus in West Palm Beach and providing transportation across Lake Worth. Joining family members and friends across the lake, Styx residents left their homes that evening not knowing that they would return to charred ruins. Later that night, after the neighborhood had emptied, a fire roared through the Styx—a fire started, local black historians say, by Henry Flagler's men—and every dwelling burned to the ground.

The Styx was no phoenix. Whether or not Flagler ordered the burning of the Styx, no new neighborhood arose from its ashes, nor was there ever again a black community on the island of Palm Beach. On the contrary, the island hangs on to this day to antiquated laws similar to those enforced under apartheid in South Africa, requiring nonresident workers to carry passes explaining their business on the island after certain hours. Flagler developed the area where the Styx burned—its center today is the nondescript corner of Sunrise Avenue and North County Road—and it bears no indication that the area was ever the site of the only black community on the island. No interpretive sign, no plaque, and certainly no statue or monument exists to honor the Styx's dozen years of resistance to Flagler's vision.

Given Henry Flagler's penchant for constructing labor forces that he kept separate from the places where the laborers worked, it should come as no surprise that the nation's longest-running guestworker program began on the western edge of Palm Beach County, less than fifty miles from Flagler's Royal Poinciana, thirty-eight years after the Styx burned. I refer to the H-2 program, or that labor-importing program that brought West Indians into

Florida as early as 1943 and today brings Mexicans, Jamaicans, and others into the United States to harvest crops, pick meat from blue crabs, clean hotel rooms, and perform several other low-wage, low-skilled jobs on a temporary basis. Florida's social and economic landscapes, like many throughout the South, have influenced social formations up and down the Atlantic coast and across the Caribbean, Mexico, Central America, and beyond. Over the past two and a half decades, I have had the good fortune to study relationships between Florida and southern history and the formation of lifestyles and labor markets in areas as far from one another as Los Mochis, Sinaloa, Mexico, and the Finger Lakes region of upstate New York. This book, focusing on the H-2 program, draws on this quarter-century of research.

The research took place in several phases. My first experience with H-2 workers was as one of a dozen graduate students who interviewed cane workers in southern Florida on a project directed by University of Florida professors Charles Wood and Terry McCoy. This consisted of ten days of fieldwork in March 1981. We took over most of the small El Patio Motel in Clewiston and spent days and early evening hours interviewing West Indian cane cutters and nights coding the interviews we had completed during the day.

Following Wood and McCoy's data, I then chose central Jamaica as a research site for doctoral research that lasted from January 1982 to December 1983. Most of the cane cutters in Wood and McCoy's study came from Jamaica's interior, so from January to August 1982 I lived with my wife and two young daughters on a small plantation north of Christiana, Jamaica, that grew coffee beans, oranges, and bananas, making daily visits to an area across the asphalt road called the Two-Meetings Watershed. In Two-Meetings I conducted interviews and observed peasant families at work in their fields and spending time in leisure or at work in their homes; in Christiana and Kingston, Jamaica's capital, I collected background information from agricultural marketing organizations, development agencies, local bookstores and libraries, and university and government archives.

In September 1982 I followed the first waves of Jamaican H-2 workers to the apple orchards of the United States, meeting with several men I had befriended in the watershed and others who worked and lived with them in Virginia, West Virginia, New England, and upstate New York. I traveled through much of New England's apple country in September and October before working my way back through Virginia and West Virginia, interviewing Jamaicans and observing patterns of labor organization and control. In November, as apple workers were either returning to Jamaica or, more often, leaving apple country to cut sugar in south Florida, I traveled back to south Florida sugar country to spend the rest of 1982.

In early 1983 I returned to Jamaica for four months, this time to Black River, on the southern coast, where I hoped to collect data from H-2 workers on a different part of the island for comparative purposes. I also wanted to index my field notes, outline and begin writing my dissertation, and visit families of H-2 workers in the highlands, filling gaps in my field notes and knowledge. During this time I became particularly interested in the ways that women, left behind when their husbands, boyfriends, and sons left for the United States, dealt with their absence and how they used the money the men sent home to them. I also became keenly aware of distinctions between coastal and highland Jamaica and the ways that people in each area cobbled together a living. Through these initial two phases of research I collected detailed data on 134 peasant households, fifty-four of which had at least one member participating in the H-2 program.

Following this research, in the mid- to late 1980s, I conducted research on food processing and rural labor markets in the U.S. South, research that led eventually to additional projects in the apple-growing regions of the eastern United States and south Florida agriculture, much of it funded by the U.S. Department of Labor and the Commission on Agricultural Labor. While working with the commission I met its research director, Monica Heppel, and legal counsel Luis Torres, and we three began planning, in the early 1990s, a second major phase of research on H-2 workers. This research phase began nearly ten years after I'd completed my dissertation, in 1993, but focused on H-2 workers in several economic sectors outside agriculture, where the workers carried H-2*B* as opposed to H-2*A* visas. People with H-2B visas work in nonagricultural seasonal jobs like seafood processing and the tourist industry, while people with H-2A visas work in seasonal agricultural jobs. During the study of H-2B workers, we interviewed 473 workers and 183 of their employers in seafood processing, shrimping, hotels, ornamental stone quarries, racehorse stables, and forestry. While information from all these sectors informs this book, I pay closest attention to the two sectors I examined in greatest detail, seafood processing and hotels. This detail was made possible by additional funding from the National Science Foundation to focus on the convergent experiences of H-2B workers from Jamaica and Mexico and African American workers who worked in seafood-processing plants and as chambermaids in South Carolina coastal resort hotels; this was my focus from 1998 to 2001. The U.S. Department of Labor and the National Institute of Occupational Safety and Health also provided funds that allowed me to investigate immigrants in U.S. rural communities and the conditions of children working in agriculture.

Monica, Luis, and I did further comparative work on H-2A and H-2B from 1999 to 2002, with the generous aid of the Ford Foundation. In combination with the National Science Foundation research, we interviewed more than eight hundred workers in Mexico, Jamaica, and the United States. The express purpose of this work was to provide a general overview of the H-2 program with Mexico and recommend ways to improve it. I was able to continue this work as I put the finishing touches on this book, as part of a multisite study of the impact of immigrants on rural communities around the United States, both as part of a research team examining the Canadian Migrant Agricultural Workers Program and as part of a working group assembled by the Farmworker Justice Fund and Aguirre International to formulate a research agenda in the wake of proposed legislation to create yet another guestworker program.

In all of these studies I paid attention to workers' and their families' experiences with programs where the management of migration was accomplished by large, highly developed state systems working with, or at times against, employers and employer associations. Yet formal guestworker programs like H-2 are not the only means nation-states use to manage labor migration. Historically, nations have used a peculiar combination of legislative activity and political will to enforce or ignore laws governing labor, housing, occupational safety, border regions, and work in low-wage, difficult jobs (Heyman 1998). North American temporary worker programs are instances of highly managed labor migration, based on premises and arguments that date to the early twentieth century—specifically, in the United States, the ninth proviso of the Immigration Act of 1917, which allowed federal labor and immigration officials to ease immigration restrictions for the temporary entry of workers who otherwise might be denied the right to work in the United States.

One of the core premises of managed labor migration programs is that a labor shortage exists, usually stimulated by political economic developments, such as war, that are clearly beyond the control of individual employers. In 1917 the immediate threat to the nation's labor supply came from World War I, and one of the solutions was to grant citizenship to Puerto Ricans, whose homeland the United States had occupied since 1898. In 1943, when the first government-to-government agreements that effectively initiated the H-2 program were signed, the threat to the agricultural labor supply, supposedly, was World War II.

Whether or not wartime labor shortages actually existed is a contested issue. Labor historian Cynthia Hahamovich argues that the agricultural labor supply, at least since the nineteenth century, has been manipulated by government agencies working in concert with private growers and labor contractors, using housing in particular as a tool to attract, retain, and control workers (1997). Like other researchers, Hahamovich argues further that the alleged labor shortages of the war years were shortages only of workers willing to work under prewar wages and conditions. They were not, in other words, absolute shortages, but shortages of workers desperate enough to accept prewar wages and working conditions while economic expansion was raising wages elsewhere in the United States.

In agriculture, farmers and farm managers who recruit immigrant workers commonly view either a shortage of highly disciplined, reliable workers, or the absence of a *surplus* of workers, as a shortage of agricultural labor. Without the discipline and reliability that H-2 workers bring to agricultural labor forces, there are several reasons why agricultural employers might desire a labor surplus, including the reduction of upward pressures on working conditions and pay, and a ready supply of new workers as jobs are abandoned because of hardship, injury, or other opportunities. Agricultural jobs, like most of the other low-wage jobs that temporary foreign workers occupy, are generally unpleasant and plagued by high turnover. As I wrote in an early work on low-wage labor: "There isn't much romance in jobs like these. They don't pay well. Often they're dirty, they're hard, they stink, they cause injury and illness, and they earn the people who work them no prestige, teach them no skill, prepare them for no promotion" (Griffith 1993, 4–5). Staffing such jobs involves actively constructing labor forces through a combination of enticement and coercion.

This process often extends beyond the work site or labor market to include controlling workers' time and space to an extent that approximates conditions of slavery or imprisonment, creating what sociologists call *total* institutions: places, like prisons, that provide everything required for bare survival, where a person can live and work for days, months, or years— sometimes an entire lifetime—without ever leaving the grounds. Constructing labor forces and quasi-total institutions often go hand in hand. In the 1920s Henry Ford built his auto factories and workers' living quarters in tandem with each other and enforced, through a private police force, lifestyles that conformed to his own vision of what a good American should be. Worker, spouse, language, diet, faith, household—all were supposed to conform to what Ford believed were healthy family values and proper ethics regarding work, marriage, and home. In the 1940s and 1950s the United Fruit Company established banana plantations in isolated regions of Ecuador's coast, patrolling them with their own police forces, building houses, schools, a hospital, and a company store, and even influencing workers' leisure time through the creation of social clubs. Workers who conformed to the company regimen lived relatively well, but those who stepped out of line were swiftly fired and shuttled away (Striffler 2002). In his chronicle of two Mexican brothers who migrated to California as young men in the 1970s, Roger Rouse shows how various institutional settings drove the once rowdy brothers toward the kind of lifestyle that feeds pliant workers to factories and fields and herds consumers into Wal-Mart (1992). Following the U.S. Civil War and the emancipation of slaves, debt peonage emerged as a means of binding workers to plantations, farms, and other highly controlled production centers throughout the South, controlling their lives so fully that they lived in a state of virtual slavery (Daniel 1972).

Florida's historical and contemporary landscapes are peppered with total institutions—not only prisons but turpentine camps in the pine barrens of the north, sugar plantations in the south, refugee detention centers, worker dormitories, labor camps of undocumented immigrants, even golf and baseball camps and the fantasy worlds created by Disney and Anheuser-Busch. Total institutions attempt to construct and control complete social contexts, yet they almost always fall short: in spite of their schedules and regimens of work, meals, and sleep, imported cultural practices gradually surface, offering residents comfort, identity, and orientation and influencing the ways that work is performed, meals are spiced, and sleep is resisted or welcomed.

Jamaicans brought into Florida's sugar fields to cut cane for nearly half a century, beginning in 1943, were housed and fed in dormitories and worked according to schedules like those of total institutions. The Immigration and Naturalization Service issued them H-2 visas, which allowed them to enter the country legally on the condition that they work, throughout their stay, for a single, predesignated employer. Despite the control that this limited access to the labor market gave their employers, these workers brought to the sugar plantations their tastes and styles of speech, and some of them settled in Pahokee, Belle Glade, Clewiston, and South Bay. Neighborhoods in communities ringing the southern shore of Lake Okeechobee began looking, sounding, smelling, feeling, and tasting more and more West Indian. Supermarkets stocked yams and Jamaican pastries, and the minibuses that transported workers between labor camps and town adopted the same flexible schedules and methods of recruiting passengers that you find throughout Jamaica.

As Jamaicans slipped away from the sugar fields, establishing a West Indian presence in southern Florida, they showed us that cultural practices nearly always leak out of and percolate up through the structures and rules meant to regulate time, space, and human interaction. Managed migration like the H-2 program can never fully dehumanize individuals, making them merely, or even primarily, workers. New, more vibrant cultural practices gradually emerged along the margins of the sugar plantations, nipping at the rules and regulations of sugar work with enticing aromas from home.

Similar patterns emerge around Disney World, Busch Gardens, and the golf and beach resorts where tourists stay for a week or two at a time. These fantasy worlds depend on large numbers of security guards, performers, landscapers, and service and maintenance personnel. Most of these people require low-cost housing because they earn low incomes that fluctuate seasonally, yet still pay the inflated prices that local businesses charge tourists for basic goods like food and basic services like medical care. It is in the best interests of the fantasy that these people disappear at the end of their shifts into neighborhoods that bear little resemblance to the fantasy worlds where they work.

I was first struck by this on a trip to south Florida's interior in 1981, when several of us graduate students from the University of Florida went into the sugar fields to interview a few hundred West Indian cane cutters for Professors Charles Wood and Terry McCoy. We stayed in Clewiston, one of half a dozen towns along the southern rim of Lake Okeechobee that served as the winter home to people who lived a hand-to-mouth existence. At least three of these towns—Belle Glade, South Bay, and Pahokee—had large sections of tenement housing occupied by refugees, illegal immigrants, and the working poor. They were two- and three-story apartment buildings with sagging balconies, torn screens, and flaking, fading paint that had once boasted bright Caribbean colors. I learned later that many of these tenements doubled as labor camps, occupied by families or single men on the condition that the residents work either directly for their landlord or for someone related to their landlord.

I'd seen slums before, in cities like Chicago and New Orleans, and once I lived in a low-rent neighborhood in Minneapolis where pimps approached my wife with offers of employment, while prostitutes approached me, but the slums of Belle Glade seemed original, unique. Belle Glade wasn't a big city. Really just a farm town, its strips of vegetable-packing sheds led to farmers' banks and nearby agricultural factories for squeezing sugarcane and juicing oranges. On the outskirts of town lay a small correctional facility. Its highway strip was similar to strips of Burger Kings and Comfort Inns throughout the South. Cheaper motels nearby, run by local or East Indian families, had been converted into labor camps for migrant farm workers or rooming houses for welfare cases and poor working stiffs earning minimum wage. Such housing stretched from the strip into the downtown and through most of the rest of the community. These deteriorating tenements and their residents distinguished Belle Glade from other small rural farm towns I knew. Belle Glade—like Immokalee, Arcadia, Pahokee, Wimauma, South Bay, and many other inland Florida towns—attracted so many immigrants and refugees that its ethnic diversity rivaled Miami's.

Florida agriculture has a history that both is and isn't like agriculture in other parts of the South. Much of Florida was only marginally cultivable before the development of water control systems, the late nineteenth-century medical breakthroughs that kept malaria, yellow fever, and cholera in check, and effective pesticides. With the notable exceptions of those pockets that Flagler's men developed, large parts of southern Florida in particular, swampy and wild, were barely habitable as late as 1900. Northern Florida saw the development of turpentine farming and distilling in the pine forests that swept down out of the Carolinas and Georgia and supplied the naval stores industry as early as the seventeenth century, but south Florida's large sugar, winter vegetable, and citrus plantations emerged more recently, attracting a mix of corporate and family farms.

The general growth of corporate agriculture in Florida did not always result in the loss of family farms but usually did replace looser, subsistence-oriented relationships with the land—combining wild and domesticated foods—with more regimented, scientific, and strictly agricultural practices. At the core of these practices was greater reliance on hired, and generally foreign or at least unknown, labor instead of on family workers or familiar hired hands. This process set the stage for foreign-born and African American workers to be diffused through Florida's farm labor force. Because Florida farms used more workers hired through labor contractors rather than under tenant or sharecropping arrangements, they encouraged the immigration of families from the Caribbean, from other parts of the South, from Texas and the U.S. Southwest, and eventually from Mexico and Central America.

Henry Flagler's labor recruiters pioneered this process. Working with laborers from the West Indies and inland Florida as well as initiating migrations into Florida through New York and West Indian labor brokers, Flagler's projects laid the foundation for future methods of labor recruitment and retention. During their first major construction project, the building of the Alcazar Hotel in St. Augustine, Flagler and his men were able to marshal impressive numbers of workers to keep the construction and furnishing of the establishment on schedule. "When the pouring of cement became a problem," writes one of Flagler's more sympathetic biographers, "Flagler had his agents recruit 1,200 Negroes from the countryside and brought them to tamp the liquid coquina gravel into the wooden construction forms with their bare feet while musicians played lively music" (Chandler 1986, 102). Later, in what would become a nagging, persistent dimension of Florida labor history, Flagler was accused of enslaving workers to perform particularly onerous tasks.

This occurred during the construction of the railway to Key West, a project whose working conditions, in addition to the common traumatic injuries that attend construction work, included battling sand fleas and mosquitoes, weathering hurricanes, and living in company camps where whiskey was allowed only among the upper echelons of workers. This last restriction reflected Flagler's condescending attitude toward those who worked the most menial jobs, an attitude that became clear following allegations that his company practiced debt peonage to deal with high labor turnover. Because New York was among the principal recruiting locations for immigrant workers, journalists for New York and other northern newspapers paid special attention to the progress of the work and conditions in the labor camps. Eventually they alleged that men working for Flagler "had forced some workers into a state of peonage by requiring them to repay the railroad for passage, before quitting the work" (Chandler 1986, 231).

Flagler's official response to these allegations, which the company denied, was most telling in what it revealed about his views of labor and labor relations. Discriminating among groups of workers by ethnic and regional background as well as immigrant status, he spoke of "Southern States Negroes" as "more or less of the floating class, working only a short time in one place before they seek new fields"; of the "Bahama Negro" as "low in efficiency"; of the "white 'Cracker,'" from the south Atlantic and gulf states, as "not adapted by training or disposition for railroad construction work, but more inclined to stick to farming or trucking and [having] no liking for any work that takes him away from his home and his 'Folks'"; and finally of "Spanish laborers from Cuba" as men that "have been a generally satisfactory type of laborer" (quoted in Chandler 1986, 232–33). According to Flagler, this last category of workers were "stayers"; they saved their money and, unlike the other groups, tended to avoid gambling, drinking, and short "junketing trips" to Miami.

One further interesting bit of information to emerge from this company missive is that Flagler's men routinely employed labor through contracting systems. These arrangements, the statement said, provided "satisfactory results," consisting of small crews of ten to twenty men contracted to perform specific tasks at set, predetermined prices. As with today's labor contractors, those of Flagler's time "seldom failed to make good wages and a profit on the work."

Segmenting his labor force by ethnicity, maintaining a condescending, company-dominated approach to his workers, subcontracting work, mixing immigrant and native workers, attributing various skills and characteristics to entire groups—these were strategies that Flagler adopted and, by extension, applied to Florida's earliest large-scale projects requiring a steady supply of labor. Flagler wasn't alone. Around the turn of the century, a fledgling winter vegetable and citrus industry developed just inland from Palm Beach, an industry facilitated and served by Flagler's railroad and the growing links between northern cities and Florida that were founded in part on networks of labor recruiters stretching from south Florida to New York (Hahamovich 1997). Many of the workers Flagler's railroad brought to Florida, after failing to show up for railroad work or leaving after a few days or weeks, found work on Florida farms. Flagler himself complained to his chief engineer, William Krome, that farmers were stealing his workers, enticing them away from the difficult work of laying ties and rails to work in fields and groves.

About the only attribute of Flagler's labor recruitment practices that differentiated them from those of agriculture, which eventually forged the nation's early guestworker programs, was agriculture's heavy reliance on the state. Cindy Hahamovich's impressive history of migrant labor along the Atlantic coast traces the constant, if uneven, role of government programs throughout the early development of a migrant agricultural labor force (1997). Whether by marshaling investigations into agricultural labor conditions, building or controlling migrant labor housing, or actively moving unemployed immigrants from urban slums to farms as part of feeble and ultimately failed population redistribution programs, U.S. state and federal governments have long been actively involved in agricultural labor.

Along with a steady, state-supported labor supply, agriculture and the food industry have needed state-supported institutions like the University of Florida's Institute for Food and Agricultural Sciences (IFAS) at least since the days of Flagler's railroad and hotels. The university land grant colleges, with their studies of such agricultural practices as fertilizer application and the breeding of more robust hogs, enable food and nutrition scientists to help make trends in food production, processing, packaging, and sales legitimate enterprises. These trends have shifted dramatically in the past fifty years, and many changes have been received with a mixture of mistrust and relief by the American public and the FDA. Recent popular texts such as Eric Schlosser's *Fast Food Nation: The Dark Side of the All-American Meal* and Nicols Fox's *Spoiled: The Dangerous Truth About a Food Chain Gone Haywire*, and academic texts like Marion Nestle's *Food Politics: How the Food Industry Influences Nutrition and Health* and Jimmy Skaggs's *Prime Cut: Livestock Raising and Meatpacking in the United States*, have leveled serious accusations against the food industry. These include environmental destruction, the manipulation of public opinion about nutrition, the lowering of bacteria's susceptibility to antibiotics, and assaults on the aesthetics of America's suburbs through the construction of gaudy and redundant fast food restaurants.

In the face of food-industry apologists and popular and academic exposés, people have become more cognizant of their bodies and the foods that go into them even as the character of meals and diets across North America has changed dramatically in recent decades. With more parents entering the workforce and family makeup changing, consumers have consented to the development of more easily prepared foods, transferring the labor costs of food preparation from the kitchen to the food industry. Food producers have responded with products like boned chicken breasts and boxed meats, orchestrating the cruel industrialization of cattle, poultry, and swine and standardizing the packaging and distribution of food in forms that are easy to prepare but perhaps less healthy than most of us would like. Food consumer advocates and other industry critics have responded with lawsuits against various branches of the industry, blaming food producers and distributors for obesity and the many health problems that accompany it, for tainting water supplies, for injuring food-processing workers, and for altering natural ecosystems.

Developing new food products involves changes that surround and influence us deeply, converting entire regions of the countryside and altering social and natural environments almost before we have time to think.

A spokesperson for the Delmarva Poultry Industry on Maryland's eastern shore once told me, "The industry rule of thumb is to have all of its production facilities—grow-out farms, hatcheries, and feed mills—within a twenty-five mile radius of the factory." Throughout the South, the heart of the U.S. poultry industry, these rules of thumb alter cropping systems, pollute groundwater supplies, and constrain farm family schedules each time a company like Tyson or Perdue builds a new chicken factory.

Because these processes are swift, and because they affect the environment and human health, most of us need to believe that the growth, development, and condition of the human body are legitimate and *entrusted* food-industry concerns. Food experts' testimony to Congress shores up at least some of that trust and legitimacy, putting politicians' minds at rest that food producers are not out to kill us with sugars and fats. Yet when food scientists and nutritionists speak up for food-industry practices, they reinforce the idea that the nation's food producers need broad powers and freedoms when it comes to the day-to-day business of producing food. They need, in particular, wide latitude in the recruitment and treatment of workers who work the land, preparing the soil, planting, caring for livestock and crops, and, perhaps most important, harvesting and processing. This has been especially so in times of war, when presumed labor shortages have allowed agricultural employers to influence, and in some cases directly craft, immigration policy (Calavita 1992; Hamahovich 1997).

Florida sugar producers, for example, were instrumental in pioneering the international agreements that led to the H-2 program. They were also deeply involved in Caribbean politics and economics through controls over sugar imports and duties and the markets and technical expertise they received in the aftermath of the 1959 Cuban revolution, when skilled Cuban technicians and rich Cubans' capital were able to take advantage of south Florida's rich agricultural lands, sophisticated water-control system, and preferential marketing agreements (Wilkinson 1989).

As part of their services to sugar growers and others, institutions like IFAS contribute significantly to debates about food and environmental safety that emerge from presidential commissions, congressional inquiries, and the nation's producers of food. Scientists attached to institutions like IFAS defended the pork industry in 1918, when J. S. Koen, an inspector for the U.S. Bureau of Animal Industry, claimed that the human influenza virus killing millions around the world was showing up in swine (Kolata 1999, 67). Meat industry scientists protested the recent development of the food pyramid—that nutritional guideline on the labels of most cereals and many other foods—for not placing enough emphasis on meat in the American diet (Nestle 2002). Historically, while such debates identify problems of food production and life in rural America and often result in a special presidential commission or congressional investigation, it usually takes national crises, like war or depression, to move people to address them.

The report of Theodore Roosevelt's Country Life Commission, released in 1909, laid the countryside's woes squarely at the feet of the land grant colleges. Listing several seemingly disparate problems, what unified them was the commission's emphasis on education. Between countryside and city, misinformation, disrespect, and mutual suspicion were rampant. While education could shrink the country-city gap, powerful barriers, both real and imagined, stood in the way. As with current cultural and physical distances between fantasylands and working-poor neighborhoods, a fringe of "undesirables" ringed the cities, creating a wall of hoboes that became, in the commission's words, "a low-class or even vicious community, and its influence often extends far into the country districts. The commission hears complaints that hoboes are driven from the cities and towns into the country districts, where there is no machinery for controlling them" (Country Life Commission 1909, 29).

Through the remainder of the twentieth century, this machinery developed in concert with the sophistication of the food industry until, today, the machinery of control in the countryside rivals and in many ways outstrips that of the city. This wouldn't be the first time agriculture's labor relations and production regimes paved the way for industry. In his history of sugar, *Sweetness and Power* (1985), Sidney Mintz argues that the time discipline that coordinated the supply of raw materials and the processing of finished products was pioneered on Caribbean sugar plantations worked by slaves, where field and factory hands came together to produce sugar and sugar-based products like molasses and rum. "The specialization by skill and jobs, the division of labor by age, gender, and condition into crews, shifts, and 'gangs,' together with the stress upon punctuality and discipline, are features more associated with industry than with agriculture—at least in the sixteenth century.... But the sugar-cane plantation is gradually winning recognition as an unusual combination of agricultural and industrial forms, and I believe it was probably the closest thing to industry that was typical of the seventeenth century" (Mintz 1985, 47–48).

Similarly, the methods of coordinating agricultural labor today, mixing temporary contract labor with longtime company employees, are more often associated with modern factory production. Company managers and supervisors often supplement a small cadre of stable employees with throngs of workers hired through agencies like Kelly Services or Manpower Inc., organizing it all under names like outsourcing, subcontracting, and flexible accumulation. Yet for more than a century, since long before modern manufacturers began moving parts of the production process overseas, the heart of farm labor has been contracting, a system of linking buyers and sellers of labor through intermediaries who recruit, transport, house, supervise, and dominate the lives of people looking for seasonal work on America's farms. Through this system, which more and more frequently engages people from different cultural and national backgrounds, the food industry extends its reach from the body at home, consuming food, to the body at work, producing it.

An additional characteristic of H-2 jobs is that they fluctuate seasonally with weather, hotel guest occupancy rates, and other factors that reduce or increase the availability of work. Unpredictable and variable pay repels native workers with alternative employment opportunities, while encouraging multiple sources of income and employment—multiple livelihoods—among those who are either forced or have little choice but to take low-wage, seasonal, temporary jobs. Here again this sector of the labor market, like labor contracting in agriculture, may be pioneering labor relations across the globe.

Many companies, institutions, and employers have increased the proportion of part-time and temporary workers in their workforces, arguing that this allows them to expand and contract their labor forces as new production opportunities arise or old markets for their products dry up (Rogers 2000). The premier example of this has been the garment industry, which relies on large numbers of seamstresses, many working out of their own homes, who can be given material and patterns as fashions shift and contractors obtain contracts, but who cost contractors nothing between production seasons or during idle times. Flexibility like this gives organizations and individuals the opportunity to take advantage of periods of sudden economic expansion while bearing none of the burden of maintaining workers during times of economic contraction. The workers who come and go with this process of ebb and flow are sometimes called "contingent workers"—a designation that implies that their work is contingent upon the needs of specific firms—and they include not only temporary and part-time workers but also leased employees, independent contractors, and, indirectly at least, what Marx called "the reserve army of the unemployed." In my own research, for example, I often hire research assistants to perform specific services such as interviewing, organizing focus groups, or drawing maps, paying them by the hour or by the task. These jobs are always temporary, depending on the availability of funding, though the more highly skilled research assistants have managed to move from one project to the next and remain employed for several years.

Thus temporary contract workers are not restricted to the low-wage labor market or unskilled positions. Over the past several decades, universities have been expanding their use of fixed-term contracts, replacing more secure tenured professors with adjunct instructors who teach one or more classes every year. Whether they receive benefits depends on the number of courses they teach per semester and the nature of their contracts, but they remain independent contractors. Many of these individuals are biding their time until a full-time, tenure-track position opens up, but the more energetic have been able to piece together highly rewarding (though still insecure) work experiences by mixing occasional teaching with research and consulting. In these cases, the freedoms and rewards of independent contracting may outweigh the (admittedly few) burdens that come with secure university employment.

Several of my relatives and friends who work in the private sector, too, are independent contractors, performing highly remunerated tasks for large corporations under temporary contracts, taking care of their own retirement and health insurance packages; and they are generally pleased with their working conditions and pay. They have sacrificed employment security for the freedom from daily supervision that most independent contracting jobs entail, yet they are paid highly enough that they tend not to view this as a sacrifice at all. These relationships are not without their problems, however. Recently one of my relatives' contracts was terminated suddenly, with neither forewarning nor any provisions for legal recourse, and he found himself unemployed in middle age, with two children in college and no retirement fund. When I visited him shortly after this occurred, he confided to me that he finally saw the value of union representation, adding that there had been no grievance procedure or even any explanation as to why his contract was terminated. They'd just let him go.

Many independent contractors avoid such a fate by establishing contracts with more than one organization, reducing their dependence on a single income stream. While this may increase one's security, among highly skilled workers the likelihood that economic contraction will threaten all their contracts is high, because their skills are usually tailored to a single economic sector. This may be one area in which lower-skilled workers are slightly better situated than the highly skilled. When low-skilled workers combine several sources of income and familial and network support to survive, these sources do not necessarily cluster in specific economic sectors and they are not always susceptible to economic contraction, particularly in the short term. Many of the Jamaicans I interviewed, for example, are active members of several households through ties of marriage, blood, and friendship. These households intermittently pool food, labor services, access to social and economic resources, cash, and other articles of survival that enable their members to withstand severe downturns in individual standards of living. While these networks often grow and mature on the basis of access to jobs, housing, and other economic resources, they may also develop more or less independently of economic development.

I discuss the use of independent contractors among professionals and the highly skilled to illustrate that contracting and subcontracting have become critical ingredients of economic practice today, influencing individual, household, network, and even national and international patterns of resource use and accumulation. In the process, work settings and the social structures of production have become increasingly fragmented, and households that supply workers to agriculture, food processing, and other production regimes requiring large numbers of low-wage workers have responded with survival practices that seem at first glance equally fragmented (Osterman 1988; Vandeman 1988; Waldinger 1986). They have relied increasingly, for example, on unpaid household and network labor, thus combining wage and nonwage work, as well as pioneering creative home-based or domestic economic activities and methods of self-employment (Collins and Giménez 1990; Benson 1990; Gringeri 1995; Smart and Smart 2005).

Such multiple livelihoods may (and I emphasize the word *may*) prevent workers from starving, but they also encourage self-exploitation and the exploitation of weaker by stronger members of families, networks, and communities. Social scientists have written about multiple livelihoods for several years, dating at least back to Lambros Comitas's observations regarding "occupational multiplicity" in the Caribbean (1974) and the work of others among Latin American peasants (DeJanvry 1983; Griffith and Valdés Pizzini 2002). Yet within the past decade, technical, social, and political developments have allowed multiple livelihoods to underwrite the formation of new economic opportunities and bases for political action. In particular, the sophisticated communications, shipping, and transportation systems that serve transnational capital so efficiently have begun serving international and interregional labor migrants as well, enabling the development of social structures and the maintenance of linkages that facilitate increased labor mobility and in some cases new opportunities for investment and political power. For example, immigrant couriers now regularly travel between the United States and their home countries, facilitating international communication, business transactions, and other opportunities generated by the growth of sister communities in two or more countries (Mahler 1995; Richman 1992; Griffith et al. 1995; Goldring 1990; Grey and Woodrick 2002; Levitt 2001).

The growth, elaboration, and changes in temporary foreign worker programs over the past six decades are very much a part of this larger process. National and local governments have developed several mechanisms that parallel the growth of multiple livelihoods, both to assist this growth and to respond to problems it engenders. These mechanisms range from encouraging more flexible scheduling ("flexitime") and home-based production systems to negotiating neoliberal trade agreements with countries where multinational corporations practice outsourcing in peasant villages. Among the principal state responses to changing labor market dynamics is the drafting and revision of immigration policy. In the United States the sweeping immigration reforms of 1965 and 1986 were developed (following the precedent of the ninth proviso) with an eye toward the labor market, the former abolishing the Bracero Program and the latter expanding visas and legal statuses to meet regional, local, and industry-specific labor shortages (Bach and Brill 1991).

In the past decade, temporary worker programs have expanded in some areas of North America and contracted in others. Particularly notable have been the growth of H-2B (seasonal, nonagricultural) visa programs in the blue crab industry of Maryland, Virginia, and North Carolina, and less dramatic growth in the tourist and restaurant industries of Michigan, Virginia, West Virginia, Mississippi, and South Carolina. Ontario's tender fruit, greenhouse, and nursery farms near the Great Lakes now import more than twenty thousand temporary workers to work for up to eight months of the year, and Quebec has expanded its program as well (Basok 2000). In these cases, foreign workers enter industries with seasonal fluctuations in labor demand and return to Mexico and Jamaica during the off-season. This allows them to engage in more than one occupation during the year, just as the native workers who formerly staffed these industries, many of whom remain on a reduced, part-time basis, must rely on alternative sources of income during times of reduced labor demand.

Historically, labor contracting in the food industry extends far beyond the simple business of matching up workers and employers. Today, primarily because first-generation Latin American and Caribbean immigrants dominate food production, the machinery of labor contracting has evolved into the very machinery of control that the Country Life Commission claimed the countryside lacked. By providing work, transportation, housing, false identification, loans, food, drugs, and a bare minimum of protection from the Immigration and Naturalization Service, labor contractors oversee the health and welfare of their crews in ways that replicate those of total institutions. In the H-2 program, labor contracting has assumed an international and state-sanctioned dimension. Labor contracting didn't begin with H-2, but with the program it has received legitimacy and altered the role of the state in engineering the agricultural and the nation's labor supply (Calavita 1992).

Relationships between labor contractors and the people in their crews begin to take shape in communities across Latin America and the Caribbean, but they become firm and binding in the links between border towns and places like Immokalee, Florida (Griffith et al. 1995). In the low-cost motels of Chandler, Arizona, on the southeast edge of Phoenix, labor contractors have been arranging passage to southern Florida for Mayan immigrants for nearly two decades. A Chuj man named Parsenal Velazquez, from Guatemala's northwest provinces (the main targets of the military's scorched-earth campaigns of the 1970s and 1980s) described the process as recently as February 2000 like this: "We arrived in Sonora and entered the United States in Arizona. We walked three days and three nights to Chandler, arriving hungry and thirsty because we went through all our food and water by the end of the second day. The trip to Florida cost us $1,000. They took us to Homestead, where we began picking tomatoes for forty-five cents a bucket. After three months of working in the fields there, the work ended and we found another month of work in the tomato fields around Immokalee."

Immokalee occupies a strategic position in the agriculture of Florida and in the food industry throughout the South. Located in Collier County, northwest of Naples and southeast of Lake Okeechobee, Immokalee is winter home to twenty-five to thirty thousand farm workers every year. Farm workers who get their feet wet in Immokalee's labor markets often work in several segments of the food industry, moving into new crops of the North during the summer and fall and, from time to time, taking more permanent jobs in chicken factories, slaughterhouses, landscaping nurseries, furniture and other factories, and on construction crews (Fink 2003). Most of these jobs are low-paying, hazardous, and unpleasant, and it is ironic that as new immigrants move into jobs outside agriculture, they contribute to the general fears that stimulate demand for gated communities. Building these communities, in turn, stimulates demand for more workers and, as the construction industry continues its practice of recruiting among the foreign-born, more *immigrant* workers.

In the food industry the irony deepens. Corporate agriculture continues to move toward standardizing crops and livestock, especially with the new genetically modified organisms (GMOs). Food science has developed, for example, a chicken with legs powerful enough to keep it off the ground, preventing fungal growth on its feathers, yet not powerful enough to encourage walking off weight. Large poultry companies like Tyson and Perdue deliver chicks with these characteristics to farmers who go into debt to build, to company specifications, chicken houses capable of delivering water, feed, vitamins, and antibiotics as systematically as intravenous feeders in human hospitals (Thu and Durrenberger 1998). Kentucky Fried Chicken and McDonalds receive the same varieties of six- to seven-week-old birds that shoppers find in poultry cases from Safeway Supermarkets in Oregon to Piggly Wiggly Supermarkets in Georgia. They are standardized birds, bearing few genetic ties to their ancestors. They are so much a part of diets across the Americas that the companies producing them wield powers that run against the grains of free speech and democracy. Scholars at land grant colleges are routinely censored or defunded for criticizing food-industry practices. Food scientists justify such repression by saying that they need good relations with the food industry to test hypotheses in food-industry theaters of science.

Yet the industry's labor practices, in particular, invite criticism. Not only are poultry plants, sugar and tomato fields, citrus groves, and other food production work sites hazardous, but highly authoritarian methods of labor control permeate food workers' lives and underwrite the industry's heavy reliance on the most vulnerable, the least likely to complain. A well-known turkey factory in southeastern North Carolina, after installing row upon row of mobile homes to house its workers, took up the labor contractor's practice of assigning housing however management saw fit, moving once again toward a total institutional context. Personnel managers at the plant believed, evidently, that providing this housing gave them license to make decisions about the composition of the Latino groups that occupied them. In one instance they assigned two Mexican men to a unit already occupied by a Mexican husband and wife, the wife working on the day shift and the husband on the night. One of the new men was to work on the day shift, the other on the night. When the husband objected to having a strange man share a trailer with his wife at night, the personnel manager seemed puzzled, observing quite simply that they were all Mexicans.

This combination of foolishness and authority might be more alarming if it weren't for the ingenuity of new immigrant workers as they elaborate their residence in Florida and throughout the South. Again and again, people interested in the welfare of new immigrants encounter incidents and practices that offer hope that they won't merely submit to the wishes of employers like the personnel manager described above. In a more recent incarnation of the H-2 visa program, the part of the program that brings Mexican women to work in North Carolina's seafood-processing plants, I have been fortunate enough to witness the resistance of thinking, breathing people to submitting to others who would control their time, movements, and physical surroundings—their very bodies—overbearingly and unjustifiably.

The resistance to which I refer occurred not in Florida but in small towns in coastal North Carolina, Virginia, and Maryland that are linked by human migration to small towns in northern Sinaloa, Mexico, and to several neighborhoods of Latinos throughout the South. In recent years, for reasons I discuss later in this book, the H-2 program has shifted its primary recruitment efforts from the Caribbean to Mexico. Thus owners of crabmeat factories along the mid-Atlantic coast have been importing Mexican women since 1988, using H-2 visas like those that Florida sugar producers used, from 1943 to 1992, to import Jamaican men. During their first seasons, many of the Mexican women were recruited by unfamiliar and unscrupulous labor contractors, housed in substandard houses in isolated labor camps, and kept in such a state of servitude that several of them eventually sued their employers so successfully that most of the abusive factory owners were driven out of business (Griffith 1999, chapter 4). News of the lawsuit and its consequences spread through the workers' small hometowns of northern Sinaloa and became absorbed into the occupational lore of others who followed these first women into the crab factories of the mid-Atlantic. Gradually, out of the hearts of total institutions, most of the Mexican women developed their own recruiting networks and engaged in occupational strategies of their own design. These have enabled them to move out from under the complete control of the crab plants while simultaneously drawing upon the social checks and balances of home.

How this has occurred is best glimpsed from their homes, in Sinaloa, in small communities called by pretty names like La Noria, Juan Luis Rios, and Gabriel La Leyva, dusty *ejidos* just off the Pan-American Highway, south of the large metropolitan marketing center of Los Mochis. In January, during one of the few months they are home, Amelia and Carlos José, a young couple in their twenties, enjoy their two-room concrete home in La Noria and its modern appliances and cabinets that they have built with money they earned in the crabmeat factories. When I visited them there, Amelia suckled a newborn girl whom she had in the hospital in New Bern, North Carolina, in the days before their return. She explained that she waited to have her child in the United States because a child born there was easier to take back and forth across the border. Like many homes in the community, their house sits in a yard enclosed by stick-and-wire fencing. Inside the fence are a few domestic animals and the house of Amelia's parents. Piped water keeps a watering pool filled, and lengths of hose run to the bases of orange and mango trees.

During this time of their lives, while working in mid-Atlantic crab factories, Amelia and Carlos José can enjoy their home for only two to three months per year. During the rest of the year the use of the new furnishings, the secure windows and door, the appliances, and the house itself are gifts that Amelia and Carlos José give to their parents. In return, their parents, and the parents of other young women and men like them, provide, from a distance, the social checks on the power that the labor recruiters and supervisors attempt to exercise at factories far from home.

Along with the other couples and single women at the factory, Amelia and Carlos José have managed to migrate into a foreign land and live among strangers without sacrificing the subtle social enclosures of home. Whenever anything interesting or gossip-worthy happens at the crab plant, it is incorporated swiftly into the daily conversations of La Noria. If one of the younger girls begins frequenting local bars, if the plant owners refuse to pay overtime or attempt to keep the women and couples too confined to the plant or its housing, or if their Mexican supervisors, Anaceli and Manuel, also from Sinaloa, attempt to enforce an edict the rest of them consider unjust, the news, quickly relayed to La Noria, is discussed and debated there until the relatives of the offenders experience shame.

Months after my visit to La Noria, I visited the open and welcoming crab factory's labor camp on North Carolina's coastal plain. It was a sunny summer afternoon, a Sunday, and the people I visited in La Noria had invited me to visit them here, listen to their stories, and share a meal with them.

Amelia and Carlos José were there with their infant daughter, and Manuel and Anaceli, their supervisors, with their own young U.S.-born son. We were sitting in the shadows of the trailers and worker dormitories, in the shade of Carolina pines. They served me hamburgers from McDonalds, food they believed Americans preferred, food whose production reshapes natural landscapes and social structures to suit its needs. Anaceli was Amelia's cousin, and while I ate she began to complain, in a good-humored way, that she had difficulty enforcing even the most basic rules of the plant without being chastised for it by her mother and her aunts at home. Feigning exasperation, she complained that they had trouble assigning rooms in the worker housing, or tasks in the plants, without hearing from elder women at home. She and Manuel, she said, really had little control over the workers at all.

And all the time Amelia, holding her infant daughter in her arms, listened, smiling wryly, and agreed.

Amelia and Carlos José have been able to resist excessive labor control through an increasing integration, or convergence, between work sites in the United States and home communities in Mexico. Similarly, the increasing reliance on foreign labor and decreasing reliance on native labor signals a convergence of the working experiences of low-wage, primarily minority U.S. workers with those of workers from Jamaica and Mexico. Because engagement in multiple livelihoods involves increased convergence between work and home, production and reproduction, and capitalist and domestic production, temporary foreign worker programs have laid the basis for a parallel convergence between the households, networks, and neighborhoods of workers in Jamaica, Mexico, and the United States. This book addresses this convergence, focusing on industries in which H-2 workers work, but also considering the ways in which these industries organize social and natural environments and the ways in which workers in general—H-2 or otherwise—comply with, ignore, resist, or aggressively revolt against such organized regimes.

Through multiple livelihoods, some poor and less empowered people have been able to move beyond the confines of low-wage labor markets, create new frontiers, assert their humanity, and insist that others view and treat them as people rather than merely as workers. This is rarely an easy, predictable process, and it often demands the concerted effort of several trusted individuals, a good deal of risk, and luck. At times it also means breaking laws, circumventing regulations, bribing public officials, and hustling along the margins of the economy. Such behaviors question and even disrupt current class and power relations. Such behaviors resist the poor and relatively powerless condition to which those relations confine most of humankind. Finally, such behaviors run deeply against the grain of highly managed, rigidly defined programs meant to feed pliant workers into onerous jobs.

ONE

ALLEGED SHORTAGES AT HOME, CERTAIN SURPLUSES ABROAD:
NORTH AMERICAN TEMPORARY WORKER PROGRAMS

At an international migration conference in Vienna, Austria, in September 2003, one of the plenary sessions, devoted to the tensions between national identity and immigration, addressed the difficulties that governments experience when integrating immigrants during periods of intense nationalism. The panelists (all but one were white men) gave as examples the use of Christianity as a cornerstone of national identity in Germany and the wave of anti-immigration laws, English-only initiatives, and the U.S. Patriot Act. During the question-and-answer period, a young Filipino woman stood to say that she was disappointed in the panelists because they seemed to conflate state policy with the success or failure of immigrant integration. The immigrants she had encountered in her travels, she said, were experimenting with new musical and literary styles, intermarrying with one another and with natives, and defying native attempts to place foreign nationals in categories of the "other." Integration was occurring, she argued, not because of state policy but in spite of it.

The tension between the panelists and the young woman, like the tension between immigration and national identity, stems from the many developments in the world today that seem to suggest that nationalism, national identity, and the nation-state itself are losing ground to competing allegiances. Assaults on nation-states range from ethnic and separatist wars to the loss of border control, the growth of multinational corporations, neoliberal trade agreements, and the European Union. Despite these assaults, the death of nationalism and the nation-state is far from assured. Some developments that seem to undermine national identity, such as transnational identities forming among international migrants, often reinforce state programs, as transnational migrants demand services from more than one local or federal government. Yet the *apparent* weakening of nations during increasing globalization threatens to weaken citizenship and the rights that citizenship entails, and these persistent and recurring challenges to citizenship and nation continue to influence attitudes toward immigration and the intersection of immigration policy, human rights, and economic policy.

In the United States, one means of shoring up citizenship and its rights has been to highlight differences among groups of people based on legal status. In differentiating citizens from immigrants—often to the point of calling undocumented immigrants "aliens"—policymakers have gone further by establishing several categories of immigrants: permanent residents, refugees, legal temporary workers, work-authorized immigrants, and undocumented or illegal workers are just a few of the ways in which the U.S. government categorizes its immigrants. Welfare reforms that exclude noncitizens from benefits, state propositions to bar noncitizen children from public schools, and English-only initiatives deepen the differences between "us" and "them." These highly visible methods of defining group boundaries are similar to the methods that ethnic groups commonly use to define themselves and to exclude or include members. They are symptomatic, too, of the tensions between globalization and the tendency to identify with smaller, often local groups based on ethnicity, occupation, class, language, religion, region, or other factors—concepts that are, ironically, often born or strengthened among native residents when immigrants move into an area.

The growth of temporary worker programs like the H-2A and H-2B class visa programs that are the subject of this book clearly reflects the growing tendency to differentiate citizens from foreign nationals in the United States. These two visa programs allow individuals from Mexico, Central America, the Caribbean, and a few other regions into the United States to perform largely low-wage, low-skilled labor in agriculture and several nonagricultural industries. The programs create a class of foreign workers differentiated from U.S. working classes by their limited access to the labor market, their temporary residence, their "nonimmigrant" appellation, and their circumscribed human rights. Historically, H-2 workers worked in agriculture, primarily because of the seasonal and onerous nature of the farm tasks they performed. Since 1988, however, H-2 workers have been recruited into other seasonal industries, notably seafood processing, tourism, forestry, and horse racing, where they work as stable attendants and grooms. This expansion of temporary worker programs took place coincidentally with a shift away from the Caribbean and toward Mexico as a source of labor, and with the increasing use of women in the H-2 labor force, in part due to the nature of work in the new industries using H-2 labor. Seafood processing and tourism, historically, have relied heavily on women.

As I noted in the Introduction, these changes in guestworker programs have occurred at the same time that temp agencies have begun playing a prominent role in staffing U.S. corporations, drawing on citizens instead of foreign nationals. As temporary workers become more commonplace in the U.S. economy, the use of temporary workers has become more acceptable to policymakers, and policies involving temporary *foreign* workers have ceased being the subject of heated public debate. Though debate persists, it has become less about the fundamentals or underlying justification for guestworker programs than about their specific mechanics. Given that growers and their associations have the most experience with guestworker programs, much of the debate over temporary foreign workers' roles in the U.S. economy draws on the history and experience of foreign workers in agriculture, where employers have successfully sculpted immigration policy to meet their needs at least since 1917.

ALLEGED LABOR SHORTAGES AND
TEMPORARY FOREIGN WORKERS, 1917–1985

World Wars I and II provided much of the initial stimulus and political will to establish relations with foreign nations specifically to import temporary workers to meet alleged farm labor shortages in the United States. Initially, fearing labor shortages with men leaving the fields for wartime service and industrial production, agricultural producers pressured the U.S. Congress to pass the Immigration Act of 1917, which included the ninth proviso: "the Commissioner General of Immigration with the approval of the Secretary of Labor shall issue rules and prescribe conditions, including exaction of such bonds as may be necessary, to control and regulate the admission and return of otherwise inadmissible aliens applying for temporary admission" (U.S. Congress 1917, quoted in Calavita 1992, 23). The ninth proviso allowed employers to import foreign workers when and where they argued they suffered from extreme labor shortages, suspending those barriers in immigration law (such as a head tax and literacy requirement) that made it difficult to import farm labor from Mexico.

The year 1917 was also important to U.S. labor markets and the military, because Puerto Ricans were granted citizenship that year, having been colonized wards of the state since 1898. Significantly, this new phase of incorporating Puerto Ricans into the U.S. economy established the first large, legal Spanish-speaking labor force in U.S. agriculture and in other low-wage, hazardous industries, initiating the back-and-forth movement known colloquially as *el vavién* (the fluctuation) that continues to define much of Puerto Rican experience today (Duany 2002; Griffith and Valdés Pizzini 2002). During the Great Depression, as large-scale deportation of Mexicans occurred from western U.S. agriculture, the continued use of Puerto Ricans maintained a Spanish-speaking presence in America's orchards and fields.

While World War I stimulated the government's intervention in agricultural and other predominantly low-wage, unskilled labor markets, it wasn't until World War II that the government-to-government agreements were forged that eventually became the Bracero Program, between the United States and Mexico, and the British West Indies Temporary Alien Labor Program (BWITALP), between the United States and Jamaica, St. Lucia, St. Vincent, Barbados, and Dominica (see Hahamovich 2001 for the most insightful historical account of the BWITALP's origins; see also U.S. Congress 1978). Mexican workers—many hundreds of thousands of them—tended to work in the U.S. Southwest and West, while BWI workers, in far smaller numbers, scattered across the eastern United States through the war years, and after the war worked primarily in sugarcane in south Florida and in apple harvests along the eastern seaboard (U.S. Congress 1978). While I met older men in Jamaica who had worked as far east as Wisconsin during the war, most workers remained confined to an eastern corridor stretching from south Florida to New England. While the Bracero Program at its peak imported nearly half a million men in one year, the BWI program never imported more than twenty thousand workers in a single year.

The Bracero Program lasted from the war years until 1964, when civil rights legislation, combined with developments in agricultural and related rural labor markets and rural society, made the program vulnerable to organized labor just when it was becoming obsolete as a source of labor for agriculture. Even though the United Farm Workers Union (UFW) was partially responsible for bringing an end to the Bracero Program, grower opposition to the program's end was probably diluted because alternative labor supplies had already developed. Migration researchers, particularly Douglas Massey and his colleagues, have argued that the maturation of migrant social networks that began during the Bracero era eclipsed the program to provide a ready supply of labor to agriculture through network recruiting (Calavita 1992; Galarza 1964). Several works on immigrant labor have shown that network recruiting, often combined with subcontracting, is among the principal methods through which low-wage labor markets become staffed (Bach and Brill 1991; Griffith 1993; Griffith and Kissam 1995; Lamphere 1994; Massey et al. 1987; Hahamovich 1997; Peck 1996; Cloud and Galenson 1987; Ngai 2004).

Although the Bracero Program with Mexico was phased out in the mid-1960s, the much smaller BWI program, also known as the H-2A program, remained in effect through the 1960s and is still in effect today. Part of the success of the BWI program was that labor union organization in southern agriculture had been weak since the decline of the Southern Farmers' Tenant Union, which was most influential during the years immediately preceding World War II but lost ground during the war years. With the exception of one successful campaign in Florida citrus, the United Farm Workers had little success in organizing southern farm workers, many of whom were African American (the UFW was primarily a Latino and secondarily an Asian union). Several other developments inside and outside the agricultural labor market occurred during the 1950s and 1960s that allowed sugar and apple producers to lobby successfully for the continued use of foreign labor.

First, the migrations of African Americans from the South into northern industry reduced the traditional supply of farm labor in the South, which had long been a combination of tenant farmers, sharecroppers, family labor, and seasonal hired hands. Many African Americans who stayed in the South rejected agricultural labor because of its associations with slavery and servitude. White farmers I interviewed in the late 1990s recalled that younger African Americans in particular, influenced by heroic acts of civil disobedience during the 1960s, refused to follow orders given by white foremen and farm operators. Other employers argued that African Americans left the fields because of transfer payments, and still others blamed the rise of alternative employment opportunities in service industries, such as tourism and fast food restaurants. While such developments did not entirely eliminate African Americans from the fields of the South and East, they did set the stage for the growth of farm labor contracting both within the rural African American community and, increasingly, among Latino workers along the eastern seaboard, a development that mirrored the growth of Latino and Asian farm labor contracting in the West (Vandeman 1988; Krissman 1999).

Prior to the 1960s, the mechanization of the cotton and sugar beet harvests stimulated new, pioneering migrations among Latino workers from south Texas and Mexico to agricultural production centers in Florida, the southeast, and eventually the entire South, on up the eastern seaboard, and into the Midwest. Similar pioneering migrations among African American farm workers, also displaced by mechanization, resulted in new migrant circuits as well as the settling out of migrant lifestyles into rural industries like poultry processing, meatpacking, and tourism (Griffith 1993). In Belle Glade, Florida, I interviewed Miles Garner, a middle-aged African American man, who recalled coming to West Palm Beach, Florida, from Louisiana in 1961. Along with forty others, all of whom had lost work in cotton, he came to pick string beans based on referrals from Louisiana and Florida employment services. He recalled, "The last ethnic group into any area was the group to get the worst-paying job and the worst housing," adding that he lived in a square tar-paper building first and subsequently in an abandoned farmhouse. The crew leader who recruited workers through the employment service, a white woman, in addition to housing them in substandard units, paid less than other crew leaders, and within two weeks Miles switched to a new crew in Homestead.

African Americans weren't alone in being displaced by technological changes in agriculture. In Immokalee, Florida, Anna Garcia and I interviewed an elderly Latino woman staffing a senior center who reported that, as a young girl, she remembered being among the first Latinos in central Florida, arriving in the early 1950s. Her family moved to Immokalee after losing work in the cotton fields, she said, and here they lived and worked primarily among African Americans. Similarly, slightly further north, during the summer of 2001 I interviewed a Latino woman who remembered being among the first Latino residents in Wauchula, Florida, in the 1960s, arriving with her parents from Durango, Mexico, to work in expanding strawberry production; the first of fourteen children in her family to graduate from high school, she and her husband have since established a real estate office and now assist new immigrant Latino farm workers who wish to settle out of migration.

Such pioneering migrations among Latinos were the beginning of what has become known as the Latinization of rural America, or the growing importance of Spanish-speaking workers from Latin America in rural communities and labor markets. This has had enduring impacts on the ways in which many H-2A and H-2B workers from Mexico experience the rural United States. The presence of Mexicans and other Spanish-speaking families has expanded the social spaces of H-2 workers, offering them alternative job opportunities outside their contracts, new avenues for resisting excessive employer control, and increased information about the abilities to live and work in the rural United States without proper documentation. Employer familiarity with Latino workers may have also had some impact on the trend, in both the United States and Canada, to shift from the Caribbean to Mexico as the principal source of temporary foreign labor (Basok 2002; Binford 2002).

H-2 EXPANSION AND CONTRACTION THROUGH THE 1980S AND 1990S

Prior to the attacks on the World Trade Center in 2001, the most recent legislative changes to influence the H-2A program were the Immigration Reform and Control Act (IRCA) of 1986 and the Immigration Reform Act (IRA) of 1990, both of which drafted immigration policy with an eye toward combining humanitarian and labor market concerns. In rural labor markets across the United States, one provision of IRCA in particular accelerated the process of Latinization of rural labor: the Special Agricultural Worker (SAW) Provision (known among Spanish speakers as *Noventa dias,* or ninety days), which authorized for work anyone who could prove that he or she had worked in U.S. agriculture for ninety days during any of the three years preceding 1986. A second provision authorized anyone who could prove—with paychecks, utility bills, and the like—that they had maintained a residence and worked in the United States for the previous five years. IRCA thus sent the message to potential migrants that the best way to achieve U.S. work authorization was to first migrate and work in the United States illegally. Current amnesty proposals send identical signals to Mexico.

Once legalized, those authorized to work, now free to come and go between the Mexico and the United States, became important sources of information about work in the United States; because most were legalized as SAWs, their employment information was biased toward rural areas. In some cases the newly authorized also became labor smugglers (*coyotes*), labor intermediaries and contractors, and *raiteros* (people who provide rides from near-border locations to work destinations), contributing to the expansion of the underground network for helping people migrate from their Mexican villages to work illegally in *El Norte.* Through the late 1980s and 1990s, then, most of the seasonal and migrant farm labor force in the United States became Spanish speaking and largely from Mexico. Many of these workers now live and work in the same communities and rural areas as H-2A workers, which influences the H-2 experience in ways I discuss in more depth in later chapters.

Ironically, H-2 workers in the Florida sugar industry were denied SAW status even though they had satisfied the ninety-day criterion and had, unlike most SAWs legalized under the program, been working legally in the United States. They had followed all the rules but were treated worse than those who had been breaking rules for anywhere from three months to five years. The Florida sugar industry opposed granting them SAW status, however, viewing it as a threat to continuing the H-2 program under conditions prior to 1986. To achieve this end, the sugar industry argued before a sympathetic judge that sugar was a dessert, not an agricultural product, and thus that sugar workers weren't *agricultural* workers but dessert workers, presumably in the same category as pastry chefs (Hahamovich 2000). The sugar companies' opposition, along with the transparency of the judge's ruling, may in turn have hardened Florida Rural Legal Services lawyers in their determination to win their ongoing lawsuit over underpayment of wages and earned support for the lawyers' cause in the U.S. Congress (U.S. Congress 1991). When they won this lawsuit and forced back payments in wages as well as wage increases, manual labor became too costly and most of the companies mechanized the sugar harvest. No longer would H-2 workers work in Florida sugar.

Even as the sugar program ended, the H-2 program was expanding across the United States in other notable ways, including shifting from the Caribbean to Mexico as the principal source of labor, expanding into nonagricultural seasonal labor, and recruiting more women from Mexico and the Caribbean. With the nonagricultural component, H-2 visas were split into H-2A (for agricultural workers) and H-2B (for nonagricultural workers). The largest recipients of H-2B workers have been North Carolina and Texas seafood producers, horse racing stable attendants in Arizona and California, and workers in coastal hotels, resorts, and casinos across the southeast (Griffith, Heppel, and Torres 1994). As noted earlier, most seafood processors and many of the tourist workers, particularly chambermaids, are women. Mexican H-2A and H-2B workers, sometimes coming from the same communities and even the same families in Mexico, routinely compare their experiences, their contracts, and other features of the two programs. H-2B workers we interviewed, for example, were particularly bothered by the fact that they paid for their own housing while H-2A workers lived rent free.

Whether H-2A or H-2B, temporary worker programs have both more modern and more primitive manifestations (Peck 1996; Hahamovich, 1997, 2001; Ngai 2004). They continue to be reinvented and reinterpreted with different drafts of immigration and labor market policy. Contract labor, in the form of indentured servitude, was an important element in the American colonies (Taylor 2003). Early on, for example, cod fishermen on labor contracts settled in New England shortly after European exploration of the New World's Atlantic coast (Sider 1987; Vickers 1994; Kurlansky 1997). These fishermen were indebted to English merchants and dependent on them for vessels, equipment, and winter provisions, and they fished with the understanding that they would sell 100 percent of their dried cod to these merchants.

Later, indentured servitude became one of the most common ways of populating and supplying labor to the colonies. The term "indenture" derived from the indentations along the edges of the pages of the contract that made tearing the copies apart easier, and the contracts tended to specify between four and seven years of service in return for passage to North America and assorted other benefits. The specific terms of the contracts varied across occupation, employer, colony, and over time, but they usually specified not only the length of time servants worked in servitude but also the nature of the work they were expected to perform, their housing and other accommodations, and what they would receive at the end of the contract period. The most generous contracts gave servants land and other capital goods for fulfilling their contracts, while the more common contracts provided bare expenses and perhaps a suit or two of clothes.

From these distant origins, temporary contract workers have altered local and regional U.S. political and economic landscapes down to the present and remain contested points of federal policy. As this book goes to press, Congress is considering a new, supposedly streamlined variation on the H-2 program. In keeping with the trend toward efficiency and flexibility in American business, some of the proposed changes, if signed into law, would strip away many of the provisions protecting workers, in an attempt to make temporary foreign labor more easily accessible to employers. These proposals began in the late 1990s and continue today without resolution because of immigration's status as a heated, ambiguous, and difficult political issue. Following original proposals in the late 1990s, talks were held between workers' and employers' representatives regarding a potential compromise that would combine the possibility for temporary workers to move toward permanent residence status with an expanded program. With a

Republican administration in the United States and Mexican president Vicente Fox's call for complementing NAFTA with movement toward an open North American labor market, a marked expansion of temporary worker programs appeared increasingly likely. Just days after Presidents Bush and Fox met in 2001, however, Middle Eastern immigrants bombed Washington and New York, and all such talks were stalled indefinitely. Not until two years later did new guestworker proposals reach the Congress, forwarded by George W. Bush himself. Not surprisingly, the proposed programs stripped away some of the current protections yet offered amnesty provisions that employers could hold over workers' heads for as long as they worked on contract. Latino responses to the proposals were leery at best, and echoed a common refrain: *El diablo está en las detalles* (the devil is in the details).

Prior to the argument that immigrants threatened national security, political opposition to temporary worker programs was based primarily on the grounds that foreign workers were taking jobs from native workers, stagnating or depressing wages and working conditions in certain economic sectors, and hindering efforts to organize workers. Popular opposition to contract labor derives from the real and perceived human rights abuses that have accompanied these programs over the years (Human Rights Watch 2003). Again and again the same or similar schemes for binding workers to specific production processes through coercive means—whether through law, policy, administrative oversight, brute force, or other manifestations of extreme power disparities, including slavery—have emerged wherever there have been onerous, hazardous, isolated, seasonal, or otherwise difficult-to-staff jobs. This is particularly true with jobs that have attracted undocumented or illegal workers, which cluster in exactly those economic sectors where contract workers find employment, such as agriculture and food processing. And H-2s are, at bottom, legally *bound* to work for specific employers.

Since the abolition of slavery, labor recruiters have funneled foreign or distant workers into labor markets, staffing such large projects as the construction of the Panama Canal or Flagler's railroad from St. Augustine to Key West, Florida, and such small enterprises as sheep farms on the high plains of the American West. Quite often these workers have little or no idea what they are getting into. At the core of these operations, even today, are networks of recruiters and labor contractors who provide services ranging from transportation loans to new recruits to supervisory tasks for employers. At the same time, however, recruiters' intermediary positions between employers and workers allow them to build up a complex system of kickbacks and bribery that prey on workers from impoverished and relatively powerless backgrounds (Peck 1996; Ngai 2004). These schemes rely heavily on formal political and corporate support as well as informal power relations, giving labor contractors and employers powers over contract workers that reaches far beyond the mere economics of buying and selling labor (Griffith 1987; Ortiz 1999). These relationships reach as far as the distant foreign communities of the workers. In addition to providing a significant inflow of cash through the remittance of U.S. earnings, temporary foreign worker programs rely on fleets of support staff in the workers' home communities—women, children, the elderly—to reproduce labor supplies and absorb workers who are injured or unemployed for other reasons (see Chapter 4).

H-2 programs, like temporary worker programs generally, remain haunted by a well-known observation that is sometimes attributed to the German minister of labor and sometimes to the Swiss playwright Max Frisch (Calavita 1992, 6): that countries that begin actively recruiting and importing foreign workers may believe they are importing only workers but soon find out they are importing people. In a fundamental and essential way, this observation points to the complex ways in which sending and receiving communities become intertwined through migration, particularly when that migration is seasonal, with people leaving and returning every year. H-2 programs link not merely economies but the daily and lifetime experiences of the migrants themselves, their families, and those who live and work near them at home and abroad. As a testament to these linkages, many have argued that the Bracero Program was terminated primarily because it had stimulated enough illegal immigration and links between U.S. and Mexican communities that it was no longer necessary (Calavita 1992; Goldring 1990; Massey et al. 1987).

Despite the complex and dynamic mix of extremely formal and deeply personal relations forged during H-2 and other temporary worker programs, far too often debates over the character of such programs leave out workers' and family members' voices from the sending countries and communities. Even when agreements are forged between participating nation-states, those drafting and signing such agreements are often poorly equipped to speak on behalf of workers and their families. Coming from different class and occasionally different ethnic backgrounds from the H-2 workers they represent, diplomats and liaison officers from the sending countries may be paternal and condescending toward the workers, at best.

At worst, they may be antagonistic and hostile (Basok 2002; Verma 2003). Even in cases where well-meaning diplomats would like to negotiate better agreements, intervene in employer disputes, and advocate for workers' rights, they are usually constrained by tenuous political appointments or because they fear losing jobs to workers from competing countries.

At a conference in Ottawa, Canada, in August 2003, several diplomats from Mexico, the eastern Caribbean, and Jamaica who deal directly with agricultural workers from their home countries met with researchers (including me) and Canadian government officials. The diplomats were well-educated, impeccably dressed, savvy political appointees occupying positions that their fellow nationals envied. During a particularly heated discussion over the ability of eastern Caribbean liaison workers to address workers' grievances, the representative from Barbados said, "If I advocate too hard for that worker, I'm liable to lose that placement to Mexico or Jamaica." While the Mexican diplomats seemed relatively complacent about the potential of losing places for Mexican workers to the Caribbean, their complacency may be short lived. In the spring of 2003 a North Carolina Department of Labor official, working closely with the H-2 program in the state, received a visit from a Laotian man who claimed he could, if given the chance, recruit Laotian workers who would work harder, and for less pay, than Mexicans. While North Carolina employers or employer associations have not yet, to my knowledge, turned to Laos as a source of foreign workers, the man's interest in the program portends a possible future in which the poorest of the world's poor compete with one another for H-2 jobs.

EMPIRICALLY GROUNDING THE DEBATE:
FLORIDA SUGAR AND EAST COAST APPLES

Historically, the evolution of the Florida sugar and East Coast apple programs, along with several related issues concerning the programs' impact on domestic labor, have shaped the debate over the H-2 program (Hahamovich 2000). Florida sugar production and East Coast apple production have used H-2 workers since World War II, or longer than any other region or industry, and both repeatedly drew the attention of the media and of state and federal departments of justice. In sugar, this attention culminated in a congressional investigation that I discuss in more detail in the following chapter; combined with a lawsuit that forced back payment of earnings to workers and pushed wages higher, the investigation led sugar companies to phase out the H-2 program from around 1990 to 1992.

Again and again, those opposed to the program raise at least three issues (U.S. Congress 1991, 1978; Wilkinson 1982). First, how do H-2 workers influence the wages and working conditions of native workers? Second, are H-2 workers truly "captive," their limited access to the U.S. labor market placing them in conditions similar to those of indentured servitude? Finally, do H-2 programs become institutionalized and, if so, effectively close employment opportunities to native workers? Among the more interesting sound bites about temporary worker programs is the catchy phrase, "there is nothing so permanent as a temporary worker." Taken at face value, it means that workers either overstay their temporary visas or return to the United States to live permanently after gaining experience as contract workers, effectively becoming illegal immigrants at least for a time. Its more essential meaning, however, points to this issue of institutionalization, implying that H-2 programs, once begun, quickly become the norm in specific labor markets or regions, eclipsing other labor processes and slowly spreading their influence over wages and working conditions. While this has been the case in some regions, notably Florida sugar, the bulk of the agricultural and much of the low-wage labor force throughout the United States is composed of immigrant, rather than H-2, workers, only a portion of whom are unauthorized. This has been the norm in agriculture even while H-2 programs have come and gone.

Framed in sound bites or in terms of either-or questions about displacing or replacing U.S. workers, the debate over H-2 overshadows the program's complexity at the ground level, from workers' perspectives, miring it in a restricted set of labor market and immigration policy issues at the same time that it ignores many of those features of H-2 programs that work for and against workers. The notorious abuses that attended the sugar program, in particular, have colored labor rights advocates' views of H-2 programs generally and have influenced the continued reluctance of employers in some regions to consider using H-2 workers. In the case against Florida sugar producers, lawyers for Rural Legal Aid were able to show that workers, fearing the loss of their contracts, routinely agreed to the undervaluing of their own labor power, assisting their foremen and the owners of the sugar plantations in meeting, annually, projected wage costs by manipulating the value of the cane workers cut (U.S. Congress 1991; Wilkinson 1982; Griffith 1986a). Lawyers also elicited testimony that the sugar companies regularly underreported the hours workers worked in the fields or spent in buses being transported to and from fields. This practice freed the companies from compensating workers for any differences between the contractually agreed hourly wage and the price per ton of cane cut.

Atop complaints over wages were piled several others: blacklisting, underreporting of injuries, illegal or unauthorized deductions from workers' pay, abuses of compulsory saving programs by Caribbean statesmen, and so forth. Clearly the sugar program, which was crafted and supported by some of the most powerful agribusiness families in the United States, illustrated how H-2 programs can become vehicles for widespread violations of human rights (Human Rights Watch 2003). Similar abuses took place in the apple orchards up and down the eastern seaboard but were more variable because they were distributed over a larger number of different-sized farms that were managed by a wider variety of people. Perhaps the oversight of the Department of Labor's regional office in Philadelphia, more vigilant about labor law violations than the southern region that oversaw the sugar program, prevented more widespread abuse.

Contract labor programs that evolve in this way take their lead from classic debt peonage schemes, preying on vulnerable workers and enlisting the aid of the state in cheating workers even as they keep them in a kind of legal bondage. In several regions of the U.S. South, particularly in extremely onerous occupations such as turpentine farming and distilling in northern Florida and southern Georgia, debt peonage persisted well into the twentieth century. In its functioning, debt peonage was similar to a local variation of an H-2 program in that it used county power structures, particularly sheriffs, to assist employers in staffing hazardous or distasteful occupations. Briefly, through the use of vagrancy laws, county sheriffs would arrest individuals for vagrancy and then hand them over to employers, who would pay their fines and bail and then force them to work off these expenses in the pine forests or in other occupations (Daniel 1972). Employee-employer relations were thus, from the beginning, extremely unequal in terms of power and were tantamount to slavery. By charging debt peons for room and board, some employers ensured that these workers never had the opportunity to work off their debt. Workers who attempted to leave before paying their debts were hunted and captured by local sheriffs and returned to their employers, often with heavier fines to work off.

Although outlawed in the mid-twentieth century, debt peonage continues in the United States today, every year binding a small yet significant percentage of the agricultural labor force to labor contractors (Germino 2003; Schlosser 2002). Over the past decade, the Immokalee Coalition for

Farmworkers has intervened in several debt peonage cases where contractors had enslaved crews of up to eight hundred workers with methods ranging from intimidation to pistol-whipping and murder, often using their own private paramilitary forces to prevent workers from leaving their crews. In one case, contractors and their henchmen began attacking independently owned and operated buses that came and went from small Florida towns, afraid that the buses were providing workers with the means of escaping their crews. They intimidated and harassed bus drivers until they altered their routes. The significance of dept peonage and slavery in low-wage labor markets is that they establish a floor of working conditions to which workers without power may, in certain circumstances, fall (see Conclusion).

While Florida sugar producers did not recruit workers through debt relations, they did routinely use their power to organize recruitment, enforce company rules, and deal with workers who disagreed with one or another aspect of company policy. Stephanie Black's documentary *H-2 Worker* contains footage of workers being deported after an impromptu strike over wages, with the direct aid of police, police dogs, INS buses, and other instruments of raw power. Thus in the sugar program, as under debt peonage, labor relations were also based on extremely unequal power relations.

"Extremely" is an important word to consider here, however. Sugar producers and their allies in Congress, the Department of Labor, the Florida Fruit and Vegetable Association, and elsewhere posed an almost (but not quite) impenetrable force against H-2 workers and *their* allies in Congress, Rural Legal Services offices, the Department of Labor, Caribbean ministries, and other organizations that fought for workers' rights. For this reason, it may be misleading to use sugar as the prototypical H-2 program. At the very least it obscures the empirical evidence that the ways in which H-2 programs influence workers and their families, in the United States and abroad, are highly uneven across industrial sectors and regions (Griffith, Heppel, and Torres 1994). At worst it leads to overly instrumentalist conceptions of state power and fatalist views of capital's dominance. Further, and perhaps most troubling, it implies that many of those working in H-2 programs today lack the ability to speak for themselves or decide what is in their own best interests in light of the broader context of their lives.

In order to achieve a more detailed understanding of H-2 and other guestworker programs, this book pays close attention to the lived experiences of workers as they negotiate guestworker labor processes, leaving home and returning year by year, always wondering whether this will be

their last season abroad. Their negotiations begin at home, with the recruiting strategies of formal and informal labor contractors, and continue
through their working conditions in the United States and the ways they
spend their earnings back home. At bottom, however, they are based on
developments in the more empowered countries where they work long
hours in jobs in which North Americans allegedly refuse to toil.

TWO

OCCUPATIONS ABANDONED, WORKERS DISPLACED:
SEASONAL LABOR BEFORE AND AFTER H-2

With few exceptions, the labor markets that foreign workers have come
to dominate once attracted domestic workers. Thus nearly every instance
of an agricultural harvest or a production line where H-2 workers work is a
story of changing labor relations. Someone either left or reduced his com-
mitment to these jobs, willingly or unwillingly, before guestworkers arrived.
This chapter looks at developments that set the stage for the genesis of
H-2 programs in two regions and three industrial sectors—mid-Atlantic
blue crab processing and tobacco, and upstate New York apple farms—and
then describes the events that led up to the end of H-2 in Florida sugar.
Together these cases illustrate how nationally crafted policies become part
of local landscapes, with specific human consequences for communities far
removed from Washington. Very occasionally, as with the sugar program in
the early 1990s, these policies have resulted in serious repercussions for H-2
employers who repeatedly took advantage of power imbalances to reduce
wages and exploit workers. I emphasize that the reasons why employers turn
to H-2 programs in the United States are influenced by local labor market
processes—including trends in power, supervision, enforcement, and general labor relations—and regional developments that result from the intersection of national policy shifts and local law enforcement practices.

That local settings condition the impact of H-2 programs on domestic
and foreign labor is evident from the highly variable distribution of H-2
labor. If the specifics of H-2 programs, as national programs, were truly uniform, we would expect to find H-2 workers wherever seasonal and onerous
occupations failed to attract a stable domestic labor force. Yet rural labor
relations range from highly enlightened and at times creative to variations
on debt peonage and slavery. Stories of how specific families and industries

began using H-2 workers offer clues to employers' motives for turning from domestic to foreign labor. By contrast, the story of how the largest and longest users of H-2 workers shifted from manual labor to machines— something they had claimed for years was impossible or economically un- feasible because of ecological constraints—illustrates the extent to which the program can become a vehicle for labor exploitation bordering on slavery.

The stories presented here, along with similar stories scattered through- out this book, suggest that employers turn to and from H-2 workers in response to an ever-changing low-wage labor market. In such a market, employers seem forever concerned with making changes that allow them to keep paying low wages while still mobilizing sufficient (or, more often, more than sufficient) and reliable, easily controlled labor. These changes inevitably draw on the unequal power relations that result from factors like ethnicity, gender, and legal status. In other words, instead of relying on market mechanisms—such as higher wages or better working conditions— to maintain a steady supply of labor, employers manipulate social, cultural, and political factors—the source of power relations—in ways that keep wages low even as costs of living and profits increase. H-2 programs fit into these strategies quite well, which is why, after the pioneering efforts of one or two employers, interest in and use of H-2 workers among similarly situated employers is generally diffused through regions and industries relatively quickly. This, of course, influences the households and commu- nities of people who once supplied workers to these industries, as they are gradually displaced and replaced by H-2 workers. We see this most explic- itly along the mid-Atlantic coast, where employers shifted from primar- ily African American to Mexican labor—and in both cases predominantly female labor—over a period of a few years.

MID-ATLANTIC BLUE CRAB PROCESSING

In the mid-1980s, visiting seafood-processing houses along North Carolina's coast, I heard the same complaint that I was to hear again and again over the next decade and a half: the main competitor for workers in the seafood plants, the plant owners said, was the government. Food stamps, energy assistance, Aid to Families with Dependent Children (AFDC), Medicaid, commodity days, and other government "giveaway" programs not only robbed them of their labor but also, in the words of one employer, "took away people's incentive to work under the big fat banner of compassion."

Since then I have conducted research in several low-wage labor markets in the South, labor markets once staffed primarily by African Americans but now staffed primarily by Latino immigrants, and in nearly every case this is one of the principal explanations that employers use for the change.

Whatever employers perceive as the underlying cause for the erosion of the work ethic among southern workers, the shift to immigrants—most of them Latino—has occurred in several low-wage labor markets across the South. Labor markets in the food industry in particular—including agriculture and food processing—have had significant impacts on recent changes in the demographic complexions of rural areas in the South, the Midwest, and the Great Plains (Fink 2003; Grey and Woodrick 2002; Griffith 1993; Stull et al. 1995). Changes in the mid-Atlantic blue crab industry share certain features with other parts of the food industry in this respect, with one important exception: the shift from African American to H-2 workers as opposed to undocumented immigrant workers.

Beginning in the late 1980s, three employers from different mid-Atlantic communities, all suffering from labor supply problems, found H-2 workers to work in their crab plants by different paths (Griffith 1999, chapter 4). One used the Virginia Employment Service, one learned of the program through a crab processor in Mexico, and the third worked with Del Al Associates, the largest contractor of H-2 workers in Mexico. In each case plant owners had long voiced the complaint that government programs had eroded the work ethic of African Americans, saying that the reliability of plant workers had dropped off so much that you never knew, from one day to the next, how many workers might show up for work. Yet was this perceived drop in reliability, supposedly caused by the federal government, the whole story? In the discussion of native crab pickers that follows, based on ninety-four interviews conducted in the 1990s, I address this question by examining several attributes of African American participation in the industry during the transition to an H-2-dominated work force.

Until the late 1980s, in many rural coastal counties of North Carolina, Maryland, and Virginia, seafood processing was one of only a handful of seasonal occupations available to workers with few skills and little education. African American women typically began working in crab plants as young girls, some as young as eleven, and many stayed in the industry throughout their working lives. Some women I interviewed reported working in blue crab nearly sixty years, though not always for the same seafood plant. In line with engaging in the multiple economic strategies that seasonal work demands, it was common for workers to rotate among two or three crab plants over the course of a season or from year to year.

In the years immediately following the arrival of Mexican H-2 workers, few African American workers severed ties to crab processing completely. This would have been difficult in any case, given how deeply work in the crab plants permeated African American communities across the mid-Atlantic. Even those who phased back or quit knew relatives or friends who continued working in the plants. Asked to name family, friends, and acquaintances who worked in the crab plants, only around one-third of those interviewed named fewer than three individuals. Instead, they said things like, "God, when I started, everybody worked; mostly everybody was related. God, I had so many relatives and people I knew working. Some picked all their life." Or, "Most everybody in this area were picking crabs." Or, "Black folks, not white folks, work there, so we know about everyone."

For as far back as they could remember, African American women were recruited into the crab-processing industry through maternal ties. This meant that most crab pickers worked beside their mothers, grandmothers, daughters, nieces, and aunts; virtually everyone came to the plants by means of female ties. Though women dominated recruiting, most crab workers didn't live in predominantly female or female-headed households but in households that, though rarely simple nuclear families, included a nuclear family unit along with one or two other people. These others might include one or two lateral kin or a grandparent or granddaughter. Households were not generally large, ranging in size and character from individuals living alone to complex households of eight individuals representing three generations and lateral kin such as cousins and aunts. More complex households tied household members into wider networks, increasing opportunities to gain access to services and new jobs, and usually reflected ongoing processes of family formation, crisis, and dissolution.

Among those workers who had quit around the time H-2 workers began arriving in the plants, or knew others who had, the primary reasons given for leaving were not *directly* related to the arrival of foreign workers. Instead, they reported such developments as health, age, or disability problems, moving, finding another (usually better) job, or family issues such as having to care for a sick relative or helping a husband in his occupation. Workers changing jobs tended to leave for work in newer coastal industries; in Pamlico County, North Carolina, the largest crab-processing county on the eastern seaboard, several workers found nursing assistant jobs in a nursing home. The growth in tourism in several coastal counties created jobs in restaurants, bed-and-breakfast establishments, hotels, motels, and marinas—sectors that, elsewhere along the East Coast, H-2 workers were already entering (see Chapter 5). Other former seafood workers took jobs in daycare centers, as domestics, in catfish farming and other agricultural pursuits, and in county and state government.

Female members of workers' households worked in jobs similar to those listed above, including, of course, crab processing, but the men they lived with tended to work in somewhat different jobs. The crab industry does provide some jobs for men, as truck drivers, maintenance workers, helpers, and the people who unload and steam the crabs, and most crabbers themselves are (white) men, but women fill the majority of picking jobs. In addition to working in the crab industry, men in crab pickers' households worked in construction, forestry, agriculture and aquaculture (catfish farming), and on military bases. Commonly, too, particularly across eastern North Carolina and the eastern shores of Maryland and Virginia, they fished, gardened, farmed, hunted, or trapped—often combining two or more of these occupations—to contribute to household income.

Clearly, families pooled resources and combined multiple livelihoods in order to survive. Although work in the crab-picking plants long constituted an important core of income and employment in many households, occupying a central role in the employment strategies of African American women with few human capital skills, rarely was crab picking a household's or even a worker's sole source of income. In line with the oft-repeated employers' complaint, households did typically rely on various forms of government assistance, particularly during the times of year when work in the plants was slow. More than two-thirds of the households reported receiving food stamps, unemployment compensation, and energy assistance.

The strategy of combining several sources of income did not change with the influx of Mexicans. Beaufort County, North Carolina, consistently falls among the poorest counties in the state, and many coastal regions of Virginia, Maryland, and North Carolina—excepting, of course, the wealthy fringe of oceanfront—have suffered from higher poverty rates than inland regions. This is true of the eastern shores of Virginia and Maryland in particular, parts of which are accessible to most by the Chesapeake Bay bridge tunnel, which charges a toll. Even with job growth in tourism and health care, most jobs in these counties are seasonal, pay low wages, or both. When asked about other jobs and income-generating activities, these workers answered that it was more common to move between crab plants and other jobs from one season to the next than during the picking season; even so,

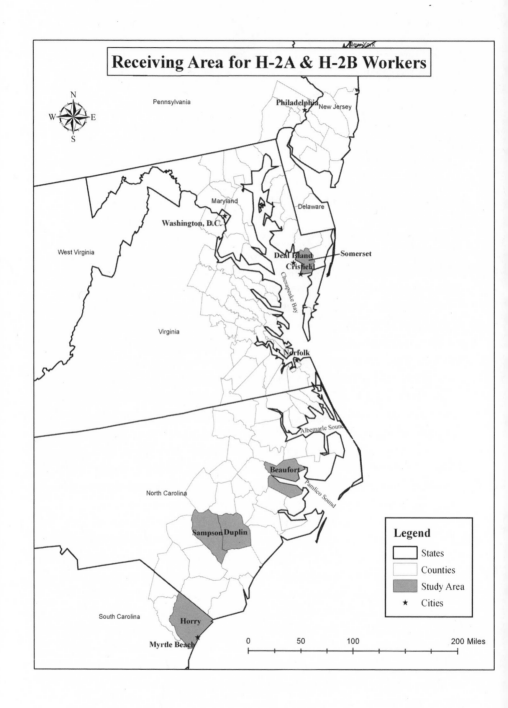

Receiving Area for H-2A & H-2B Workers

Legend

▢ States
▢ Counties
▨ Study Area
★ Cities

one-third to one-half reported moving into other industries during the picking season.

During the early years of the H-2 program, the arrival of Mexicans influenced the economic and employment strategies of domestic workers in two ways: first, among those who continued to rely on crab picking, this work became less important in their overall income-generating activities; second, younger workers reconsidered crab picking as an occupation, let alone as a lifetime career—as their mothers might have done—and moved into other economic sectors. Overall, African Americans began working more sporadically in crab houses after foreign workers arrived. Although some crab plants did not import Mexican workers and continued to provide employment for domestic workers under conditions similar to those of the past, the arrival of ready and willing foreign workers in neighboring plants increased competition for blue crabs. This effectively constricted the supply of crabs at all plants, reducing the amount of work available to each individual employee, whether foreign or domestic.

Coincidentally, during the early years of H-2, crab supplies to plants (and therefore the amount of work available) were further squeezed by the development of a "basket" crab market (hard-shell crabs shipped live) and a market for soft-shell or "peeler" crabs. These developments highlight the far-reaching implications that fairly localized factors have for H-2 workers. In the new basket market, crabs previously sold to picking houses were now shipped live to Baltimore. Plant owners attempted to compensate by importing crabs from other regions, primarily Louisiana, South Carolina, and the Chesapeake Bay, and more recently from overseas, as well as by establishing or expanding their own crabbing fleets. Interestingly, the practice of establishing crabbing fleets initially took advantage of the H-2 program, with some processors teaching male H-2 workers how to trap crabs and putting them on boats. When local crabbers complained about this practice, which was illegal under the terms of the H-2 contract, these crab house owners replaced H-2 workers on the boats with Mexicans who had been authorized to work as Special Agricultural Workers (SAWs) under the Immigration Reform and Control Act (IRCA). Around the same time, again in an only marginally related, local development, families of Vietnamese fishers moved into Virginia's and North Carolina's crab fisheries, further differentiating the seafood industry's labor force. While the development of new fleets of Mexican and Vietnamese enabled some crab plants to maintain and even expand production of processed crabmeat, work in other plants became more sporadic and less predictable.

As all of these changes converged, crab-picking employment in most African American households was reduced or eliminated altogether. Elderly pickers took this especially hard. "Malcolm [plant owner] didn't need them [the Mexican workers]," one said. "They were full of workers, excellent workers who picked fifty pounds a day, even with bad crabs. They made their living, built their houses off this money. . . . It's like they said, 'You black people, we are through with you.'" Another claimed, "That's what messed it up [the arrival of the Mexicans]. It took all the work from the people. Those Mexicans work all the time." Yet another, pointing to reductions in work, said, "When the Mexicans came, we worked less days. Not enough work for us. Some days I would get home at 9:00 or 10:00 [A.M.]. I'd come home and say to him [her husband], 'Honey, we're picked out.'" Her husband, present at this interview, nodded, adding, "They might as well stay at home." Echoing this, another said, "Only Mexicans worked the evening shift. That cut us out of working at night."

Comments like these are more telling when viewed in the context of household survival strategies in counties with limited economic alternatives. A brief account of one woman's experience illustrates how the program affected some who continued to depend on crab picking after foreign workers arrived. Toni Thule, born in Pamlico County in 1930, began working in the tobacco fields as a youth but in 1975 moved into the seafood industry, shucking oysters and picking crabs. She worked in the crab house with her daughter and several other friends from the community; her daughter predated her as a crab picker, staying with it for twenty-six years. From 1975 to 1990 Toni worked for four different crab plants, one of which went out of business. During this time, in her household of six, her husband was a logger, one of her daughters picked crabs, and her other children took summer jobs in agriculture.

In 1990 Mexicans began arriving at the plant where Toni worked. Between 1990 and 1993 several developments reshaped the composition of her household and her employment strategies. Worst of all, her husband died. Then all of her children but one left home, and the daughter who worked in the crab plant left and took a job in a restaurant. Work in the crab plants became more sporadic. Toni worked on and off between 1990 and 1993. After her husband's death, she moved in with a man who collected disability payments and picked up odd jobs, primarily repairing cars for neighbors and friends. Then one of her sons moved in with them after being released from jail. In attempting to help him find work, she recommended that he apply at the local drugstore instead of the crab plant where she worked. Leaving work in crab altogether, she began subsisting primarily off her husband's Social Security, food stamps, and the generosity of her children and boyfriend.

Toni's case illustrates how crab picking gradually disappeared from the core of her family's livelihood. Not only did work in the crab plants become more sporadic following the arrival of Mexicans, but the social support of having her daughter with her in the plant disappeared as well. Her case, while extreme and complicated by household changes, was similar to that of many women who stayed in the plants with the Mexicans.

At the other extreme were younger women who moved on to other jobs following the arrival of foreign workers, in some cases improving their economic situation. Anna Ipock, at age twenty-nine, secured two jobs in the two years after leaving the crab plants. Both improved her economic position, yet she has continued to seek additional employment. She works from eight to twelve at the Department of Social Services and from three to eleven as a nursing assistant at a local nursing home.

Until 1994 Anna worked for ten years in crab processing, in the same plant where her mother worked. She also held a job with Head Start for ten years while she worked in crab picking. In 1991 the plant owner began importing Mexican workers, causing a reduction in everyone's workload. While many of her co-workers complained, Anna used the extra time to improve her human capital skills. "We worked the same," she said, "but we had more employees, double what was there before, so work was cut to four and a half days." From 1992 to 1993 Anna attended classes at the community college, earning certification as a nursing assistant. In 1994, after ten years in crab picking, she got a job in the nursing home where her sister worked.

Anna's work history and continued job-seeking behavior suggest upwardly mobility, and she viewed the arrival of Mexican workers as yet another opportunity to improve her job skills. In her case, the arrival of temporary foreign workers allowed increased flexibility, while her work in the plant provided income to meet college expenses. Others fared less successfully. The same age and from the same county as Anna, Marcia worked in crab picking from the age of eleven, from 1967 to 1993, three years after Mexicans began arriving in the plant where she worked. Although initially she just picked crab, eventually she took a second job, working in a restaurant at night. She also cleaned houses, lived with a man who worked as a logger, and received food stamps. Over the years she worked in six crab houses. She had a tenth-grade education and took one year of training to learn how to become a bricklayer, but she never found work in that field.

Marcia left crab work in 1993 and concentrated exclusively on working in the restaurant, citing childcare responsibilities as the principal reason for leaving the crab plant. She left the restaurant in 1995 and is currently awaiting receipt of unemployment and living off food stamps and AFDC payments. Both she and her boyfriend, a former logger, are now out of work. She has adopted a far more casual approach to the job market than she used to have, taking odd jobs when she needs to. She believes she could work again in the crab plants if she wanted to—that they would "find her a seat," she says—but currently she spends most of her time taking care of her young children.

These three cases illustrate the varied experiences of crab pickers during the shift from African American to Mexican workers. Generally, those who left the plants found work in tourist-related jobs, nursing and health care, and restaurants. In some cases these jobs improved income security and provided benefits, which the crab plants had never done. About one in five workers quit crab work without finding another job; most of these claimed they were injured at work, and injuries on the job were one reason that workers moved among various crab plants and between crab plants and other economic activities. Some of this movement is due to the relief and recovery time it provides injured workers, which is not uncommon among low-wage workers who work in hazardous industries (Griffith and Valdés Pizzini 2002). Networks among female kin enabled most workers to find employment in other economic sectors.

The profiles of these three women both contradict and lend limited support to plant owners' contentions that domestic workers reject crab-processing jobs because they are receiving welfare benefits. Interestingly, however, fewer African American workers reported collecting welfare benefits in the early 1990s than during the mid-1980s, when I conducted my initial research on the crab industry (Griffith 1993). At that time, too, workers relied more heavily on crab picking than they did ten years later. This suggests that, instead of undermining their labor supply, welfare benefits actually subsidized crab plant owners, allowing workers to accept jobs that were insufficient to lift them above the poverty line. Even so, workers' receipt of these benefits allowed plant owners to justify the shift to Mexican workers, at the same time shifting the burden of subsidizing workers to Mexican families and communities.

One incentive for African American women to leave the plants came from local community colleges. During the late 1980s and 1990s community colleges marshaled extensive outreach programs among women, minorities, and nontraditional students like retirees. Interviews with five community college recruiters in eastern North Carolina counties suggest that the enrollment of African American students in most counties remained relatively constant over that period, accounting for between 8 and 17 percent of total enrollments, yet in Pamlico County, the county with the most crab plants in the mid-Atlantic region, community college recruiters reported that African American enrollment increased. These recruiters also reported that African American women had historically been the second-largest group (after white women) to attend Pamlico County Community College.

The workers we interviewed expressed an interest in education as well. Even those with little formal schooling placed a high value on education, encouraging it in their children; many viewed it as a necessity for finding and keeping a job, even though more than half of the African American women we interviewed had not finished high school. Around one-third, however, had had some community college training, including training in nursing, child care, business administration, upholstering, auto mechanics, computers, and cosmetology. Most women who had taken or were taking these courses were between twenty and forty years of age. Clearly, younger women viewed education as a necessity more often than older women, but even many of the older women we interviewed made comments such as this one, from a woman born in 1931 who had only a tenth-grade education: "I plan on going to Pamlico Tech in January. I might take up nursing. You have to go to school for everything now."

Such comments, combined with the tendency of many of the younger workers to pursue certification at local community colleges, suggest that younger African Americans in rural North Carolina were more upwardly mobile than their parents, perceiving a wider range of economic opportunities and rejecting crab-picking jobs. For them, crab plants provided work only until they found something better. At the same time, younger women rejected crab-picking jobs because working conditions in the crab plants and chances for advancement did not usually compare favorably even to work at local fast food restaurants. Although tourist jobs tend to be seasonal, other coastal jobs are year-round positions with more pleasant working conditions. While many viewed work in crab as "easy money," potentially paying more than minimum wage, this was true only as long as there were enough crabs to pick: the higher earning capability of skilled crab pickers, that is, became threatened as fewer crabs were available per worker. Further, many younger women objected to the quality of supervision in the crab plants, where labor relations were paternal in Gerald Sider's

(1987) sense of the word: customary benevolence interrupted by sporadic and irregular mistreatment. As with industries comprising several small-scale, family-run firms, labor relations were, however, highly variable, with some employers far more benevolent than others, and mistreatment, at least in the years before H-2, tempered when labor was in short supply.

A final note regarding reduced work in the plants concerns its role in the erosion of the authority of elder women over younger female kin and friends. Historically, when crab jobs were the main source of income for poor young women in rural areas, the plants became a setting in which groups of elder women taught and disciplined the younger women whom they brought into the production process; in the community at large, their role in network recruitment provided them with some material means of controlling younger women. The erosion of this control was, of course, liberating from the perspective of younger women, reflecting their increased employment opportunities, but some elderly women lamented the loss of this source of discipline from the lives of youth. One even went so far as to blame younger workers' lack of enthusiasm for crab-picking jobs as the principal driving force behind bringing in Mexicans in the first place, saying, "Now there was a time when the young blacks wouldn't work, so they brought in the Mexicans. So it was the young blacks that hurt the faithful workers." Another blamed the shift to Mexican workers on a somewhat more far-reaching range of problems, saying, "I think they [the Mexican workers] should go back where they came from. We need the work around here. These young girls around here need to go to work and quit getting welfare. They know how to pick. They're able. They can work, but they just mess around."

That younger workers were rejecting these jobs, however, may have had less to do with a desire to escape parental discipline than with resistance to workplace discipline, which became more rigid with the arrival of foreign workers. As ethnic segmentation theory would have predicted, once Mexicans began working in the plants, labor relations deteriorated. "The boss makes it hard on the blacks," said one African American. "He tells you what you are going to do or else he will give your job to a Mexican. I have a few Mexican friends. It's the bosses, not the Mexicans, that treat you bad." African American workers agreed that plant owners began treating them differently after the Mexicans arrived, threatening to replace them with Mexicans and reducing their hours. Plant owners became more demanding, insisting on higher standards of performance and increased worker reliability. This came as a blow particularly to workers who were used to meshing plant schedules with home production schedules, coming to work when they pleased. Of course, from the employer's perspective, operations became more efficient and planning became easier as they pushed African Americans out of the industry.

"They separated us," said one worker. "The blacks worked on one side and the Mexicans on the other. He [plant owner] didn't care if you came to work [before the Mexicans arrived] and then he would say, 'If you don't come to work, you will not have a job.' Also he started grading our work harder, checking our backfin buckets for quality." Another said, "To me personally, everything changed [after the Mexicans came]. It went down for Americans. That's why I left. Days got shorter. Crabs were scarce and there were so many extra workers that it was squeezing out the original workers. Money was short. . . . It hurt the loyal dedicated workers—cut their hours because they brought in so many workers. They can't get new American workers because they know they won't make enough to survive." "We picked more days when they first came, but then crabs slowed down and they we worked less," said another. "As long as the Mexicans are here, we work. When they go back, we don't work. They try to keep work for the Mexicans." Finally, said another, "Crabs were getting scarce anyway and we picked slow, but when they came in it cut us down to a few days. They didn't need all those extra Mexicans. They took our hours."

Most African American workers tended not to blame Mexicans for these changes as much as they did the plant owners. A few admitted that employers attempted to buy more crabs after the Mexicans arrived, to compensate for the imbalances created by labor surpluses, and clearly this would have been in the interests of workers, too. Statistics on production of crabmeat from the Division of Marine Fisheries show, in fact, that in North Carolina at least crabmeat production did increase in the first few years after the arrival of the Mexican workers, from around 8.9 million pounds to 10.8 million pounds, or an increase of around 21 percent (North Carolina Division of Marine Fisheries 1995).

By the mid-1990s, then, Mexicans dominated the crab-processing labor force. The few African American women who stayed on tended to have alternative sources of income (primarily working spouses), were highly productive pickers, or were those elderly workers for whom work in the plants had become tightly interwoven with their social lives. By the summers of 1998 and 1999, we had stopped hearing the kind of negative comments from African Americans who still worked in the crab industry that we'd heard during the transition years. Instead, they commonly spoke of the Mexican women with warmth and praise: "Barnes [pseudonym] was the first one to get Mexicans here to the factory. Some of them had to have had experience in Mexico. But seem like they'd much rather be here. I don't know why. I reckon [to make more money]. Because I'm telling you, they did act like they was tickled to death and they were very sweet, as sweet as they could be. I mean they'd see me on Saturday and they'd all come to me and start hugging me."

A few African American women were instrumental in teaching the Mexican workers how to pick crabs in ways preferred by North American plant owners, adding that they were impressed with the Mexicans' speed. They seemed to hold nothing against them. By 1998, though, for the most part only those African Americans tolerant of the new cultural environment worked in crab.

The shift to Mexican workers may have prompted initial negative responses from African American women, and in some cases left behind a legacy of income insecurity and other forms of economic difficulty, but African Americans weren't alone in these problems. They may have sympathized with the young Mexican women precisely because they saw that they were forced to comply with the new terms of employment. Although I discuss this in more detail later in the book, here I point out that some plant owners took workplace discipline a step beyond what most of us— and certainly what the African American women—consider justifiable, isolating Mexican women in company housing, controlling their transportation, and otherwise keeping them tied closely to the production regimes of the plants. This in turn led to several charges of indentured servitude, legal disputes, Department of Labor investigations, and other problems that forced some plant owners out of business, shaking out some (but not all) of the most exploitive of the employers (Griffith, Heppel, and Torres 1994; Griffith 1999, chapter 4). As a result of these problems and market developments, some crab plants went out of business, and capital became concentrated among those that remained. It also taught some H-2 workers that they need not follow the terms of their visas.

MID-ATLANTIC TOBACCO

A second story comes from the tobacco fields of North Carolina and Virginia. In tobacco, employers began turning to Latino workers in the 1970s and 1980s, in part because of perceptions—similar to those of crab plant owners—that African American crews were becoming less reliable and creating disciplinary problems in the workplace (CAW 1992). Tobacco owners often turned from African American to Latino workers out of racism, yet racism alone cannot account for the shift. Historically, racism has been a crucial ingredient in the *use* of African American labor, justifying extreme power differences, undermining labor unions and labor unity across color lines, and supporting corrupt judgments in court cases that challenged white authority. Like crab plant owners, tobacco farmers routinely blamed government welfare programs for the decline in the availability and reliability of African American labor, but several factors seemed to account for the shrinking supply of and demand for African American workers in southern agriculture.

As mentioned in Chapter 1, the expansion of the service sector, attributable to changing consumption habits and demographic trends over the past forty years, played no small part in increasing employment opportunities available to English-speaking citizens with little education and few skills, including agricultural workers. The mid-Atlantic region experienced rapid population growth from 1970 to 2000, in line with the general shift in population from the Midwest and Northeast to the South. Population growth stimulated the job growth that accompanied the so-called "selling of the South" (Cobb 1982). Employment in the service sector in North Carolina grew from slightly more than 592,000 jobs to more than 993,000 jobs in the 1990s, and Virginia and North Carolina together added between 900,000 and 1,000,000 nonfarm jobs during the same time period (U.S. Bureau of Labor Statistics, 2000).

Job growth in construction, tourism (hotels and restaurants), and health care, linked directly to population growth, as well as the expansion of military duty and employment during and after the Vietnam War, drew African Americans out of agriculture at the same time that Latino crews based in Florida were becoming more organized, more diversified, and more familiar with a wider range of harvests. The Latinization of the South that began in Florida in the 1950s after the mechanization of cotton and sugar beets was far advanced by the mid-1980s in much of the rural South (CAW 1992a; Heppel 1983; Griffith 1993; Griffith et al. 1995; Hahamovich 1997). In Pitt County, North Carolina, where I live, one of the largest tobacco-producing counties in the world, Mexican migrants began to appear in considerable numbers around 1985. This was an uneven process, however, as Florida-based Latino crews had been working in various locations up and down the eastern seaboard beginning as early as the 1970s, and African

American crews remained in harvests well into the 1990s (Hahamovich 1997; Heppel 1983). During two studies of the impact of the immigration reforms of 1986 and 1990 on the poultry and meatpacking industries, we found these industries largely responsible for enabling Latinos to settle out of agriculture and remain in communities in the rural South year round (Bach and Brill 1991; Griffith 1993). Throughout the 1990s, in nearly every small mid-Atlantic town with settlements of Latinos, Latino entrepreneurs established businesses catering to Spanish-speaking patrons, including grocery stores, restaurants, newspapers, radio programs, video rentals, wire transfers, and bus service. Such businesses have facilitated the exchange of information about employment across transnational and transregional space. They have also furthered class differentiation among Latinos that becomes the foundation for more elaborate labor-contracting relations linking the rural South and Midwest to ever more distant and isolated rural communities across Mexico and Central America.

Job growth and Latino immigration help explain the decline in African American workers in agriculture as a response to external developments, yet within African American communities forces took shape following the civil rights movement that contributed to this decline as well. School and neighborhood desegregation had many far-reaching repercussions throughout southern African American communities, not all of them positive. Many African Americans argue that desegregation dealt a significant blow to secular leadership and disrupted African American life in other ways, a charge that historical and social research supports (Cecelski 1994). Businesses that once catered exclusively to African Americans, such as tourist homes, had trouble competing with more powerful, white-owned businesses as both sought African American commerce. The emigration of African American teachers, school administrators, businessmen, and other professionals from historically black neighborhoods and schools furthered class differentiation within the African American community while opening neighborhoods to influxes of other ethnic groups. Those left behind became targets of increased police surveillance and arrest, deepening ties between specific African American neighborhoods and the criminal justice system (Gibson 1990).

These developments left a residue of hostile relations between longtime employers of African American labor and the sons and daughters of African American workers, in part due to stubborn legacies of debt peonage and sharecropping that haunted labor relations between blacks and whites (Daniel 1972). Notes from an interview with a North Carolina tobacco grower illustrate this lingering hostility:

Melvin Garner grew up farming tobacco, surrounded by African American aunts and uncles who used to farm for his family under tenancy and sharecropping arrangements. Unlike many of his neighbors, his family, he said, didn't use "the white man's pencil," or create a system of debt peonage. On other farms, typically, at the end of the season, after deducting for credit and items for the store, workers would be in debt $10. Overcharging for fertilizer was common.

His family never considered this morally correct behavior, and eventually, on his family farm, the elder African Americans became liaisons between him and the African Americans who were younger. Blacks his age, he said, during the 1960s, wouldn't take orders from a white man, but would from an elder black man. When black foremen got too old to work, he had to shift to Latino workers, first using workers legalized under the SAW program and eventually turning to the H-2 program. (Field notes, July 1998)

Melvin's use of SAWs before H-2 workers was common throughout southern agriculture in the years immediately following passage of IRCA. As SAW workers began taking work outside agriculture, many southern growers, now used to Latino workers, shifted to hiring illegal workers from Mexico and Central America. For another North Carolina tobacco grower, the H-2 program merely allowed growers another means, one similar to the SAW program, of legalizing their workers:

Joshua Yellin uses six H-2 workers, a father and his five sons, but these are the same six workers that he has used over the previous three years. Prior to the 1998 season, they were illegal workers, but he converted them to H-2 status after they approached him with this request. Previously, it cost them $1,000 apiece to travel from Mexico to North Carolina, paying *coyotes* and *raiteros,* and they traveled in cramped, dangerous, and unhealthy conditions. In years past they arrived at his farm tired, thirsty, and hungry, after riding in a cramped van for several days and fed, he said, "like dogs."

The workers themselves prefer the H-2 status, because now it costs them only $500 and they take an air-conditioned bus to North Carolina from the Mexican-U.S. border. Yellin deducts the costs of transportation from their pay, along with the $50 per worker he pays to the North Carolina Growers Association. He would like, in particular, to circumvent the Growers Association, but as long as he believes he has to use them, he will, taking the fees (illegally, under the terms of the contract) out of the workers' pay. (Field notes, July 1998)

In both North Carolina and Virginia tobacco, developments both within African American opportunity structures and external to them accounted for the erosion of African American labor in agriculture at the same time Spanish-speaking workers trickled into the region as migrant farm workers. Growers replacing African Americans with Latinos, principally Mexicans legalized under the SAW provisions of the 1986 IRCA, set the stage for the use of H-2 workers. This did not occur overnight, but over a twenty- to thirty-year period and unevenly across the southern landscape. The eventual nearly complete replacement of African Americans by Latinos—which took place primarily in the 1990s—was further bolstered by the elaboration of the Latin presence in and around food-processing plants and the expansion of Latinos across the South in general. Information from upstate New York suggests similar trends with significant differences. There, growers' and packers' long time association with Puerto Rican workers, and their use of Jamaican H-2 workers since the 1940s, complicated the transition from African American to Latino crews.

UPSTATE NEW YORK

In the Finger Lakes region of upstate New York, where the use of *Mexican* H-2 workers is relatively new, I encountered a case of a Mexican workforce replacing an African American workforce almost completely in roughly ten years. Historically, this area has used H-2 workers from Jamaica (a practice that spread from the Hudson River valley further south, where Jamaican H-2 workers still harvest most of the apples), in addition to African American migrants from Florida, southern Georgia, and other parts of the South. The use of Mexican H-2 workers evolved out of a combination of a somewhat bizarre transition within the African American workforce, an entrepreneurial former grower turned labor contractor, and active growers' association advertising in the season following increased INS activity on local farms.

The apple farm where these changes took place in rather extreme form was a family farm owned by the McMillan family (pseudonym), just south of Lake Ontario in Wayne County. This county attracts around six thousand migrants per year for its fruit and vegetable harvest. Until recently these workers originated principally in the band of tomato and onion production of northern Florida and southern Georgia. According to the McMillans, until four or five years ago the crews that arrived each picking season were predominantly specialized harvest crews. Instead of migrating slowly up the eastern seaboard, following crops, these crews worked only the Florida and Georgia harvests, traveled directly to upstate New York to pick apples in the fall, then returned to Florida and Georgia communities like Quincy and Waycross.

Gradually, as the ethnic compositions of the crews in Florida began to change to include more and more Latinos, similar changes occurred in the apple orchards of upstate New York. As elder crew leaders dropped out of the harvest, the younger crew leaders who replaced them were more often than not Latinos themselves, usually Mexican Americans with ties to border families in Texas or to Latino families around Immokalee, Wauchula, Belle Glade, or Homestead, in central and south Florida. The McMillans watched as many other apple growers around them hired Latino instead of African American crews. In time, they too decided to try a Latino crew themselves: first one crew, then another, and another, until all their crews were composed of Latinos.

Coincidental with this transition—and here the story gets bizarre—the character of the few remaining African American crews began to change. According to the McMillans, first a few members of the African American crews were rowdy and cantankerous, challenging Latino workers to fights in the labor camps at night. From one season to the next, more and more of the remaining workers on the African American crews became, in varying ways, more difficult to have on the McMillan farm. The crew leader himself, a man with whom the McMillans had dealt for several years, had taken a transvestite wife, hired a cross-eyed prostitute to travel with the crew, and replaced many of his workers with either gay workers or workers indebted to him because of advances from the prostitute who traveled with the crew. There were, the McMillans claimed, other forms of sexual enslavement going on about which they had only sketchy details but which clearly bothered them. "It was an annual freak show," Jan McMillan said. "The wife, he, she—whatever it was—had hands like baseball mitts and wrists like polish sausages. She had a high, pretty voice and showed porn films with an 8-milimeter projector to entice young men into the crew. Once, when a white man named Champ called him queer, she gave him a roundhouse blow that knocked him across the room. When he came to he was looking up at the plumbing fixtures under the sink. She'd put his head through the cabinet."

Violence in the camps became common. Once, during a fight with a Latino worker, one of the men in the gay crew was so high that he held on to the blade of the Latino's knife until it cut through to the tendons. The McMillans reported that they worked under false names, they shot and beat each other, and they littered the orchard with MD 20/20 and Wild Irish Rose bottles and tall cans of malt liquor.

The McMillans just couldn't understand it. This crew leader whom they had hired for so many years, over the span of two or three years began bringing to their farm crews that were violent and, at least to the McMillans, bizarre. And at the same time the crews were gradually changing from African American to Latino. In one final blow to that last African American crew, the McMillans called the sheriff to arrest several of the crew after a particularly violent fight. When the crew leader learned that the sheriff was coming and tried to leave, Bud McMillan, the young son, poured brake fluid into the crew van's crankcase. "This mixes with the engine oil and produces sulfuric acid," Bud explained, "which causes the engine to fail about two hundred miles down the road." He wanted them to get some distance away, in other words, but not far enough that they wouldn't be caught. After this incident, in 1996, the McMillans fully changed over to Latino workers. Shortly after the shift, they appealed to a special government loan program to build new housing, reporting that much of the old housing had been destroyed during the transition. At this time, however, their crews were not yet H-2 workers but were composed of predominantly undocumented Mexican workers, hired and supervised by a Latino who achieved legal work status under the SAW provisions.

In 1997, the year before the McMillans turned to H-2 workers, an incident involving the INS caused a great deal of debate and labor contractor activity in the area. The incident involved an INS official allegedly firing on an allegedly undocumented immigrant fleeing a field. The local farming community objected strongly to this act of violence, with newspaper coverage of the incident sounding much like coverage of Chicago mayor Richard Daley's infamous "shoot-to-kill" order during the 1968 Democratic convention. According to some sources, this incident stimulated the shift to H-2 workers on several apple farms in Wayne County.

While INS activity may have been a precipitating factor, several developments in the area suggest that the social and physical infrastructure and the psychological predisposition to use H-2s had been forming over several years. This was not the only INS raid or the only action against a grower for hiring unauthorized workers. At another apple farm, the Cormishes claimed to have used H-2 workers in the mid-1980s, more than a decade before the 1997 incident, but shifted to undocumented Mexicans after being sued by lawyers representing H-2 workers and being forced to pay $100,000 in back wages. They hired from the migrant stream for several years thereafter, suffering INS raids and deportations, yet reported that, ironically, "each time the INS raided, more of our workforce became illegal." They still used a core of non-H-2 workers in 1998, supplementing their work force with H-2s during the height of the season.

Other growers who used Mexican H-2 workers had experimented with the H-2 program, on and off, for several years prior to 1997. One of the vegetable producers in the area reported hiring Jamaican H-2 workers after an INS raid in 1996, but after one year of using Jamaicans he shifted to Mexican H-2 workers. "From the walk-ins we were getting," he said, "we thought the Mexicans were better at stoop labor. The Jamaicans were more suited to fruit."

As in other parts of the U.S. South and East, Mexican workers had been showing up in upstate New York for agricultural work for several years prior to the use of Mexican H-2 workers. Increased numbers of Mexican workers began traveling to upstate New York after gaining legal status under IRCA. One local labor contractor, Christian DeLoach (pseudonym), brought in a significant number of the Latino workers, using his ties to labor contractors in Florida to arrange work for his crews in several states before the autumn apple harvest. DeLoach also assisted farmers in obtaining loans to build new labor camps. And DeLoach had been around for more than a decade; when Heppel and Amendola (1992) interviewed growers in Wayne County, New York, in 1989, they found that a grower's first response to a labor shortage was to call DeLoach to arrange for a Mexican crew.

Growers in the region, even if they hadn't used Latino crews, were familiar with them. Indeed, farmers had been using Puerto Rican workers in the area's processing plants for several years, and were still using them in the late 1990s. The use of Spanish-speaking workers was thus well known, and many of the Puerto Ricans could act as translators and intermediaries for the new Mexican workforce. By the time of our research, as the McMillans' experience suggests, Mexican workers had experience harvesting every crop

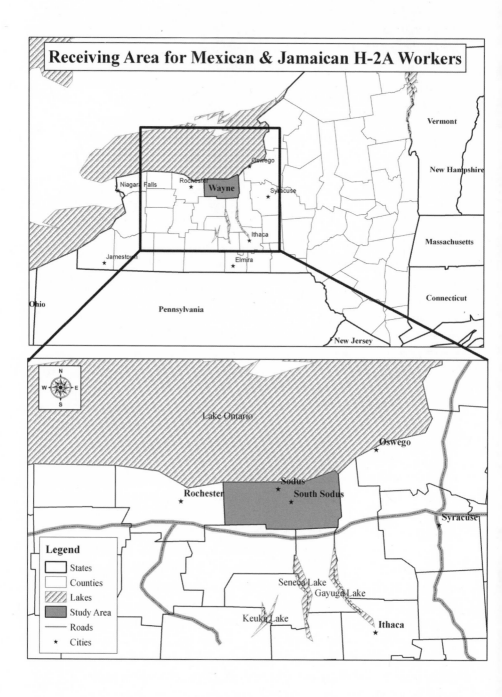

Receiving Area for Mexican & Jamaican H-2A Workers

Vermont

New Hampshire

Niagara Falls

Rochester

Wayne

Oswego

Syracuse

Massachusetts

Ithaca

Jamestown

Elmira

Connecticut

Ohio

Pennsylvania

New Jersey

N
W E
S

Lake Ontario

Oswego

Sodus

Rochester

South Sodus

Syracuse

Seneca Lake

Gayuga Lake

Keuka Lake

Ithaca

Legend

☐ States

☐ Counties

▨ Lakes

▨ Study Area

— Roads

★ Cities

in the region, and large local labor contractors like DeLoach had already established good working relations with Latino crews in Florida and Georgia for the region's vegetable and fruit growers.

Finally, in addition to increasing familiarity with Mexican workers, developments in housing helped set the stage for the use of H-2 workers. The McMillans built new housing only shortly before bringing in H-2 workers. Like most of the labor camps we visited, these units were designed primarily for single males rather than families. Local observers of the farm labor market suggested that the transition from family to single workers was accompanied by an emphasis on housing only productive workers. Rooms that contained unproductive workers, such as children who wouldn't or couldn't work, were viewed as wasted space. We have observed this elsewhere in the United States, including the tobacco-growing regions discussed earlier, and several observers of farm labor practices have written extensively about the role of housing in the social composition of farm labor (CAW 1992a; Griffith et al. 1995; Hahamovich 1997; Heppel and Amendola 1992).

While the shift to dormitory-style housing may not have been a direct precipitating factor in the use of H-2 workers (all of whom are males traveling without families), it did accompany the transition from African American to Mexican labor. Once Mexican workers were employed, housing built for single men rather than families eased the shift to the use of H-2s.

If H-2 programs seem to emerge from the rubble of real and perceived problems with workplace discipline and more general ethnic changes in labor supplies, once in place they seem to become institutionalized rather quickly. The adage that "there is nothing so permanent as a temporary worker" points to this, and in fact, in the region and crop that used H-2 workers longest—Florida sugar—growers' use of H-2 labor did evolve to make the harvest off limits to domestic or other non-H-2 labor even during times of widespread unemployment. Events in the wake of IRCA, however, proved otherwise, and we can find in the story of the demise of H-2 in Florida sugar production important clues to the nature of contract labor in the world today.

AN END OF H-2: JAMAICANS CUT FROM FLORIDA SUGAR

In the early 1990s Florida sugar companies, after more than half a century of importing thousands of British West Indians every year for the sugarcane harvest, abandoned the use of temporary foreign labor. Ironically, the British West Indies Temporary Alien Labor Program stopped providing labor to the sugarcane harvests during a time when, elsewhere in the United States, the use of H-2 workers in agricultural and nonagricultural industries was increasing. Further, the program ended at a time when U.S. immigration policy was being crafted more and more with an eye toward the labor market. Nevertheless, the heightened public debate over immigration reform, particularly over the Seasonal Agricultural Worker (SAW) provisions of the 1986 Immigration Reform and Control Act, laid the foundation for a series of lawsuits that eventually made importing British West Indian labor too costly.

Legal Challenges to the Sugar Program

The successful lawsuit brought against sugar producers on behalf of British West Indian workers was but one of several legal challenges to H-2 programs around the United States. Over the course of the program's history, legal services corporations, acting on behalf of plaintiffs (some of whom were aggressively recruited) challenged the program on several grounds: its use during periods of high domestic unemployment (when, presumably, U.S. workers needed the jobs that sugar companies provided to immigrants), its tendency to create conditions of servitude, the prospect that the program lowered wages and undermined working conditions, and its promotion of dormitory-style housing for single males, a practice discouraging families from farm labor (Griffith et al. 1995).

During their many years in Florida sugar, West Indian workers grudgingly complied with industry practices as long as alternative employment opportunities did not exist in the Caribbean and the hope for alternative conditions did not develop in the United States. One practice particularly symbolic of the power imbalance between capital and labor was the industry practice of undervaluing rows of sugarcane and, by extension, customarily underpaying workers (U.S. Congress 1991, 11–13). Industry representatives called "ticket writers" accomplished this by determining how much a row of cane was worth based on their estimate of its yield in tons of cane. Workers were paid based on the number of rows cut and hence the tons of cane they produced for the factory. Problems arose in discrepancies between what workers considered the worth of rows (i.e., how much cane they would yield) and how ticket writers valued rows, and in productivity levels. Sugar companies expected its workers to cut enough cane in a day to earn the contracted hourly wage rate. If they failed to cut this amount, companies were contractually bound to make up the difference in pay—between earnings according to hours worked and earnings based on the piece rate. Workers who could not reach the designated productivity level—one above that which required the companies to compensate them—were cut from the program and sent home. Knowing the consequences of failing to achieve these levels, workers routinely agreed to underreport the number of hours they worked per day.

What is important here is not only that underpayment of wages was customary but that the sugar companies set productivity levels so high that achieving them was both nearly impossible and dependent on the judgment of the ticket writer. This reduced company wage bills while solving one of the principal threats to the H-2 program: the occasional attempts by non-H-2 workers to work in the cane fields. In a complaint against the sugar companies, a Haitian refugee, seeking work cutting cane, was hired for five weeks, fired for not achieving the standard productivity level, and subsequently blacklisted from sugarcane-cutting employment in the future. Part of his complaint reads: "After about five weeks, I was fired for not cutting cane quickly enough. It was never explained to me exactly what production would be required of me in order to keep my job. Toward the end of the day, the 'fieldwalker' [ticket writer] measured my row. At that point, I was only five feet away from the stake that the company had placed in the ground designating the finishing point for my day's task. The 'fieldwalker' told me I was fired, even though I was almost finished with the task" (*Cebonet v. Florida Fruit and Vegetable Association*, U.S. Department of Labor, ETA, Case No. 2-83, March 8, 1983). The following season, when Cebonet attempted to apply for another cane-cutting job with another company, he stated, "I was informed that if I was on the sugar companies' list of unsatisfactory workers [a list maintained by the Florida Fruit and Vegetable Association], no Florida sugar company would hire me as a cane cutter."

Blacklisting and underpayment of wages may have been the most opprobrious manifestations of the capital-labor power imbalance, but they were only two of several. On both sides of the border West Indian H-2 workers were cheated out of millions of dollars of wages annually through payroll deductions. Workers and their advocates disputed both a 23 percent compulsory savings program and a 2 percent insurance deduction that were established by the West Indian Central Labour Organization (WICLO), the organization that managed the program in the Caribbean. WICLO was made up of government officials, usually from the Ministries of Labour of the various participating companies, as well as a few permanent staff. They negotiated the contract on behalf of the workers, assisted in recruiting and transporting workers, and supposedly represented workers in grievances against the companies. Several incidents in the mid-1980s brought to the foreground the ways in which WICLO officials and others used their positions to profit from worker deductions. First, investigations reported in Jamaica's newspaper, the *Daily Gleaner,* raised the possibility that Jamaican Ministry of Labour officials were using the compulsory savings monies to purchase durable goods in Canada and the United States for resale in Jamaica. While they reimbursed these accounts following the sale of these goods, the accounts themselves paid workers no interest (*Queen v. James Smith,* Resident Magistrates Court, Kingston, Jamaica, 103,117, quoted in U.S. Congress 1991, 9–10). Second, the 1991 congressional investigation found that a 2 percent insurance deduction generated more than $600,000 over and above the cost of the insurance policy covering the workers, and that the policy's benefits were "so minimal as to be meaningless in the U.S. health care system" (U.S. Congress 1991, 10). Additional deductions for food and transportation were also illegal.

West Indian sugar workers were mistreated in other ways as well. In several letters attached to questionnaires returned to lawyers suing the sugar companies for back wages, as well as on film in Stephanie Black's award-winning documentary *H-2 Worker,* West Indians lodged complaints ranging from workplace injuries and their lingering complications to having to drink polluted water. In one incident that Black captured on film, several workers, following a dispute over pay, were herded by police and police dogs into buses, immediately shuttled to Miami, held in detention centers, and returned to Jamaica. In one of the letters to attorneys for Florida Rural Legal Services, one Jamaican, probably an unwitting participant in the dispute (whose identifiers I have changed), wrote:

> "Dear Sir Madam: Greetings in the Mighty name of the Lord Jesus our Soon Coming King. Yes I have this Problem. I am a Jamaican farm worker I have Been up to the State Eight times, work for the Okeelanta Corporation. Last year I went up the 20th of October I work three weeks and there was a dispute witch took place Concerning Some Cane price some five hundred of us was force to leave and send home. Some of us did not get a chance to take any of our Belonging with us. When we reach at Miami at the holding Center some Liason officer came there and take names of those

who leave thing Behind. I gave him my name and until now I dont hear or reseave anything from them so I am asking if you people could help me out in this problem. I leave at the Camp four pants and four shirts and there was $150 I had in a key wallet in the pant pocket on my Bed and that's where it was at the time of the incident on my Bed. I did not know what was taken place out side until the Security came in side the Building and told us to get out side. We had was to do as we were told. I have two pay stub with my saving the first one with $36.69 and $93.57 and I haven't reseave any pay ment as yet. OK my contract no is J-50253 Rafael McWest with the above address. I am looking forward to hear from you soon. With thanks, R. McWest."

In preparation for the lawsuit that eventually ended the program, lawyers for the workers collected more than two file cabinets' worth of letters like McWest's, volunteering information above and beyond what the lawyers requested. Many of these letters revealed similar concerns packaged in similarly effusive tidings and salutations, reflecting the willingness of workers to join a complaint against the sugar companies while still expressing lingering hopes for help. These letters and the newspaper coverage also relate the fear in which H-2 workers occupied U.S. soil. "Security came in side the Building and told us to get out side. We had . . . to do as we were told."

The incident at Okeelanta that Mr. McWest described occurred in November 1986. News articles in the Jamaican press focused on issues similar to those raised by McWest: the exercise of raw power and the workers' loss of money and clothes. "Nearly 200 Jamaican farm workers who were fired from their jobs in Florida," one report began, "returned home yesterday afternoon saying that dogs and soldiers were used to chase them from the camp where they were staying, and at least two workers say they were bitten by dogs. . . . The obviously depressed and frustrated farm workers said that they were forced to flee the camp leaving behind their money and other personal belongings" (Pixley 1986). Following the incident, as the initial public disgust and bitterness faded, *Gleaner* articles and editorials raised the issue that problems such as this could jeopardize the H-2 program at a time when the U.S. Congress was debating immigration reform—including the potential reform of the program or the replacement of Jamaican workers with either Mexican or Chinese workers. News coverage in this vein tended to suggest that Jamaican Ministry of Labour officials failed to act as effective liaisons for Jamaican farm workers, and ministry officials responded with visits to the United States to meet with sugar company officials and others with interests in the program.

In the years after the 1986 Okeelanta incident, at least four developments further undermined the program: (1) U.S. immigration reforms, which stimulated the sugar companies' opposition to legalizing Jamaican cane cutters (1985–87); (2) Stephanie Black's 1991 film documentary, *H-2 Worker*, which captured part of the Okeelanta incident and received awards and widespread news coverage; (3) the revelation, in 1992, that Jamaican Ministry of Labour officials were misusing farm workers' savings accounts; and (4) a flurry of social research on immigration in the wake of the reforms of the late 1980s and early 1990s.

Throughout the 1980s and 1990s, successive waves of immigration reform created political and economic conditions that helped legal services attorneys mount successful challenges to the sugar industry and its labor practices. In 1986 immigration reform raised the possibility that Jamaicans might become authorized for work under the SAW program of IRCA. Again, as noted earlier, agricultural workers who could prove they had worked in U.S. agriculture for ninety days in the three years prior to the passage of IRCA would be granted work authorization. While many thousands of Jamaican workers who had cut sugarcane for several years prior to 1986 fulfilled these requirements, the sugar companies used their influence to exempt Jamaican workers from SAW status, a change that would have jeopardized their control over this labor supply and perhaps threatened the H-2 program itself by flooding south Florida's labor market with obviously skilled cane cutters whom the Florida Fruit and Vegetable Association would have trouble blacklisting for low productivity. It is likely, too, that an authorized labor force with free movement within the U.S. labor market would have been more militant in their opposition to underpayment of wages, unfair deductions, and other abuses, happily lending their depositions to the lawyers who were challenging the sugar companies.

Jamaican sugar workers were well aware of the changes in U.S. immigration law and the possibility that they might be able to apply for SAW status under IRCA. In addition to coverage of IRCA in the Jamaican press, lawyers for the workers, in letters updating them on the status of the lawsuits, indicated that the new reforms might result in resident status for them but that the sugar companies were opposing these provisions:

> We would like to tell you about the new immigration law in the United States. This law passed in November and it may give green

cards (permanent resident status) to farmworkers who have worked for the past few years in the United States on the contract. Workers with a green card are permitted to legally live in the United States with their families and may work at any job in the United States. The government of the United States has not yet decided which workers will be able to apply for these green cards. . . . The sugar companies are fighting very hard to stop the contract workers from getting green cards, but we have hope that all contract workers will be eligible. (Schell 1987)

Given the emphasis on continued work in the United States in letters received by workers, workers very probably viewed the sugar companies' opposition to their legalization as cruel and immoral, particularly when juxtaposed to the lawyers' work on behalf of Jamaican farm workers. Again and again workers emphasized their appreciation for the lawyers' work, nearly always expressing their appreciation in the first person plural, as members of a class rather than as individuals, as seen in the sample passage below:

> I have received your letter and read through the contents carefully and everything is clearly understood. I must inform you without further delay that I am VERY grateful for whatever you are doing for me and the other Farmworkers. I must also say I appreciate it very much that you find time to respond to our letters. . . .
> Thank you very much for your concern for us workers. . . .
> Good day in the Presus name of Jesus I was very happy when I received your letter for this thing we were looking for and we thank God that it come through. I thank you and all your teem that work on this case to make it successfully may God Bless you.

While the sugar companies eventually won the battle to deny SAW status to Jamaican H-2 sugar workers, the victory was short lived. Shortly after this, the lawyers' efforts to recruit Jamaican workers into their lawsuit began to pay off. Within five years of the passage of IRCA, as the H-2 program began expanding in other parts of the country, the sugar companies, after paying millions in back wages and having to increase their wage bills because they could no longer underreport workers' hours, began shifting slowly from Jamaican H-2 labor to machines.

As noted above, the decision to force the sugar companies to pay back wages did not occur in a vacuum. In addition to increased attention to the program due to the 1987 strike incident and Stephanie Black's film, this was a time of a flurry of social scientific research on immigration, much of it funded by the U.S. Department of Labor and the Commission on Agricultural Workers in direct response to immigration reforms passed under IRCA. Anthropologists, economists, political scientists, sociologists, interested policy scribes, and worker and employer advocates took part in these research efforts, meeting in a variety of settings either to exchange ideas or to influence the direction of immigration policy. Several published works, government documents, and technical reports resulted from these endeavors (e.g., Papademetriou et al. 1988; Bach and Brill 1991; CAW 1992a, 1992b, 1992c), including many that became important to lawyers suing the sugar companies.

SUMMARY

In New York apples, North Carolina and Virginia tobacco, and North Carolina crabs, the shift from African American to H-2 workers did not occur overnight, nor was it a smooth, even process. Factors within and outside African American communities disrupted decades-old ties between employers and workers, and the process of moving from one workforce to another did not happen without turmoil and pain. In each of the regions and industries, it would be difficult to characterize the arrival of H-2 workers as the direct cause of the widespread displacement of native, usually African American, workers. Among the elderly this may have been the case, but most younger African American workers were turning their backs on these jobs before H-2 workers arrived. Instead, in New York apples and mid-Atlantic tobacco, H-2 workers seem to have replaced unauthorized Latino workers who make up most of the agricultural labor force today (NAWS 2000). Nearly a decade and a half after IRCA's legalization program, the proportion of SAWs in the agricultural work force has fallen, while the proportion of unauthorized workers has risen. A perceived threat of INS raids, heightened by recent reports from the Social Security Administration showing the number of suspect social security numbers among their workers to employers, has provided employers the rationale for the use of H-2A workers.

Clearly, H-2 workers stabilize production by assuring a predictable supply of labor in the wake of what employers perceive as workforces that are deteriorating from within. Yet the benefits of H-2 to employers extend beyond this. As we have seen, they also allow employers to keep wage levels separate from the pressures of a free market economy, as employers continue to rely on political solutions to economic problems. In the cases of H-2 workers in the Florida sugar industry, employers undoubtedly exploited political conditions to control and underpay workers. This may have contributed to the program's precipitous decline after half a century.

Florida sugar companies may have set the stage for the use of H-2 workers in U.S. agriculture, but their exercise of power, shown most clearly in the systematic underpayment of wages over many years, could not continue under the critical mass of information that emerged in the late 1980s and early 1990s. Similarly, during an earlier period, the much larger Mexican Bracero Program came under fire as part of the broader civil rights legislation that moved the country toward more humane treatment of workers in general, a period the British West Indies Temporary Alien Labor Program survived (Calavita 1992; Griffith 1987; U.S. Congress 1978). The victorious lawsuit, of course, proved a mixed blessing among Jamaicans. Many still want to work in the sugar program, and that many still wish to work in the United States is evident in the popularity of those H-2 programs for Jamaicans that continue: the apple program in the northeastern United States and the growing use of Jamaicans in the tourist industry as chambermaids and waiters. When Luis Torres and I interviewed the Jamaican minister of labour in 1994, he defended his predecessors for their use of H-2 workers' money, claiming that "Not a single penny was missing from workers' accounts," and he lamented the growing use of Mexicans in the H-2 program, citing, specifically, the crab-picking program. Though Jamaica has no blue crab industry similar to the one in which many Mexicans receive their training prior to coming to the United States, the minister nevertheless saw this as a relatively unskilled job, adding, "Our people could do that."

PART II

JAMAICAN EXPERIENCES, 1981–2001

THREE

FROM BEAUTY TO TRUTH

> I died for Beauty – but was scarce
> Adjusted in the Tomb
> When One who died for Truth, was lain
> In an adjoining Room –
>
> He questioned softly "Why I failed"?
> "For Beauty," I replied –
> "And I – for Truth, – Themself are one –
> We Brethren, are," He said –
>
> And so, as Kinsmen, met a Night –
> We talked between the Rooms –
> Until the Moss had reached our lips –
> And covered up – our names –
>
> —EMILY DICKINSON

In central Jamaica, near the lip of the Yankee Valley, through a small opening in the bush, a well-worn footpath dips to a narrow creek and climbs up the opposite bank to a gravel road. The creek winds through fields of yams, red beans, and potatoes and a tropical understory of large, leafy root crops like cassava and dashien before emptying into the Yankee River. It is one of many small runnels and streams that make up the Two Meetings watershed, named for the meeting of the Yankee and Cave rivers. Throughout Two Meetings, first Norwegian and later U.S. government funds encouraged the local people to control soil erosion with terraces, drainage ditches, and pine trees. When I worked there in the early 1980s, bunches of pine saplings sat at irregular intervals on the high gravel road connecting the footpaths crossing the valley. Each seedling was wrapped in black plastic and available to anyone to take and plant for free. All across the valley were cement-lined ditches and fields terraced with local labor, foreign capital, and freshly cut bamboo.

For eight months in 1982 I crossed this network of ditches, streams, and terraced fields nearly every day, wearing down the same footpaths that Jamaicans had traveled for generations, climbing into and out of the valley. I visited people who farmed and inhabited the valley—households of families I called peasants in my notes and in the articles I published, using the term in the way A. V. Chayanov, Eric Wolf, William Roseberry, and Theodore Shanin had done. The families I visited *were* peasants, at least in the sense that they used family labor to farm small parcels of land primarily for their own subsistence, yet they were of course much more than that. As the sunlight waned late in the day and I approached that narrow opening in the bush, at that narrow nameless creek, I often encountered the same man wearing a black beret and goatskin vest and smoking a cone-shaped, five-inch-long marijuana cigar. He was a goatherd, driving five or six goats into the valley I was just about to leave, to tether them on long ropes and

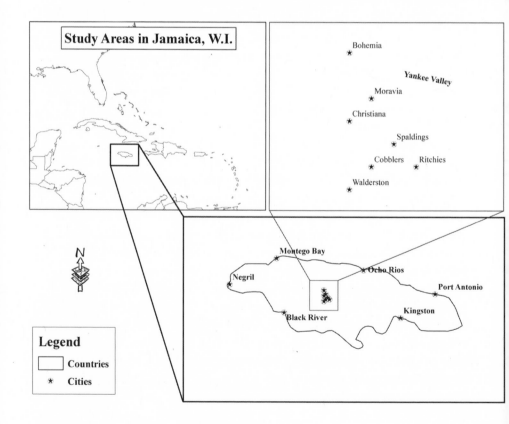

let them forage and feed through the night. We always exchanged a word or two in greeting, but rarely more. I was tired of talking, exhausted from fieldwork and my daily climb, and he was performing what may have been one of his last tasks of the day. I never knew any more about him until one day when our landlady's maid, Tina, agreed to make my family curried goat.

While chicken, beef, and pork sold in the Friday and Saturday markets in the nearby town of Christiana, goat meat sold on a hillside outside of town on Sunday. I don't know why, exactly, but it may have been that curried goat, like akee and saltfish, is a signature Jamaican dish. Perhaps goat meat's special place in the Jamaican diet demanded a special place for its sale. That Sunday I saw the man with the beret and goatskin vest again, only this time with his goats tethered to stakes in the clearing on the hillside. Beside him was a long collapsible table with stainless steel mixing bowls full of goat meat, plastic bags, and a portable scale. Near the table stood an iron apparatus with legs and a crossbar even with the man's beret. We exchanged a simple, familiar greeting—the same we exchanged almost every day near the lip of the Yankee Valley—and I asked for five pounds of goat meat. He looked at the meat in bowls on the table, calculated quickly, and then in several deft moves swept up the smallest of the live goats, tied it to the crossbar by its hind legs, slit its throat, and, as the blood drained from the goat's twitching body, began methodically cutting away the hide for my five pounds of meat.

I had never before seen an animal slaughtered and butchered so swiftly and efficiently, but it was all second nature to the goatherd. This was how he made his living. Or at least part of how he made his living. Like other Jamaicans I have come to know over the past twenty years, the goatherd's work with goats was only one of several livelihoods. I happened to see the goatherd in the evenings, as my own day's fieldwork was drawing to a close, because he had spent his day in other pursuits—farming, helping a friend build a house, unloading concrete from trucks at the hardware store—and now was "finishing" his day with yet another activity that helped him make ends meet.

My goatherd acquaintance was by no means alone. Changes in the nature of work, combined with the erosion of subsistence security around the world, encourage people everywhere to string together multiple ways of increasing their incomes and reducing their costs of living. Quite often, for people from places like Mexico or Jamaica, engaging in multiple livelihoods involves migrating and working low-wage, seasonal, and hazardous jobs. These jobs are often so difficult and taxing that, once they are finished, workers need prolonged periods of rest. In my work on seafood and poultry workers in the U.S. South during the 1980s and 1990s, I found that it wasn't uncommon for these workers to quit their jobs periodically for relief from the debilitating muscular disease called carpal tunnel syndrome (Griffith 1993). Mark Grey's work in midwestern meatpacking plants recorded similar behavior among workers from various parts of Mexico (Grey 1999). In our recent book on Puerto Rican fishers (2002), Manuel Valdés Pizzini and I argue that Puerto Rican fishers who work in difficult jobs in agriculture and industry on the U.S. mainland return to fishing in the beautiful waters of the Caribbean as a therapeutic response to occupational injury. Should we expect similar behaviors from Jamaicans returning from difficult labor in the orchards, fields, and greenhouses of the United States and Canada?

At a meeting at the University of Guelph, Canada, in the winter of 2003, Jamaican researcher Roy Russell, summarizing preliminary findings from a study of Jamaicans who work for part of the year in Canada as legal seasonal farm workers, remarked that it puzzled him that the same Jamaican who received high praise for his hard work on a Canadian farm could return to Jamaica and spend most of his time in lazy activities, smoking ganja, gambling, and drinking rum (Russell 2003). For me, Roy's comments resonated not so much with my own previous findings about injury and therapy among Puerto Rican fishers, because fishers work hard while at home, but with Kenneth Carter's book on the Jamaican working class and with an article I'd just read, by Ilka Thiessen, on the work ethic among highly trained engineers in the former socialist state of Macedonia (Carter 1997; Thiessen 2002). In her paper, Dr. Thiessen suggests that many Macedonian engineers work extremely hard in foreign settings specifically because one of their greatest desires is to live, quite publicly, lifestyles that appear leisurely—the lifestyles, frankly, of the rich. They live a paradox of deriving their status from both very, very hard (and at times degrading) work for foreign firms and very, very leisurely living in the open-air coffee houses and cafés of Skopke, Macedonia, lending a new empirical twist to Thorstein Veblen's understanding of conspicuous consumption—a cornerstone of leisure. Yet the engineers Dr. Thiessen studied hardly belong to the leisure class. While working abroad, they struggle in positions that their peers consider beneath them and in some cases are as exploited as the world's most vulnerable workers: immigrants, children, young women working under authoritarian male regimes, and so forth. Yet their fellow Macedonian engineers deeply desire, and envy, their foreign jobs.

While Thiessen's work focuses on highly skilled workers, Kenneth Carter's book analyzed nearly all segments of Jamaica's working class in virtually all formal sectors of Jamaica's economy. Through surveys with eight thousand workers and two thousand supervisors, Carter suggests that Jamaican workers are at least as concerned about respect and control of the workplace as about wages and benefits. By directing attention to other facets of the work experience and its relationship to leisure, both Thiessen and Carter offer at least partial explanations of why Jamaicans returning from Canada might be less likely to work as hard as they had worked prior to entering the program.

If such behavior is common, it raises questions about the impact of the program on Jamaica and, by extension, the importance of migration and guest work abroad to sending communities' cultures, societies, and economies. Clearly, in the daily lives of the migrants, participation in guest-worker programs generates ambivalence, and that ambivalence often engenders other behaviors that are difficult for an outsider to interpret. For one thing, the work is often so difficult that those of us who write and read books like this have little idea what their bodies take day in and day out, for months on end. A Jamaican woman I came to know relatively well through the late 1990s and early 2000s, Victoria Barrow, was a widow with five children when she first migrated to Kingston Plantation, in Myrtle Beach, South Carolina, to work as a chambermaid under the H-2B program.

A magnet for tourists with its golf and beach vacations, Myrtle Beach's popularity during the height of the tourist season made Victoria's workload grueling. On a typical day she cleaned between a dozen and sixteen rooms, with more than 90 percent "checkouts," which required deep cleaning and several additional tasks. She had trouble believing the messes guests made—bloodied sheets, wine stains on cushions, chicken bones thrown in the corners, vomit around the commode. Guests used the linens and towels like rags, shining shoes, cleaning windshields, mopping up barbeque sauce. She worked well beyond five o'clock every day, usually six to seven days a week, waited for a bus after work, and cared for an ailing man in the evening as payment toward her room and board.

Back in Jamaica, was it any wonder she rested? She believed she deserved it. During her long stay abroad she sent cash to her eldest daughter, Paula, and her sister Catherine, who used it to meet household expenses, buy the children food, clothing, and supplies for school, and attempt in other ways to maintain or improve their economic circumstances. In this regard, Victoria, Paula, and Catherine were no different from other women I met in

Jamaica years earlier, when I was visiting the families of men working in south Florida's sugar fields and the apple orchards further north. They too used their remittance largely to feed people in their networks, maintain their households, and send their children to school. In his 2002–3 study, Roy Russell found that the 5,081 workers who went to Canada in 2002 supported 19,563 dependents, or an average of close to four people per worker, most of them women (2003). In this sense, women, as the principal recipients of wages sent home from abroad, participate in North American temporary worker programs, though indirectly, in greater numbers than men.

WOMEN, REMITTANCES, AND REPRODUCTION

Understanding women's participation in the programs is crucial to understanding who finances the reproduction of working people and their social and economic conditions and how that reproduction is accomplished—central issues in understanding poor households, like Victoria's, that supply labor to capitalist business as part of multiple methods of making ends meet. Investigating how reproduction occurs—how, that is, people reach working age in good enough health to work for wages themselves—is especially helpful in explaining how and why poor households remain tied to specific production regimes, such as peasant farming, even in the face of multimillion-dollar development packages like those at work in the Two Meetings watershed. Peasants are particularly important in this regard, because even households like Victoria's benefit from peasant or small farm production. Many of the chambermaids who worked in the H-2B program, including Victoria, had extensive ties to the Jamaican countryside and its produce.

That peasant households subsidize the expansion or continued strength of capitalist industries is something that social scientists have known since the early 1970s (Painter 1984; Collins 1984; Griffith and Valdés Pizzini 2002; Meillassoux 1972; Long and Richardson 1978; Long 1977; Deere 1983; Deere and de Janvry 1979; de Janvry 1983; Striffler 2002). Peasant households produce inexpensive foodstuffs and other products to satisfy household members' subsistence requirements and to sell to urban markets, providing part of their own household income and thus making up for any need that their wages fail to meet. Assuming wages were sufficient to meet the household's total income needs, of course, peasant production would return a surplus to the household, generating an investment fund, yet most empirical research suggests that this is not the case. Wages are usually insufficient, and household production must thus make up the difference between the total household income needs and the needs that wages cover. More important here, however, is that peasant production allows household members to accept jobs at wages below the costs of maintaining and reproducing their households.

Through social and trade networks with people like Victoria, peasants often contribute to the subsistence needs of urban workers by providing low-cost or free foodstuffs, free labor and services, and house construction materials (Portes and Walton 1979, 88–91). Another chambermaid I met in 2001, Janice Wingate, drew on contributions from four different households—three rural and one urban—to support her participation in the H-2B program. One household, her aunt's, was in a new urban neighborhood in Black River, on the southern coast, while the other three—one belonging to her and her children, another belonging to her parents, and a third belonging to an uncle—were thirty minutes from her aunt's place, in a small town called Ramble. In the compound that included her parents' and her own residence, there were a few head of livestock, a small kitchen garden, and a small store where her brothers repaired stereos and other electronic equipment. Within walking distance of the compound were small fields of beans, yams, and other crops that the father of her children tended.

Janice used her aunt's address in Black River as her principal contact point for the Ministry of Labour because of its phone and urban address. She relied on her rural uncle, who had been an H-2A sugarcane worker in Florida in the 1970s and 1980s, for the initial political connections that got her into the H-2B program, and they were able to appeal for the placement in part because Janice's father was incapacitated. From her parents' and her own rural household, she, her brothers, and her children's father relied on the produce from the garden, livestock, and fields, the small income that the repair shop generated, and of course Janice's earnings from the United States.

By pooling resources in this way, households absorb much of the cost of producing working people and maintain the unemployed, unproductive, and less productive members of the labor force. These arrangements are not without their difficulties; in the next chapter we'll see that drawing on such a wide network of resources demands returning value to members of the network and the network itself. This is particularly difficult when members of the network are, like Janice's father, incapacitated, requiring nearly constant attention and care. Under these conditions, development efforts like those in the Two Meetings watershed, designed to control soil erosion and make Jamaican farmers more successful and self-sufficient, contradict the logic of capitalist production. Yet by maintaining and reproducing their production regimes at modest levels, peasants bear the majority of their own reproductive costs, resulting in savings to those industries, like Gulf & Western Sugar or Radisson Hotels, that hire them. As oxymoronic as it may sound, by putting some of their earnings into peasant agriculture, these workers, in a way, finance their continued impoverishment.

The issue of reproduction versus development is especially important when workers from poorer and underdeveloped countries migrate to work in richer, highly developed ones. Many view labor migration as one way that wealthy nations offer a helping hand to their poorer neighbors. Immediately after World War II, scholars and politicians commonly assumed that international labor migration from poor to rich countries would benefit the sending countries in a variety of ways (U.S. Congress 1978; Rasmussen 1951; Reubens 1979; Spengler and Myers 1977). First, emigration would reduce unemployment in the sending countries. Second, migrants would send back portions of their paychecks regularly, helping those they left behind make ends meet and invest in businesses, farms, and other enterprises. These remittances would help, too, with the poorer nation's need for foreign exchange to service debt and pay for exports. Later the migrants would return with skills and savings that they would put to use in their home countries, facilitating capital formation, and remittances would aid in reducing balance-of-payments deficits.

As is now relatively well known to analysts of international labor migration, these predicted consequences materialized unevenly (Binford 2002; Basok 2000; King and Strachen 1980; Magnarella 1979; Brandes 1975). In most cases, migration either exacerbated or created the very problems that inhibited development. Though migrants did remit portions of their earnings, instead of stimulating investment this created a dependence on remittances (Rubenstein 1983), helping to institutionalize migration and create transnational migrants who draw on material and emotional support from two or more nations and communities (Basch et al. 1994; Glick-Schiller 1999; Levitt 2001; Reichert 1981). Higher overseas earnings relative to local incomes have inflated local land prices (Dinerman 1978), increased the demand for imported goods (OECD 1978; Richman 1992), and removed land and other resources from production (Cohen 1999; Rhodes 1978). These findings, based on empirical research rather than assumptions, observed in the sending countries rather than deduced by the receiving countries, led to the revision of earlier assumptions about the impact of international labor migration and raised a new generation of social scientific inquiry. Analysis of international labor migration shifted, at first, from the receiving to the sending countries and subsequently to both, with increasing interest in transnational migrants (Basch et al. 1994; Gmelch 1980; Grasmuck and Pessar 1996; Mahler 1995; Rouse 1992; Glick-Schiller 1999). In an effort to address questions of the costs of producing labor, as opposed to the benefits of development brought about by labor migration, many of these studies sought to determine how the earnings of the migrants were used at home. Were migrants' earnings used for savings, investment, primitive accumulation, capital formation, or capital accumulation? Or were they used primarily to reproduce labor and the social and economic conditions that make transnational migration a necessary and even desirable economic alternative?

I devote most of this chapter to examining the impact of remittances of Jamaican H-2 workers on reproduction and development based on how women in Jamaica use those remittances. The focus on women derives from their being, as noted earlier, the principal recipients of remittances not only in Jamaica but around the world, even if they receive those remittances from other women, as Paula does from Victoria. I argue that seasonal labor migration, as a common means of incorporating poor households into capitalist labor markets, allows families in sending countries to meet the costs of reproducing themselves and their social and economic conditions. Women play a crucial role in this process by bearing and raising children, by keeping network ties and income-pooling strategies alive, and by overseeing farm production operations while male household members are gone for extended periods to work abroad.

Most of the data for this discussion come from two phases of fieldwork, the work in central and southern Jamaica in 1982–83 and the more recent work with H-2B chambermaids from 1998 to 2001. Whether the families were engaged directly in agriculture or benefited from Jamaican peasant production indirectly, as Victoria did, mattered less than the fact that their links to Jamaican farming and other economic activities were critical to meeting their household subsistence needs. In any case, most studies have found that more than 90 percent of the farm workers to Canada and the United States come from peasant or small farming backgrounds, though more of the H-2B hotel workers come from urban areas with links to the countryside (Russell 2003; Griffith, Heppel, and Torres 1994). More commonly, through ties to children, parents, and significant others, chambermaids like Janice Wingate participate directly in two or more households and rural and urban areas in Jamaica, thus drawing directly on both rural agricultural produce and urban services. At an international level, transnational connections take advantage of national services and economic disparities (Glick-Schiller 1999; Richman 2005).

The characteristics of Jamaican peasant agriculture and the distribution networks for its produce make it clear that small farms rarely provide enough income to meet all of a household's consumption needs but that they are nevertheless capable of meeting bare household caloric needs through the year. Agriculture throughout most of the Caribbean has been dominated by plantations since the early days of European colonization, monopolizing most of the flat, fertile coastal plains and leaving the more marginal, hilly interior regions for small or peasant farming. Jamaicans' farms tend to be so small—between one and five acres—that they measure them in tenths of acres, called "squares." Each household usually raises one or two head of livestock—a goat, most frequently, or a cow or pig—keeping them as "savings accounts" in case of emergency or, among guestworkers, selling them just before traveling to the United States or Canada to cover traveling expenses.

Where I worked in central Jamaica in the early 1980s, most farms occupied slopes along valley walls. They tended to be fragmented, families farming several small plots that were sometimes many miles apart. While this increased the time it took to get from field to field, widely separate fields also gave farmers access to different soil types and mixes of bush and cleared land for tethering livestock. Most households had access to a variety of fruit trees, including papayas, jack fruit, coconuts, oranges, and bananas. Their house-and-yard compounds, usually swept dirt, typically contained a smoky scrap-wood kitchen and house of concrete block or wood with a zinc or thatch roof (Mintz 1974). Slightly fewer than half the people I interviewed lived in houses with electricity, though only one in ten had indoor plumbing.

The household's kitchen garden was usually near or within this compound—called a kitchen garden because most of its produce supplied the household's kitchen needs for fresh vegetables, onions, garlic, thyme, ginger, some fruits like pineapple, and assorted other herbs and spices. Often these gardens were beautified and perfumed with bougainvillea, begonias, small orchids like yellow buttercups, and other ornamental flora. Women gardened near the house. I have not altered the spelling or punctuation of this letter from Rupert Herriot, describing the division of labor between his mother and father in a letter to me: "My father and mother was very poor and They have it very heard in life and They have to plant a Little Long Fearm Crop like yam, CoCa, and banana, and a Little Catch Crop Like Corn. Red Pease. and Sweet Potata. yes he did farming only he sometimes hired Three men for the week, and my brthers and sisters were old enought to help them them sleives at That time (she have five of us). She Plant her Little garden around the house. She Cook. Wash. and Cleane. She also do domitic job outside to help us to go to school."

Rupert eventually inherited a part of his father's farm, sharing it with two sisters, three brothers, two half-sisters, and one half-brother, but when I worked in the Two Meetings watershed his father hadn't yet died. On his own, he had managed to gain access to five plots of land to farm, two of which he owned and the other three of which he gained access to through rental and other arrangements. The first was his house plot, one of his largest, 2.5 squares in size; this sat next to the road running along the top of the valley. On this land he built his house, planted a small garden, and had enough land left over to put in a small "catch crop" (a crop grown quickly for sale) of carrots or onions, along with his staple crops of red peas, yams, and corn.

The second plot, far down the valley, only a few yards up the slope from the Yankee River, was three-fourths of a square in size and good land for planting potatoes. This particular plot belonged to an elderly gentleman named James Franklin who owned and farmed several large plots around the watershed. A shrewd man, Franklin allowed Rupert to plant potatoes on this land as long as Rupert made sure that some of the fertilizer he used for his potatoes also fertilized the pine trees around the plot. The third plot, one square in size, was about halfway up the valley. Rupert rented this land from the Franklin family at a reduced rate in exchange for clearing the land the previous year. Clearing away the bush was a costly, time-consuming process, involving his own, hired, and exchange labor, making Rupert's reduced rent less of a bargain than it might have seemed. He planned to transfer yams onto this freshly cleared land from the fourth plot, a square of land he owned just across the road from his house, next to the house of a Rastafarian named Leon.

Finally, the fifth plot, also belonging to the Franklins, was new that year, high up the opposite wall of the valley. Unfortunately, while Rupert was in the process of clearing this plot and preparing it for planting, he found out that it adjoined a plot of disputed land—land claimed by both Leon and the Franklins—and Leon suggested that maybe some of the land the Franklins were letting him farm didn't rightly belong to them. As Leon's neighbor and the Franklins' tenant, Rupert was trying to stay neutral in the dispute, though he worried that the dispute might spill over onto some of his acreage and jeopardize the work he had put into the land.

Jamaican peasant farms like Rupert's are similar to peasant farms described throughout the social scientific literature and to many small businesses that involve small inputs of labor and cash for generally small rewards (Cohen 2001; Wolf 1966; Mintz 1974; Pearse 1975; Painter 1984; Deere 1983; Durrenberger 1979; Chayanov 1966; Buitrago Ortiz 1973; Russell 2003). Production is organized around the survival and reproduction of the household and includes subsistence production as well as production for the payment of land rent and taxes. Rupert wasn't alone in farming sloping, often rocky fields under a variety of more and less tenuous land-tenure arrangements and in areas accessible only by foot or mule. Nor was he unique in planting the area's principal cash crops of Irish potatoes, red peas, bananas, coffee, carrots, lettuce, cabbage, tomatoes, cocoa, and peanuts. Nor were his concerns about losing precious cleared land to a property dispute far from other Jamaicans' experiences in areas where small, fragmented farms predominate. Commonly, too, peasants throughout the watershed planted marijuana. Rupert's yellow yams, which were grown for both home consumption and sale, were perhaps the most common and reliable crop of the watershed. They were not only flavorful and nutritious, they grew well in the watershed's soil, could remain in the ground for months on end, and could be harvested to meet household needs or for sale. As should be obvious from the above discussion, monocropping does not conform well to household food and cash needs, and most fields of Two Meetings were intercropped to some extent.

For crop production and other labor needs, households drew upon the common peasant pools of family, exchange, and hired labor. Often during my treks across the watershed I was invited to share a meal of the thick, rich soup that the men who organized work crews were cooking for the noon meal. (I admit I often sought out the familiar fragrances of pepper and thyme while observing work crews planting or harvesting a crop, hoping to be offered a bowl.) These work crews tended to work for a single peasant farmer who was either planting or harvesting his crop. He may have had an emergency order for yams or Irish potatoes and needed a group of five to ten men and women to help him get the crop to market in a single day. The workers who gathered for these tasks could be receiving day wages or repaying favors, or they might simply be members of the farmer's extended network of households—his own, his parents' or siblings', those of his "outside" children (children born to former wives or other women), and so forth. In addition to the noon meal, these work crews had two breaks—one, called "chocolate," in the midmorning, when they served hot chocolate and smoked marijuana, and a second in the late afternoon, where marijuana and rum were nearly always enjoyed.

Nearly all peasant households used the famous marketing women known as higglers for marketing their crops. Even today higglers constitute the principal human link between country and city, buying, packaging, and transporting small amounts of farm produce from a number of farmers to sell in several near or distant, usually urban, markets. They are usually women, cultivating relations of trust among farmers, who give them their produce free of charge and take what cash they bring back. Many of them occupy stalls at regional open-air markets or sell their produce from stands along the street. Similar women from fishing households buy and sell fish—raw, whole, cleaned, or cooked on the side of the road, the poorer-quality species ending up in stews or teas. About half of those I interviewed used the government marketing board called the Agricultural Marketing Corporation. A few more belonged to the potato cooperative. Even with these marketing options, gross annual farm incomes were quite low. When I conducted fieldwork in 1982–83, it was not uncommon for people to report making less than US$100 per year; Russell's 2001 figures show annual incomes of around US$1,350 per year, although both he and I agree that these incomes are highly variable and that they are particularly influenced from year to year by weather, markets, theft of crops and equipment, and other factors.

Leaving these low-income environments for the United States, working as cane cutters in south Florida, picking apples in the Northeast, or working in resort hotels in South Carolina, Michigan, or Virginia, Jamaicans can net between $3,000 and $4,000 apiece annually (Russell's figure for 2001 was around US$3,200). Not only is the pay considered high relative to farm earnings, the program provided and still provides additional benefits of travel to the United States and Canada and access to the relatively inexpensive "pretty pretty" goods there (for example, tape decks and jewelry; see Binford 2002; Basok 2000; McCoy and Wood 1982; Griffith 1983b; Russell 2003). To participate in the program, men must get one of the few hundred job cards distributed along lines of political patronage and informal social networks throughout the island (Russell 2003); women in the H-2B program need recommendations from their Jamaican employers as well. While the sugar program has been terminated, these practices still prevail among Jamaican farm workers to Canada and the U.S. apple-growing regions.

Job card distribution is only the first step in a complex recruitment process that often skirts official policy. During the sugar program (1943–92), U.S. employers, representatives of the Jamaican Ministry of Labour, and men with the Florida Fruit and Vegetable Association traveled from parish capital to parish capital over a two-week period, screening up to three and four hundred men per day. In Mandeville, where I witnessed the process before a Ministry of Labour official asked me to leave, more than three hundred men stood in a public park waiting for more than an hour for the recruiters to arrive. Most, like me and the men I had come with, woke around 4:00 A.M. to catch minibuses to the parish capital from small outlying villages with names like Silent Hill, Pedro's Cross, and Succeed. We arrived around 5:30 A.M., expecting the recruiters to arrive at any time, but it wasn't until around 7:00 A.M. that four identical new Honda Accords pulled into the park, each carrying two or three U.S. employees or FFVA officials, following a van with the Ministry of Labour insignia on the side. Setting up their tables and lists, they began interviewing the men around 7:30 A.M.

The word "interviewing" glorifies the process. The term the Jamaicans used to describe it was "the hand test," referring to the recruiters' practice of grasping and examining the workers' hands for calluses. In addition to checking their hands, the recruiters examined the workers' teeth and eyes, very much as slave traders examined slaves for sale, and asked questions like, "Can you eat rice and pork three times a day?" Those who passed these screening sessions were then put on a list of men called to cut cane and pick apples in the event of an opening.

While the sugar program was operating (i.e., prior to 1992), workers who succeeded in making it into the program remitted around one-quarter of their earnings to their spouses, unmarried partners, mothers, and a few others back home. Today the total Jamaican migrant farm worker population remits around US$5 million and around Can$6 to $8 million (US$4 to 6 million) to Jamaica annually (Russell 2003). Based on my sample, during the early 1980s women accounted for more than 90 percent of the principal recipients of remittances, wives and girlfriends receiving an estimated US$40 to $60 every fortnight, or a seasonal total of around US$400 to $600. Their monthly incomes for the five to seven months their husbands and boyfriends were in the United States came to around US$100—equivalent to nearly a year of the cash income generated from farming. Mothers, the second-most common category of recipients, received anywhere from US$30 to $50, but usually with less frequency than the girlfriends and wives, around every second or third fortnight. For the total season the amount sent to mothers averaged around US$200 to $300. Although money orders were occasionally sent to fathers, children, grandparents, and siblings, these were infrequent and generally smaller than those sent to wives, girlfriends, and mothers. Russell's data suggest that similar remittance behavior occurs today.

Jamaican women tended to spend cash—whether remitted or earned in other ways—on the nutrition, health, and general well-being of their children. As in impoverished communities everywhere, spending money on children is equal to making payments into social security. Most obviously, this practice helped reproduce the peasantry—literally, in the biological sense. Less obviously, the practice aided in the reproduction of the social and economic conditions of remittance recipients' households and the households around them. This occurred because the social context of small farming in Jamaica, oriented toward combining subsistence with commercial production, is derived from social relations of production within male-biased marketing and other institutional frameworks, placing female remittance recipients in contradictory roles.

First, while male members of their households were abroad, female recipients of remittances assumed management of household farming, working with men in their families or their local communities. This management generally did not include managerial or technical innovations or expansion of the acreage devoted to cash or subsistence production of crops or livestock. Instead of expanding their farms, they kept agricultural output at levels that characterized the farm prior to the absence of the migrating male. In some cases they cut back production of cash crops. I describe below the demographic, political, and cultural reasons for this lack of agricultural innovation and expansion among peasant women, though here I want to point out that virtually no migrant households in my sample planted an early spring crop of Irish potatoes during the years their male members migrated to the United States in the program. In cases where years of migration to the United States overlapped with potato cooperative and Agricultural Marketing Corporation sales records during the same time period, household potato sales fell during the years of participation in the program, rising again to previous levels thereafter.

Diane Roberts, for example, whose husband, Lewis, was a successful migrant farm worker in both Canada and the United States, maintained his farm under its premigration levels of production during the three seasons he traveled to Canada and the three to the United States. While this allowed Lewis to move easily back into subsistence farming during the months he was home, it forestalled investment in land or other capital goods until Lewis believed he was close to being cut from the program. After his sixth year of migration, fearing it would be his last, Lewis purchased land to expand his farm, but Diane let this land lie idle during the seventh year of Lewis's migration. Lewis put this land into production only after he stopped traveling. It was also notable that, at the time he purchased this land, only two of Diane and Lewis's eight children had reached an age, between ten and twelve, where they could provide very much labor to farming. Like most farm workers, Lewis was traveling at the very time that Chayanov's theory of peasant economy predicts he would have attached a high subjective value to labor and, very probably, produced a surplus—a time, that is, when the ratio of consumers to workers in his household was five to one.

Although women tended not to expand production, they did maintain the level of agricultural production, usually by hiring labor with earnings from abroad, thus infusing the local agricultural economy with overseas earnings and contributing to local employment. This didn't result in the development of local highland farming systems, however, any more than it resulted in the farm's ability to generate higher incomes. Jamaican women continued channeling their energies to the care and well-being of their children. Again, given the nature of social relations among Jamaican households, this was the most feasible course of action.

Although most Jamaican peasant households maintained exchange labor relations with one or more households, women receiving remittances tended to hire day laborers from other, neighboring households. Part of the reason for hiring labor was that these women had young children to care for. But fully understanding why these women hired rather than exchanged labor requires some elaboration on the dynamics of labor relations in Jamaican peasant farming systems. Despite the ubiquity of exchange labor in societies short on cash, Jamaican peasants repeatedly told me that they preferred hiring paid day laborers to relying on exchange labor relations, for several reasons. They complained that exchange laborers showed up late, left early, took frequent breaks, and were often unreliable; hired laborers, by contrast, put in a full day's work. Also, exchange labor was not without cost: earlier I described how the host producer must provide two break-time snacks, chocolate, rum, and marijuana, at least one and sometimes two meals (usually that peppery, starchy soup of potato, green bananas, chicken backs, garlic, and thyme). Finally, hired labor conferred prestige, as labor was among the most costly resources in Jamaican peasant farming. Without machinery capable of operating on steep, rocky, bamboo-choked land, labor was the primary means by which new land could be brought into cultivation and existing land more intensively and efficiently cultivated by terracing, digging irrigation ditches, applying fertilizers evenly, and so on (Edwards 1961; Goldschmidt and Blustain 1980; Russell 2003).

In addition to the high value, both perceived and actual, placed on labor in Jamaican peasant farming systems, seasonal fluctuations in labor demand influenced whether or not women needed to hire workers while their husbands and boyfriends were away. Edwards's (1961) comprehensive study of small farming in Jamaica showed that, in five out of nine areas studied, planting and reaping, the two most labor-intensive activities on Jamaican peasant farms, occurred primarily between October and March—the very months that sugar workers were in the United States. In the other four areas, around 50 percent of the planting and reaping was done during these months. For the sugar workers, therefore, households' agricultural labor requirements were thus highest while the farm workers were in the United States. Resort and hotel workers spend some of this time in the United States as well, generally leaving in March and staying well into November or December.

The practice of hiring day labor on Jamaican farms raises several questions about the economic impact of remittances—questions of crucial importance to developing economies and central to the justification of managed migration programs. How much, for example, is paid in wages to meet agricultural labor requirements? How many jobs do remittances generate back home? What are the multiplier effects of this earned income? At a more general level, what are the class and gender implications of women employers?

The purely economic questions are the easiest to address. Based on data I collected in 1982–83, the daily wage in agriculture was around J$9.00 (US$4.50), which included the costs of feeding workers and providing them refreshment for breaks, and the average number of days of hired labor on migrants' farms was 107. Around three-fourths of the remittance recipients reported hiring day laborers. Based on a stable seasonal migrant population of around 6,200 (Jamaican Department of Statistics 1982a, 25), calculations suggest that the sugar and apple programs generated around J$4.5 million annually (US$2.25 million) in wages paid to day laborers in Jamaica, or around half a million days of work. Russell's (2003) more recent figures about the use of remittances found that only around 4 percent of remittances (or around US$220,000) were used to invest in the migrants' current income-generating activity, which could include hiring labor, yet he reported around US$4.5 million in an "other" category, which could also include hiring labor (the largest single expenditure was on schooling for children).

As is typical with simple economic calculations, these measurements tell only a small part of the story, understating the effect of these remittances. As we have seen, the women who used part of their remittances from abroad to hire workers hired day laborers. These were temporary, part-time workers, not full-time hired hands. Moreover, these women usually hired neighbors (not necessarily or even usually friends) who were peasants themselves and who managed their own small farms. Their farms were in the same ecological zones as the women's farms, and they were subject to the same seasonal schedules. They needed cash income at the same times of the year that the women needed cash. While able to rely on family and exchange labor for their labor needs, peasants who hired themselves out as day laborers needed cash, in order to plant and reap their own crops, for things such as seed, fertilizer, pesticides, rent, transportation to market, and chicken backs and rum for exchange labor partners. They could hire themselves out and still devote time to their own household economic activities, since they usually worked no more than a day or two as hired labor. Remittances from abroad thus helped keep agricultural production levels stable on these day laborers' peasant farms as well as on the remittance recipients' farms, which further supported the reproduction of labor.

On migrants' farms there are demographic, political, and cultural reasons why hiring day labor tended not to result in farm expansion or innovation. First, most of the wives and girlfriends of migrants were at a time in their lives when their families and domestic responsibilities were increasing, primarily because alien labor programs select strong, young workers, most commonly between the ages of twenty-four and forty-six (McCoy and Wood 1982; Griffith 1983b, 1985). The people they leave behind are thus caring for young children and overseeing the management of the household, without time for the detailed observations and practices that agricultural experimentation requires. Second, agricultural expansion in Jamaica has been and remains oriented primarily toward males. The female component of the Integrated Rural Development Project (IRDP), sponsored by USAID, consisted of classes in nutrition, breast-feeding, childcare, and the preparation and care of family gardens (Jamaican Ministry of Agriculture 1979; Goldschmidt and Blustain 1980; Kruijer 1967).

Two additional observations support the finding that agricultural production undertaken by Jamaican women was oriented more toward subsistence than toward production for a market. First, Jamaican women traditionally cared for family gardens, raising crops grown primarily for home consumption like sweet potatoes, cassava, pumpkin, corn, and pok chow. One of their major roles in the growing and marketing of cash crops was in processing the products for market—washing vegetables, separating ginger root into smaller pieces, bundling garlic and thyme together, drying coffee beans. Yet the sexual division of labor on the farm wasn't strictly observed. Women provided crucial support services on a daily basis for the production of market and subsistence crops. They often cooked the mid-day meal for the field hands. At planting and harvest time, when the need for labor was high, women and men worked side by side. Ideals of women's and men's work crumbled under the pressure of getting a perishable product to market or meeting a lunar planting schedule.

Second, the records of the Agricultural Marketing Corporation (AMC), the major government market for agricultural produce, contained a disproportionately small number of female sellers. From a sample of 946 AMC receipt vouchers from three different years (1974, 1978, and 1981), I found that 739 vouchers were made out to men and 207 to women; the male sellers outnumbered the women 3.5 to 1.

To those knowledgeable about Caribbean women's roles, these findings may initially seem strange. Commercial activities among women are deeply rooted throughout the West Indies, as the famous studies of "pratik" and "higglering" relations show (Mintz 1961, 1971; Katzin 1971). However, the AMC was the formal government marketing board, reflecting an overall orientation of agricultural extension and policy and demonstrating, as noted above, a male bias. Peasants and small farmers who sold to the AMC had first to obtain an order for their product from AMC officials, except under situations of high demand for one product or another. According to peasant men, obtaining an order from the AMC usually involved political patronage, especially for crops, such as yellow yam, that are in high supply throughout most of the year. Although women traditionally channeled their entrepreneurial skills into marketing rather than production, they tended to sell small quantities and wide varieties of produce in peasant markets, as opposed to government marketing outlets such as the AMC.

Finally, the tradition of strong mother-child bonds in poor Caribbean households has been well documented in the social scientific literature (Ho 1995; Clarke 1957; Lowenthal 1972; Gonzalez 1969). Especially since emancipation and the beginning of large-scale, predominantly male emigration, the development of these bonds has served as a valuable social investment among Caribbean women, providing much-needed social security in old age. In both word and deed, women and men throughout Jamaica express deep obligations to their mothers—far greater than the obligation to their fathers, as is evident by the extreme disparity between mothers and fathers as recipients of remittances. The strength of these bonds underlies a great deal of the instability of sexual and marital unions between Jamaican men and women (Roberts and Sinclair 1978), since a woman's primary allegiance is to her children and her parents' household and a man's to his parents' household and the households containing his children.

I point out the importance of these mother-child bonds here for two reasons. First, that this tradition exists further explains why peasant women use remittances primarily on their children. Second, although there are a variety of intellectual, emotional, and material aspects of the development of these bonds, part of maintaining them involves satisfying the nutritional well-being of the children through subsistence agriculture. The result of the bias toward subsistence agriculture is that the household literally consumes the money spent on farming, facilitating the physiological reproduction of people who may become sources of labor.

Like assuring the nutritional well-being of children, schooling constitutes an investment in human capital and a possible delayed, indirect means of upward mobility and prestige for the parent generation. Although public education in Jamaica involves no tuition, schooling children requires money for lunches, uniforms, books, supplies, and so forth. An excerpt from a letter written by a migrant mother to her daughter in Jamaica shows the value mothers place on education.

> Hello my dear sweet darling daughter Michelle. . . .
> I hope you are all doing your lesson Michelle remember if you do not have a P.H.D. and masters degree you will not be able to get a job or even to find something to do into this world and to get a degree you have to be able to go through high school, through college and university and to go all these places you must be able to read and write well in order to pass your exam, so please see to it the other children do their lessons. . . .
> Take care and Write soon always loving mother. (Griffith 1983b, 59)

Many of the Jamaican women I interviewed shared this woman's sentiments (Roberts and Sinclair 1978). Yet there was no evidence that the schooling of children depended on the receipt of remittances. Comparisons between the migrants' households (n = 45) and a control population of peasants (n = 83) showed that around 90 percent of both groups had children of school age attending school (90.6 percent and 87.1 percent, respectively).

Despite the perceived importance of education, without broader employment growth there is no guarantee that schooling children will yield dividends of prestige and upward mobility. This is not to say that putting money into formal schooling is a wasted effort. Certainly a literate population will facilitate more economic and social development than an illiterate one will. And an educated population may be more likely to perceive various forms of subordination, engage in collective organization, and enlist the aid of actors like Rural Legal Aid attorneys in airing grievances against employers (with the unfortunate consequence of laying the foundation for shifts such as the one from the Caribbean to Mexico in H-2 programs). In any case, schooling is not necessarily highly correlated with improved income opportunities, nor do remittances seem to substantially increase the proportion of educated children in the Jamaican countryside.

One final point concerns the long-term returns of investing in children and its probable role in reinforcing the importance of motherhood among Jamaican women (Pessar 1999). I have argued that remittances provide women in Jamaica with additional means to invest in their most promising source of social security: their children. That mothers of farm workers constitute the second-largest category of remittance recipients suggests that this investment strategy pays off in the long run. The strategy is so widespread, in fact, that it influences decisions of others who are directly or indirectly related to the functioning of the H-2 program. I found an interesting example of this while investigating the ways in which seasonal migrants received their job cards. This case involved two households related to each other through a man whom I refer to as Samuel Evans.

In his first relationship with a woman, Samuel and the woman had five daughters and two sons. He later moved in with another woman, Gloria, who had two sons of her own from a previous relationship. When he moved in with Gloria, her two sons were twenty-one and twenty-six years old. The elder son had already moved out of the household and the younger was soon to leave. Samuel's own biological sons were, at that time, eighteen and twenty-four. Samuel was more of a social as well as a biological father to his children than he was to Gloria's. Bonds between him and Gloria's children were not strong. Yet after the move, when Mr. Evans became a Peoples National Party committee member and began receiving job cards (committee members usually receive one per year), he gave the first card he received to Gloria's elder son rather than to one of his own sons. The following year he gave his second job card to Gloria's second son, again passing over his own sons in favor of the son of the woman with whom he was then living. Only after he had given cards to both of Gloria's sons did he give the third card to his own son.

One can readily see the material basis of Samuel's choices. Gloria's two sons remitted money to Gloria; Samuel's sons, by contrast, would remit money to their mother, a woman with whom Samuel no longer lived. The men to whom Samuel gave his first two job cards thus remitted money to the household where Samuel lived. Samuel's own son did remit money directly to him, but with far less frequency than he did to his mother. By giving job cards to Gloria's sons rather than his own, the household in which Samuel lived benefited.

While the suggestion that motherhood remains an important part of women's lives may run against the grain of feminist scholarship that views the burdens of childcare as confining and oppressive, Samuel's story and others like it suggest that motherhood may be marshaled as a tool in gender relations, influencing the decisions that men make vis-à-vis other men. In the long run, such behavior may undermine patriarchy and contribute to women's empowerment even as it creates conditions for the continued dependence of women on male earnings. Whatever this may mean for feminist scholarship or theories about gender's role in migration, in the end Gloria will always be her sons' mother, but perhaps not always Samuel's wife.

FOUR

ASPECTS OF THE MACHETE

They hold the handle. We hold the blade. Any way they move it, we get cut.

—Jamaican sugar worker, characterizing labor relations in the sugar program

Women weren't the only recipients of foreign earnings who had trouble investing them in ways that might have improved rather than reproduced their impoverished conditions. Despite the male bias of agricultural extension in central Jamaica, men returning from the United States in the 1980s, prior to the end of the sugar program, were faced with several barriers to expanding their agricultural production. Even before draconian economic policies associated with debt crises and the new neoliberal trade agreements of the mid-1990s, structural factors prevented investment in peasant or small-scale agriculture or other household-based, labor-intensive businesses available to those with limited resources.

For several years there has been a growing consensus in the social scientific literature on international labor migration that suggests that migration is far more likely to generate more migration than significant investment in the underdeveloped countries from which migrant labor comes. Not only do more and more individuals from countries like Jamaica see migration as their principal hope for a solid future, but more and more individuals already in migrant streams seek to lengthen their stays as opportunities at home seem less and less promising. This was certainly the case with the H-2 workers I interviewed. At around the time they believed their contracts were to expire, they overwhelmingly sought ways to prolong their stay in the United States rather than seek alternative income opportunities at home. Workers with several seasons of experience often began considering leaving the program. Whether because they hadn't received pay increases in all their years of service or because they witnessed their co-workers cut from the program after three to four years, many workers worried that if they didn't leave the program soon, they would find themselves back in Jamaica without a request to return or any other means of finding work in the United States.

This behavior reflected prevailing patterns of the use of foreign earnings at home, and the scholarship of the day documented a similar set of behaviors across several social and cultural terrains. Rubenstein (1983), for example, argued that remittances to the West Indies from migrants living abroad, although voluminous, are used primarily to meet consumption needs and finance more migration rather than to create employment and income opportunities at home. Studying in Mexico, Joshua Reichert (1981) found that migration between Michoacan and the United States led to a "migrant syndrome," in which migrants became dependent on migration to maintain their standards of living instead of using foreign earnings to alleviate economic problems in a long-term, sustainable fashion. Rhodes (1978, 141–42) found that return migrants were oriented toward consumer spending that would enhance their ability to generate income.

These trends have changed in subtle ways, in part owing to changes within migrant streams generally, but the basic difficulties facing migrants remain. In recent work, for example, Basok (2000) and Binford (2002) concurred that Mexican guestworkers to Canada, working primarily in flower greenhouses and on farms in Ontario, did not earn enough to make significant capital investments in Mexico. Work on transnational migrants over the past decade has enriched Reichert's observations about migration becoming its own end, leading to such effects as increases in national import bills as migrants create demand for consumer goods, and the tendency among return migrants to inflate land prices, to open small grocery stores and bars in areas with surpluses of such businesses, and to use their earnings for little more than the construction, expansion, and furnishing of their homes (OECD 1978; Dinerman 1978; Grasmuck 1982; King and Strachen 1980).

These findings seem to support dependency theorists' early contentions that the articulation of productive modes, quite personally through labor migration, failed to address severe structural and historical obstacles to sustained economic development. Instead of a development-fostering process, migration was seen as yet another form of the exploitation of labor by capital within the historical-structural paradigm (Rhodes 1978; Wood 1982; Pessar 1980, 1999; Bach and Schraml 1982). The theoretical roots of this perspective reach back to Marx, and though dependency theory has been diffused throughout the social sciences, it ultimately failed to achieve its political objectives and either moved in new directions or was displaced by more humanistic models that emphasized agency, often manifested as resistance, over structure (see Frank 1966; Wallerstein 1970; Amin 1974; cf. Ong 1989; Scott 1979).

Despite their fall from grace, dependency theorists were able to show that structural and historical relationships between developed and underdeveloped countries often created obstacles to capital accumulation. Histories of colonialism, neocolonialism, uneven development within underdeveloped countries, and dependent development between developed and underdeveloped countries often resulted in highly unequal distributions of material and social resources, restricting access to capital, education, health care, and markets for many (Striffler 2002; Ortiz 1999; Stein and Stein 1970; Furtado 1976; Wolf and Hansen 1970; Wolf 1982). I argued in the last chapter that households and communities that contribute individuals to migrant streams absorb the costs of reproducing labor, maintaining workers during their youth and years of declining productivity, while the benefits of their labor accrue to those who hire them (Meillassoux 1972). Under such conditions, international labor migration thus constitutes a means by which poor nations subsidize capital accumulation in wealthy nations (Amin 1974).

The last chapter dealt with how this occurred through remittances from abroad. Another question arises about returning migrants: are they, unlike their spouses, able to accumulate the capital necessary to free them and their replacement generation from the migrant stream? Men in Jamaica don't face the same gender discrimination that women experience in agriculture. The buying cooperatives, marketing corporations, and agricultural education and extension services are oriented toward men (Russell 2003). Equally important, various opportunities to acquire cash or forge productive relationships with others are available to men through short-term contracts with local agencies interested in agricultural development. These contracts, which may involve clearing hillsides to plant pine trees, building terraces, or digging drainage ditches, provide cash to men while fostering the formation, development, and maintenance of predominantly male work groups. Participants in these groups can then draw on these relationships for agricultural production on their own farms.

The differences between women receiving remittances and men returning from overseas jobs with money to invest are profound enough that they warrant separate investigation. Over the past two decades, the theoretical basis for such an investigation has changed from an emphasis on structural impediments to capital accumulation to one that includes agency, which I take to mean individual initiative seasoned with subaltern consciousness that tends toward resisting domination. When I first entered the field in the early 1980s, the two competing paradigms used to characterize and represent the impacts of international labor migration on sending communities were microeconomic modeling and historical-structural approaches. Microeconomic models direct our attention to individuals' decisions, overlooking or downplaying they ways in which social, cultural, or historical factors constrain or support economic choices (Spengler and Myers 1977). Historical-structural approaches, by contrast, ask us to place individual outcomes in the context of long-term processes that have caused labor migration and that undermine returning migrants' abilities to accumulate capital, overlooking or downplaying individuals' economic decisions (Wood 1981, 1982).

Neither of these paradigms emerged without some basis in observed human behavior. Clearly, individuals make decisions, and historical-structural processes influence those decisions. What was needed, then, were intermediate areas of inquiry that could account for individual behavior without losing sight of big structural processes. Early attempts to identify intermediate areas suggested using the household, rather than the individual or the migrant stream, as a unit of analysis (Wood 1981, 1982; Pessar 1980). The household, defined as the "group that ensures its maintenance and reproduction by generating and disposing a collective income fund" (Wood 1981, 339), could be seen as a unit that mediated individual decisions concerning employment and disposal of income, and adapted to broader socioeconomic and political processes by combining a variety of strategies for survival and reproduction. The household was thus conceived as an intermediate arena of behavior between the individual and wider social, cultural, and historical processes that affect opportunities and choices. As an immediate unit of analysis, the household offered the greatest potential for the development of more accurate conceptual models of the causes and consequences of labor migration. Further, the household was usually the principal social and economic unit among dominated social groups that supplied labor to capitalist production (Brandes 1975; Griffith and Valdés Pizzini 2002; Magnarella 1979; Wolf 1966; Chayanov 1966). Finally, households were seen as hubs of diffuse social and economic networks that originate with the migrant, with his or her wife or husband or sexual partner, with children, or with other residents.

As ideal as households seemed to social scientific inquiry, scholars during the late 1980s and 1990s began to question some of the assumptions about them, particularly their apparent unity of purpose as they went about generating and disposing collective funds (Pessar 1999). Much of this criticism came from feminist scholarship and its attention on the divergent views of men and women regarding the reasons for and outcomes of labor migration. Some noted that, in contrast to solidarity among members, household power disparities based on gender and age undermined how much members behaved for, against, or indifferently toward migration and other endeavors that involved making demands on or contributing to collective funds (Pessar 2004; Mahler and Pessar 2001). One need look no further than the statistics on divorce and domestic violence to question household solidarity.

The quest nevertheless involved an intermediate unit: a social location where structure and agency met. One of the most successful intermediate units became the network, a structure based in connections among individuals that spanned geographical regions, linked many households, and served several informational and financial functions that facilitated migration and influenced the outcomes of migration, including abilities to invest in agriculture at home and consumption behavior at home and abroad. Networks were central to the influential work of Douglas Massey and his colleagues, in their *Return to Aztlán* (1987), which also opened a theoretical pathway to a focus on process without losing sight of structure.

Another promising approach focused on transnational migrants and communities. Work within this field has since eclipsed much of the writing on international labor migration, despite cautions against this from its seminal thinkers (Glick-Schiller 1999, 96), shifting the emphasis toward agency through examinations of cross-border networks that migrants maintain and their relationships to migrant identity, albeit an identity enriched, molded, fueled, and influenced by global cultural images in food, dress, expression, and so forth (Appadurai 1992). Though the emphasis has shifted, those who write about transmigration or transnational communities haven't left structural concerns behind. Indeed, one of their principal insights has concerned the links among nation-state composition, political processes, and migration, and their work has contributed to the emergence of self-conscious attempts by leaders of migrant-sending states to embrace transnational migrants as political constituents.

Unfortunately, some of this writing tends to conflate academic writing and other forms of discourse, such as the speeches of politicians or the observations of statesmen captured in the popular press, with the lived experiences of migrants. Because of this, however compelling the work on transnationalism and networks has been, it is a misrepresentation of migration to fail to acknowledge the importance of economic motives—work and investment, at home and abroad—in shaping and sustaining migrant streams. Thus, through all these theoretical developments, the importance of work in the migration experience has not faded from view. By far the vast majority of migration in the world (as distinct from refugee flows) is *labor* migration. Thus migrants are entangled in broader relations of class that form and change in sending, receiving, and transnational settings, and that migration may itself influence the accumulation of capital, consumer goods, or other resources. Without work and investment opportunities abroad combined with a dearth of the same at home, it is doubtful that either transnational sentiments or structures, or network ties, would be sufficient to sustain migration over long periods of time. Even within areas that have relied heavily on migration, such as Jalisco, Mexico, opportunities for work often reduce emigration. Developing models that capture the experience of migration are therefore most accurate if they situate the economic dimensions of migration at the core of the richer ethnographic contexts of households, families, networks, and transnational migration.

In this chapter I attempt to do this through an assessment of comparisons between migrant and nonmigrant households in Jamaica's interior that I made in the early years of fieldwork. With few exceptions, these comparisons revealed that the capital holdings, production levels, and marketing activities of the migrants were neither qualitatively nor quantitatively different from those of neighbors who had never migrated. I explain the lack of investment and capital accumulation among the returning migrants by situating their behavior within their households and their social relations with other households in the Jamaican countryside. Finally, I present information on those returning migrants who have accumulated capital, showing that capital accumulation occurred only among migrants who traveled abroad long enough to satisfy obligations to other members of their households and social networks.

THE STATISTICAL EXPERIMENT

When the sugar program was still operating, Jamaicans working in south Florida for the four- to five-month season were netting an average of around US$3,200, and the total Jamaican farm worker population earned around

$20 million per season in U.S. currency. Twenty-three percent of this amount was deducted from each paycheck and sent back to the island under a compulsory savings program, which generated between $4 and $5 million in foreign exchange for the government of Jamaica; those Jamaicans traveling today to the United States and Canada still have this 23 percent returned to the island, awaiting their return (Russell 2003; Griffith 2003).

While the benefit of guestworkers as sources of foreign exchange for Jamaica is obvious, until my research, how the program influenced the workers directly and the local areas from which they emigrated were not readily apparent. In their south Florida study, McCoy and Wood found that 91 percent of the Jamaicans were operating small peasant farms while at home (1982, 30). Given the predominance of peasants in the migrant population, my research task became one of assessing the program's impact on Jamaican economic development by comparing randomly chosen populations of migrant and nonmigrant peasants, focusing in particular on their agricultural production and other economic activities common among Jamaican peasants.

Before leaving for Jamaica, I had the good fortune to become friends with a statistician named Sammy Suisse, a Jewish French Canadian who had been born in Morocco but whose family fled to Canada when it became dangerous for Jews in northern Africa. He was a brilliant fellow, so talented a statistician that he was eventually able to acquire an H-class visa himself because he'd developed a statistical method or theory—I'm not quite sure which—that was so innovative and complex that only he and a few others in the world were qualified to teach it. Thus he eventually became a guestworker himself, though one admitted not because he was willing to take a position that allegedly no one else would take, such as cutting sugarcane, but because he was so gifted that he was filling a position that very few others were qualified to fill.

I was lucky to have befriended him when I did. Not only did he help me in the design of the comparative experiment I had in mind, but, more important, he helped me make sense of the results. The experimental design was straightforward enough: I was to randomly select a large enough number of households—I shot for 200 and settled for 134—some with migrants (45, it turned out), others without (89), and then collect data related to agricultural production. As is nearly always the case with anthropological research, the first problem that arose was how to select households at random. Central Jamaican peasants weren't listed in any directory, license list, phone book, or other official list. And if the description of Rupert's farming practices in the previous chapter were any guide, selecting agricultural parcels from the tax rolls wouldn't work very well either.

I settled, then, on what has become a favorite sampling method of mine: cluster sampling. Cluster sampling consists of sampling in stages, first mapping a region, then dividing it into meaningful clusters (in this case, clusters of between fifteen and twenty peasant households), and then randomly selecting clusters, mapping them in a more detailed fashion, and finally randomly selecting households within selected clusters. The rule of thumb with cluster sampling is that you select a large number of clusters and a few households per cluster; for a sample of two hundred, for example, you'd want to select, say, forty clusters and then elicit data for about five households per cluster.

The benefit of cluster sampling is not just that you generate a random sample but that during the mapping phase of the project you become familiar with the area from which you will be collecting your data. Equally important, the people of that area become familiar with you and with your study. Thus, the first few weeks of my study, I trekked daily across the Two Meetings watershed, counting houses, encountering peasants in their homes and fields, annotating published maps and making crude sketches and maps myself, meeting the families who lived there, and explaining my presence. The principal obstacle I encountered during this early phase of research was that, when I mentioned the sugar program, people assumed I was a recruiter; nearly every young man wanted to sign up, nearly every mother wanted her sons to sign up, and every girlfriend or wife tried to offer her male partner for work. When I finally convinced them that I was just *studying* the program, not recruiting for it, people usually said something like, "So you find de men dem and reason with dem and discover their story?" It sounded close enough to the truth.

A second side benefit of my sampling strategy was that I was making mental and written notes about the families I would encounter, noting in particular where guestworkers lived and farmed, what their houses looked like, how they differed from families without migrants, and what kinds of crops and livestock they raised. It was during this time and later, as I began collecting data on cropping strategies, production levels, marketing strategies, and the like, that I began making the comparisons I would subsequently make with the aid of a computer and statistical analysis. Before analyzing the data, I thought that the agricultural production statistics weren't that different between the migrant and nonmigrant groups. It seemed to me that guestworkers' farms simply weren't much larger than those of workers who weren't participating in the program, and they didn't seem to grow many more bags of potatoes or hills of yams—the two most important cash crops in the watershed—than others living in the same area, with access to the same lands but not access to the same large amounts of money.

When I returned to the United States, ran the statistics, and found that this was indeed the case, I lamented to my statistical consultant and friend Sammy that the statistics revealed no surprises. The figures, I told him, were coming out exactly as I suspected. He said he wasn't surprised, adding, in his endearing French Canadian accent, "You've been doing the statistics all along, in the field, just in your head. You should be pleased you're not surprised."

I tried to be pleased, but I felt cheated. I had wanted the statistics to reveal something I hadn't suspected, wanted the exercise of coding and analyzing the data statistically to be more than just a confirmation of my hunches. I was asking, I know now, too much. The facts were just facts. It was true that nonmigrants and migrants produced, more or less, the same amount of crops, owned, rented, and cultivated about the same amount of land, and hired more or less the same amount of labor (see Table 4.1).

As Table 4.1 shows, the comparisons between the two populations suggest that participating in the guestworker program does not seem to benefit migrants in terms of their productive capability; if anything, in fact, it reduces their production. The data in the table show that the differences between the two populations are either not statistically significant or favor the nonmigrants. These findings emerged again and again in both qualitative and quantitative comparisons of the two populations. Differences that existed did not influence production. For example, access to a relative's land was more important to nonmigrants, suggesting they owned less land, yet land use was not significantly different between the two groups. By the same token, higher hired labor inputs of the migrant households, partially a result of the migrant's absence, did not translate into higher production levels or more land cultivated. Production statistics revealed, too, that the migrant and nonmigrant households raised almost identical average numbers of cows, pigs, goats, and donkeys or mules. Migrant household crop production was no higher than that of nonmigrant households; for Irish potato production, the primary cash crop in the area, their production levels were lower.

Why should this be so? At first I wondered whether significant differences might exist between the two groups in terms of numbers of workers per household, age of household head, or other demographic variables that might give one group an edge over the other, but this wasn't the case. Nor was it the case that there were no investment opportunities in the Jamaican countryside relative to the amount of money that these migrants earn in the United States. Farm workers' U.S. earnings were more than sufficient to take advantage of investment opportunities in rural Jamaica, capable of generating future income and local employment (Griffith 1983a, 1983b). Neighbors and friends they knew were opening small transport services or taxis, becoming effective market liaisons, financing cash crops, or using earnings to expand or begin small construction firms. In fact, some of the farm workers, discussed below, did manage to accumulate capital with their U.S. earnings. Hence I couldn't explain the lack of investment among returning migrants as the result of a lack of opportunity in rural Jamaica. Through a close examination of the social environment from which these migrants were drawn, however, a more accurate explanation of the lack of investment behavior among returning migrants emerged.

Table 4.1   Migrants and Nonmigrants Compared

Variables	Migrant Households (N = 45)		Nonmigrant Households (N = 83)
Land rented and owned (acres)			
Mean	3.05		3.76
Standard deviation	2.63		4.11
		p = .15*	
Land cultivated (acres)			
Mean	2.26		2.64
Standard deviation	1.62		2.38
		p = .17	
Person-days of hired labor annually			
Mean	107		75
Standard deviation	148		79
		p = .12	
CWTs of Irish potatoes			
Mean	5.2		10.6
Standard deviation	4.1		10.1
		p = .01	
Hills of yam/farm/season			
Mean	726		521
Standard deviation	745		265
		p = .11	

* Probability levels are the results of t-tests.

JAMAICAN PEASANT SOCIAL ORGANIZATION

Early ethnographic depictions of Jamaican households and communities characterized them as unstable, loosely organized, structurally weak, and fragmented (Cohen 1954; Gonzalez 1970; Clarke 1957; Wagley 1957; Solien 1970; Mintz 1974). Contrary to the impression one gets from some of this literature, several aspects of Jamaican peasant social organization create cohesion within and between households, and more recent work on child sharing and other dimensions of Caribbean social organization has reinterpreted earlier characterizations in line with the increased attention given to networks and other social fields noted above. The Jamaican peasant households I encountered during fieldwork were usually based in concrete or wooden houses surrounded by one or more other structures, a yard, and often a fence and small garden. Its adults, or adults and children collectively, contributed, through labor and income, to its survival and reproduction, thus making the household much like others depicted elsewhere (cf. Wood 1981, 339; Gonzalez 1970, 232). The household members' relations with each other and with others outside these households tended to channel migrants' U.S. earnings into consumption rather than investment, thereby reducing the benefits for economic development that could issue from the annual transfer of around US$20 million from the United States to Jamaica.

Jamaican peasants returning from south Florida sugar or East Coast apples maintained a number of interdependent relations with members of other households. Three such relations were symptomatic of the instability of relations between male and female partners for sex or marriage. First, half of the migrants had fathered children with women whom they no longer lived with. These children, called "outside children," in all cases lived in households separate from their biological fathers' households, yet nearly all the men with outside children contributed to their welfare and to the welfare of their mothers, whom they called "baby mothers." In return for these contributions, both the outside children and the baby mothers contributed various services (farm labor, cooking, laundry, etc.) to the father. Anyone who has lived in rural Jamaica is familiar with the common practice of children carrying pots and dishes of cooked food between houses and yards, a visible and touching expression of the interdependency of these households.

The second and third types of interdependent relationships between households were relations between the woman and her parents' household(s) and relations between the man and his parents' household(s).

Women and men in rural Jamaica typically maintain strong ties with their parents, especially their mothers, throughout life. Migrants to the United States materially recognized these ties by remitting about $160 per season to their mothers and, less often, to their fathers, about half as often as they remitted money to their current wives and girlfriends, the women they lived with while in Jamaica, whom they were sending around $500 to $600 per season (Griffith 1983b). Women also contributed to their parents' household(s) when they migrated or obtained cash through other means, including remittances their husbands or boyfriends sent from abroad. I was moved (though not to action) when prostitutes in Negril and Port Antonio, as part of their sales pitch, told me that part of their earnings went to support aging parents or grandparents. Parents' households also served as convenient residences for women and their children between partners.

The tendency of Jamaican men and women to maintain strong ties with their parents' and outside children's households reflects unstable family relations between women and men that are common among people who suffer from difficult financial circumstances. These ties bind households to one another, within and between generations, creating diffuse social networks through which cash, goods, services, affection, and information flow. Created at a household rather than an individual level by several household members, they influenced spending patterns among these seasonal agricultural migrants returning from the United States.

These relations further reflect the economic behavior of participants in the H-2 program, because these migrants are without exception men. Writing about the West Indies, Gonzalez pointed out that "men, particularly, tend to be placed in positions in which potential conflict between households devolves upon them, thus putting strain on the individual in one or both units" (1970, 232). She argued further that the strongest bonds within households, as among African American women in the United States who worked in the seafood plants and hotels, were matrilineal: "Relationships among other family members tend to be defined in terms of this original mother-child relationship. Thus, ties are stronger among uterine siblings than among those sharing only a father. The protective male, if present at all, may be important to ego primarily as 'mother's husband,' whether he is ego's father or not. Other relationships will also be defined in terms of the mother" (Gonzalez 1970, 233).

In other words, Jamaican men, occupying tenuous positions in the network, nevertheless provided critical links between two or more households specifically because they'd loved different women without severing ties with their children and past loves. Jamaican women, moving between different loves as well, enhanced those ties through mother-child relationships. As noted earlier, men maintained strong ties with their mothers and their households, an emotional closeness expressed in remittances to mothers and occasionally grandmothers, sisters, aunts, or other female relatives of their birth household. Still, a man's relationship with his children was mediated through his relationship with his current or previous sexual partners, and most migrants maintained and acknowledged these relationships as well, contributing cash and goods to households containing their children. The returning migrant, being the sole connecting link between his mother's and children's households, occupied a delicate position. Whatever he gave to his mother came from what he might have used for the welfare of his children. Often this caused strained relations between a man's mother and the woman or women who had given birth to the man's children, as each of these individuals competed for U.S. cash and goods. This tension deepened, too, as women attempted to channel some of these resources to their parents' households and to the households of their former partners.

Migrants returning to Jamaica with money in their pockets and suitcases full of U.S. goods thus often found themselves in a position similar to that of the fellow in the rowboat with his mother and wife. When the boat overturns and both are drowning, which one should he save? Participants in the alien labor program solved this dilemma by tossing a life preserver to one and swimming after the other: they sent cash and carried back goods to both.

Not only did the migrant's position within his household and in relation to other households influence the dispersal rather than concentration of his earnings; the specific time of life when migrants tended to participate in guestworker programs undermined their ability to invest overseas earnings as well. Most guestworkers—whether women or men from Jamaica, Mexico, or elsewhere—participate in guestworker programs when they are relatively young and of childbearing age. According to McCoy and Wood's data from south Florida (1982), for example, 90 percent of the Jamaican workers in the program fell between the ages of twenty-four and forty-six. More recently, Russell (2003) found that more than 80 percent of workers were under forty-five, and Verduzco, working among guestworkers from Mexico to Canada, found that around three-fourths of workers he interviewed were under forty-five, adding that the Mexican government encouraged only workers with dependent family members to participate in the program. These are times of life, in other words, when their households are growing, and growing in ways that usually result in more consumers than workers.

Anyone familiar with the literature on peasant households, from Chayanov and scholars as insightful as Marshall Sahlins and Paul Durrenberger, understands that consumer-to-worker ratios in these households play critical, at times determining roles in motivating household production. Put simply, high numbers of consumers who are not fully workers (young children and the elderly, for example) relative to able-bodied workers force those who can work to work longer and harder. When several households are involved in production and consumption, as was the case in Jamaica, relations between consumers and workers *and* between consumption and production become more complex.

When I returned to Jamaica in the late 1990s and early 2000s, and when I visited the offices of the Florida Rural Legal Services in Belle Glade, Florida, the group that sued the sugar companies, I had the opportunity to piece together more complex household and network histories, see how they influenced consumption and production, and place them in the larger context of the demise of the sugar program. These histories illustrate not only the extreme challenges facing Jamaican workers but the importance of guestworker programs to merchants in U.S. communities where guestworkers shop. I will turn to them in a moment, after assessing migrant spending in the United States and at home.

PATTERNS OF EXPENDITURE AMONG MIGRANTS

The migrants' positions in their networks and their age and family circumstances during their participation in the program directly influenced how they spent the money they made abroad. Along with remittances, migrants most commonly used their earnings to purchase consumer goods in the United States and construct or expand houses for their growing families. West Indians were famous for their consumer behavior in U.S. host communities. During the sugarcane harvest, Belle Glade, Florida, the major shopping center for most of the workers, became a bustling commercial core catering to West Indian needs and tastes. Cuban markets stocked yams and Jamaican pastries. Kentucky Fried Chicken offered a Jamaican special. Winn Dixie and other supermarkets kept supplies of pepper sauce, canned goods, soap, and other goods West Indians purchased. Strings of downtown shops stocked clothes, shoes, radios, tape decks, stereos, speakers, and small and large appliances. Dickering and haggling over prices characterized commerce. During the sugar harvests, merchants estimated that roughly 80 to 100 percent of their business came from the cane cutters. Signs in their store windows boasted that they shipped to Jamaica any item in the store.

It really was an amazing thing to watch. During the harvest the whole town came alive in the manner of a resort area during the peak of the tourist season. From the end of October to the end of March, for three hours every evening the streets of downtown Belle Glade filled with West Indians with money in their pockets. Drifting in and out of stores and restaurants, they exchanged buying experiences and swigs of liquor and beer, shopped, checked out prices, compared product qualities, planned future expenditures, and wheeled carts through the supermarkets. Discreet drug transactions occurred here and there. Patois was the language of the street. Even the most casual observer could tell you that the West Indians did not come to town to window shop. Almost no one left the downtown without making at least some small purchase: jeans, a T-shirt, a chicken sandwich. Between seven and eight o'clock the cane cutters gathered in small groups of three or four or stood by themselves on corners, their crates, boxes, and sacks resting at their feet, waiting for transportation back to the camps. Taxis and minibuses cruised through the downtown with the same flexible scheduling of the Jamaican minibus system, the drivers yelling the names of labor camps and the passengers flagging them down, stuffing boxes and sacks under the seats or into the trunks, and piling in. In the first hours of darkness at the labor camps, these vans and taxis unloaded and the men returned to lock up their goods in lockers next to their bunks. By nine o'clock the cultural complexion of downtown Belle Glade returned to native Floridian.

The communities of the U.S. Northeast where Jamaicans worked were less dependent on their consumerism than the merchants of downtown Belle Glade, but the workers there went on similar buying sprees. By Jamaican standards, the products they bought there were reasonably priced. A pair of tennis shoes, which in Jamaica cost around US$30 to $40, cost between $9 and $12 at K-Mart. In Jamaica, tape decks sold for as much as seven times what they cost in New York or Boston. Designer jeans and T-shirts cost about half as much in the United States as in the islands. Watches, jewelry, televisions, motorcycles, refrigerators—virtually anything in the "durables" category cost less in the United States than in Jamaica, especially after fluctuating currency exchange rates had crippled the buying power of the Jamaican dollar. Coming across bargains like these at a time when they have steady income from farm work, with the needs of a growing household back home, was it any wonder that these men spent 30 to 40 percent of their total gross seasonal earnings on U.S. goods? From their net earnings, after deductions for board and insurance, the proportion spent on U.S. goods was even higher, between 40 and 50 percent. In conjunction with deductions for food, just over half (51 percent) of the workers' total seasonal earnings never left the United States in cash form.

The remittances and cash that did make it back to the island also yielded to the consumption demands of farm workers' households. These consumption demands included clothing, footwear, and entertainment, but most important housing. More than half (61 percent) of the farm workers designated house construction as their first or second use of the funds that make it back to the island, and half used the money in the compulsory savings accounts primarily for house construction or expansion. Russell (2003) and Verduzco and Lozano (2003) found a similar emphasis on housing among guestworkers they interviewed, and our more recent studies of Mexico, where we visited women from the seafood plants and men home from working in U.S. tobacco fields, found that it was routine for workers to channel money into housing. The use of money from migration for the purchase of real estate has been documented among returning migrants all over the world (Levitt 2001; Magnarella 1979; Brandes 1975; Dinerman 1978; Reichert 1981; King and Strachen 1980; Hill 1976).

CAPITAL ACCUMULATION AMONG RETURNING MIGRANTS

As noted earlier, these patterns of expenditure among migrants reflected the migrants' positions within relatively diffuse social networks, binding several households together. Such relations drew upon the migrants' earnings in ways that undermined their ability to withhold cash from consumption for investment and capital formation. By extension, of course, these relations undermined the program's ability to serve as a vehicle for economic development in the Jamaican countryside.

Yet this is a static portrait, a cross section. Workers' households pass through the various stages of the life cycle, each ushering in changes to its members' wants and needs, their relations with other households, the conflicts they endure, and their consequent methods of negotiating gender and age relations and making ends meet. Young girls and boys who once were nothing but consumers gradually mature and become productive. They can tend bar, handle livestock, help with plantings and harvests, or drive or maintain the car for a transportation business. Their outgrown clothes, purchased in New York or Belle Glade, become their younger siblings' hand-me-downs.

As such changes occur, one would expect the household to recombine its resources, redirect its energies, and adapt its strategies to changes in household size, composition, and relations with other changing households. The disposal of migrants' U.S. earnings should reflect these changes. To test these assumptions, I turn to detailed considerations of households that I pieced together with additional information during my later fieldwork in Jamaica, focusing in particular how production and consumption patterns changed over time.

Most migrants, it is true, spent their U.S. earnings in the ways described above, yet a few acquired land and other resources with the money they earned working in sugar fields, apple orchards, or hotel rooms. Though in the minority, these deviant cases nevertheless demonstrate that it is possible to overcome, at least partially, the constraints on investment that arise from life cycle and network positions. The principal variable that seems to allow for the transcending of these constraints is quite simply the length of time one works in the United States: those workers who participate in H-2 programs for four or more seasons seem able to acquire capital. Although slightly more than one-third of the workers I came to know had accumulated capital, twice that proportion of long-term migrants accumulated capital during or after participation in the H-2 program. This capital was spent on a variety of things, including land purchases of more than one-half acre, twenty or more head of livestock, a taxi or truck for a transport business, or it could be used to open a rum shop or expand a merchandising business, or invested in another business, such a construction firm. Again, these expenditures were dynamically linked to migrants' consumption patterns.

William Hubert was a case in point, migrating to the United States for eight seasons over ten years. He first received a job card with another person's name in 1970; on that card he worked three seasons before sitting out the program for a year and then returning under a different name to work five more seasons. Working under others' names was part of William's strategy: a thin man, around five-feet-nine, with a close-cropped beard sprouting from his chin, William had a history of forming and dissolving relationships with an eye toward investment opportunities. Born in the neighboring parish of Trelawney, he and his brothers inherited six and a half acres from their parents, which they kept in contiguous plots and farmed jointly. He married Zora Hollowell and they had their first of seven children. It was 1961. They began farming primarily for the family's subsistence at that time.

While sharing his land with his brothers provided basic subsistence to him and his young family, he negotiated a deal to buy a few head of cattle shortly after his second child was born, throwing access to land along with a little labor and cash into the bargain. A year later his third child was born, and he entered his peak household consumption years, with another child being born every year or two and the firstborn still five to six years away from contributing valuable labor to the farm. It was no wonder that William looked for a way into the H-2 program.

When he was unable to get a job card himself, he made a deal for another man's card, again by combining access to land with labor and a loan, and in 1970, just as his first son began to shift from a consumer to a consumer-worker, William entered the program. Although he hoped to work in the program for at least a decade, after the third season, for reasons unknown to him, he wasn't called back. Home now, with three years' earnings under his belt, he made a small investment, purchasing half an acre of land in the Two Meetings watershed; for the first time in his life, he began farming on land he owned outright, without having to share with his brothers.

By the time William received his second job card and entered the H-2 program, again under a different name, his household was beginning to change in important ways. His eldest son had reached an age where he could be an almost fully productive worker on the farm, working beside his mother and even supervising minor tasks that could be delegated to his younger brothers and sisters. For the next few years, as a new baby entered the Hubert household every year, another child was entering his or her productive years. The time was ripe for farm expansion. Still, William traveled to the United States another three seasons before adding to his holdings again, this time renting three acres near his half-acre and beginning to plant more cash crops while still covering his subsistence needs from his own and his family's lands.

These investments paid off. By the time he finished working in the H-2 program (again because he wasn't called back), he was able to buy a house and another plot of land in Silent Hill, moving his family from Trelawney. In Silent Hill he was, he said, a "stranger." His neighbors reacted to him with bitterness, a common emotional response among those who envied his success and were perhaps suspicious of someone who seemed to have severed ties with his brothers to improve his circumstances. Nevertheless, William continued expanding his farm, seeking assistance from the Integrated Rural Development Project, hiring a lawyer to gain secure titles to his lands, and even renting some of his land out to his neighbors.

What is notable about the Hubert family's case was their ability to marshal their human resources *after* they had satisfied the immediate consumption needs that characterize migrant families during their early years of travel. The birth and maturation of children coincided with specific capital investments at a time when William had access to U.S. earnings by means of his (technically illegal) participation in the H-2 program, altering the dynamic between consumption and production through time. At the same time, his renting land to others placed him in an advantageous class position relative to his neighbors, who responded with bitterness.

A word about this bitterness: Jamaicans often told me that this or that person was "bitter," usually referring to people they believed disliked them for their accomplishments or, in other words, who envied their success, however modest. In another case, for example, people in the watershed often compared two guestworkers who had both worked for more than fifteen years in the program, but only one of whom, Vernon Hamilton, had much to show for a decade and a half of wage work. Of the other, Jonah Sharp, who neighbors claimed could have made as much of himself as Vernon, they said, "Jonah's bitter, bitter," meaning that Jonah expressed a dislike of Vernon for accomplishing more than he with what others perceived as the same opportunities. Of course, there is a rich literature about institutionalized envy acting as a leveling mechanism among peasants and the poor, dating to George Foster's work in Mexico, yet in Jamaica bitterness carries additional weight and meaning. Accumulating resources alone, as we will see in the profile of Vernon Hamilton below, is not sufficient for bitterness to take root. Instead, people toward whom others are bitter are perceived to share less than others, and stinginess coincides with reducing the strength and importance of—or constricting and redirecting—one's network ties. Removing himself from his brothers by moving to Silent Hill, while establishing new ties with people through rental and legal arrangements, made William the object of bitterness.

Vernon Hamilton, by contrast, was an object of admiration among nearly all of his neighbors. Although Jonah may have been bitter toward him, many people in the watershed viewed Vernon as a man to emulate. As the most successful guestworker I encountered, Vernon's business holdings included a three- to four-hundred-square-foot rum shop and dance hall, a one-truck transportation business, and a productive farm. In the program from 1958 to 1975, he was able to last as long as he did because he was promoted early on from the more backbreaking task of cane cutting to fireman, responsible for burning the cane fields the day before the crews cut the cane. Vernon and his wife, Carmen, had eight children, the eldest born the first year Vernon began traveling to the United States and the youngest born the year he finished traveling; their peak household consumption years thus began around ten years after Vernon first entered the program. Vernon's expenditure patterns were typical: after using his first three years' earnings to meet pent-up consumption demands, buying clothes, shoes, jewelry, and so forth for his wife and child and other family members, he purchased a house-and-garden plot and built his house. Three years later he added a small rum shop.

It wasn't until his first three children made the shift from consumers to consumer-workers, however, that Vernon significantly expanded his farming operation, transitioning, in his own words, "from gardening [subsistence farming] to farming." After this his main investments consisted of adding to his rum shop with U.S. purchases of a sound system and a freezer (for making frozen confections) and expanding his food selections. The store, bar, and dances, run by his wife and children in his absence, were among the family's principal sources of revenue until after he finally stopped traveling, when he purchased more land, some of which he rents, several head of varied livestock, and a truck for transporting his and his neighbors' farm produce to distant markets.

While I focused on the accumulation of productive resources and capital, it is worth pointing out that in these cases and others changing production and consumption patterns altered the family's ties to the watershed and its relations with others through the region. William's rental agreements with others placed him in a position of dominance, while Vernon's rum shop and dance hall provided his neighbors with a place to shop, congregate, and enjoy themselves, tempering his rental arrangement with his neighbors and thereby reducing the chance of his becoming, like William, an object of bitterness. Vernon's success may have been envied, but it was also admired, and Vernon himself was well liked throughout the watershed, his ties with his neighbors enhanced though marketing arrangements in addition to providing local entertainment. On Friday and Saturday nights families certainly benefited from his dances; without them they would have had to walk into Christiana or take a bus to Mandeville for similar amusements.

Much of the point here, however, is that not everyone in the program was as lucky as Vernon; just the opposite, in fact, is true. What differentiated the long-term migrants who accumulated capital from those who did not? Not surprisingly, all of those who hadn't accumulated capital came from poorer households. No household member had inherited any land or had access to the land of an emigrant relative. None came from families that financed either the migration of at least one member or the education (beyond high school) of one member. Those who owned land owned only house-and-garden plots of no more than half an acre in size.

This tendency for extremely small landholdings or no landholdings among this group suggested two other tendencies that inhibited households' potentials for economic growth. First, they had trouble getting loans. Although some tried to borrow money from a local bank or the USAID-funded Integrated Rural Development Project (IRDP), they had no collateral to speak of. Some succeeded in getting aid from the IRDP, but their lack of collateral restricted their credit alternatives to this single source. Second, with credit restrictions and small landholdings, individuals in these households oriented agricultural production primarily toward production for use rather than cash cropping. They hadn't, as Vernon said, made the transition "from gardening to farming."

At this point one could ask why these individuals did not, like Vernon or William or other farm workers who worked for four seasons or more and who also came from poor households, use their U.S. earnings to buy land, improve their creditworthiness, borrow, and expand production. Again we turn to their networks: simply, they were extensive, including kin distributed across several households and several generations. All of these individuals supported three or more households because of outside children and partially supported parent households as well. Whether or not a migrant household was able to accumulate capital thus depended on the social relations of all its members, the obligations associated with those social relations, and the access or lack of access to agricultural or other economic resources that accompanied those social relations.

FIVE

GUESTS AS HOSTS:
JAMAICANS IN THE TOURIST INDUSTRY

From archaic times down through all the length of the patriarchal regime, it has been the
office of the women to prepare and administer these luxuries, and it has been the perquisite of
the men of gentle birth and breeding to consume them. Drunkenness and the other pathological
consequences of the free use of stimulants therefore tend in their turn to become honorific,
as being a mark . . . of the superior status of those who are able to afford the indulgence.
Infirmities induced by over-indulgence are among some peoples freely recognized as manly
attributes. It has even happened that the name for certain diseased conditions of the body arising
from such an origin has passed into everyday speech as a synonym for "noble" or "gentle."

—THORSTEIN VEBLEN, *The Theory of the Leisure Class, 70–71*

According to the beautiful young desk clerk, Sonya, Black River's Waterloo Guest House was the first establishment in Jamaica to receive electric
light. Facing the Caribbean Sea across the main road entering town, on the
island's arid southern shore, the blue-gray guesthouse is a large two-story
wooden structure owned by a woman named Mrs. Allen and surrounded
by variegated crotons and tall, prolific breadfruit trees. The guestrooms are
upstairs. On the ground floor are a restaurant, bar, kitchen, the front desk,
and a small gift shop that opens very occasionally and stocks so little inven-
tory that one wonders who would ever shop there. Adjoining the courtyard
in back is a swimming pool and two floors of newer, air-conditioned rooms
made of concrete.

The Waterloo is the kind of place that attracts Canadian, British, German, and Dutch tourists along with the occasional U.S. anthropologist
looking for a bargain. In 2001 its rooms ranged from US$25 to $40 and its
meals from US$5 to $10. Its atmosphere and personnel are casual, tranquil,
and so different from the scripted performances and amusements of the
gated resorts or the desperate street people of the island's largest resort
cities that you might think you were on another island.

Yet it is far more likely for a Jamaican chambermaid to work in a place like the Waterloo than in one of the thirty or forty gated resorts outside Montego Bay, Ocho Rios, Runaway Bay, or Negril, and thus it is far more likely for a Jamaican chambermaid recruited to work as an H-2 worker in South Carolina, Virginia, or Michigan to come from a place like this than from one of the sprawling, exorbitant, exclusive resorts. In a study Monica Heppel, Luis Torres, and I conducted during the mid-1990s, we found that slightly more than two-thirds of Jamaicans working with H-2B visas did come from resort areas, although only a handful worked for places like Sandals, a chain of exorbitantly priced resorts in the Caribbean. As much as possible, many continue to work in Jamaica during the months they are home, but many also reported that Jamaican employers tend not to rehire workers who have entered the H-2 program.

In each of Jamaica's heavily visited tourist areas, for every expensive re-sort there are several smaller, independently owned, less expensive, quieter establishments whose desk clerks, chambermaids, cooks, and other ser-vice personnel work under both less desperate conditions than the street people and less structured conditions of employment than their fellow Jamaicans at the resorts. And for every one of those smaller independent establishments, there are several other Jamaicans who depend in some measure on the tourist traffic—growing and peddling ganja, carving wood, fishing, farming, diving for and selling shells, weaving baskets and tams, or engaging in any one of dozens of hustles in which people make from a few cents to a few dollars per day. It is these people who give the tourist areas of Jamaica their desperate feeling: these are the street people against whom the gated resorts are gated, for whom the cruise ships are off limits, and out among whom the patrons of the resorts venture, usually, only in guided vans.

The sense of desperation surfaces especially whenever a crisis, however minor, occurs. A problem with a cruise ship left the crafts market all but empty one day when my wife and I walked among the stalls. The merchants, most of them women, were hungry. They came at us like barkers at a county fair, cajoling, goading, even pulling at our shirts, pushing us toward their wares. They never stopped begging for our attention. Swarming around us, persistent and aggressive, they didn't let up even after we'd purchased as much of their merchandise as we could carry.

This was Montego Bay in January, the height of the Caribbean tourist season. The market women weren't the only Jamaicans so desperate for a sale that they plucked at our shirts or pressed a gentle hand against our backs. In the hotels, the desk clerks arranged car rentals with an eye toward kickbacks from the rental company. On the streets were young men selling packs of chewing gum, buns and cheese, individual cigarettes, and endlessly offering ganja, the services of a guide, a young girl. When they could offer nothing you desired they fell to begging. On one of the public beaches I watched a tourist refuse to buy ganja on the grounds that he already had plenty, at which time the man selling the marijuana begged for some of the tourist's.

Both the scripted, structured amusement of the gated resorts and the desperation of the street people—in many ways reflections of each other—influence the ways that Jamaican tourist personnel learn their trade and transfer these lessons to the tourist industry in the United States as H-2 workers. Tourist areas attract tourists precisely because, unlike most of the locations where H-2 workers find work, they are, or at one time were, pleasant places to visit. Their pretty vistas, comfortable temperatures, and many human and natural amenities—waterfalls, rafting, golf, exotic cuisine—bring tourists by the thousands even as they push and squeeze many permanent residents into small, less desirable neighborhoods or away from tourist areas altogether.

This process, usually called gentrification, often coincides with locals' migrating into places like Montego Bay, Jamaica, or Myrtle Beach, South Carolina, for employment—a process that adds to the desperation as too many people chase too few jobs. Inevitably, this combination of job prospects and the squeezing out of permanent residents influences local patterns of survival. Precisely how people survive depends on the wider economic and ecological setting in which gentrification takes place, and how patterns of survival have evolved in Jamaica are thus quite distinct from how they have evolved in South Carolina or the other U.S. destinations of H-2 workers.

At the Waterloo Guest House, for example, Sonia and the other desk clerks, cooks, and bartenders typically work long shifts that are broken by lengthy periods of time off. Sonia's schedule consists of two seventeen-hour shifts beginning Friday, followed by a fifteen-hour shift and then a five- to six-hour shift, adding up to fifty hours or more in four days. On Monday, her short day, she overlaps with Rebecca, another young woman who works a ten-hour shift on Monday, followed by three to four fifteen-hours shifts, depending on guest occupancy rates or other, more personal factors. These personal factors may include working in other jobs or combining paid tourist employment with other activities critical to household well-being. Places like the Waterloo let workers share jobs, live with their children on the grounds or bring them to work, or otherwise combine multiple livelihoods.

In cases where tourist workers work under more rigorous schedules, or migrate for extended periods, as in the H-2 program, they often rely on other household members or members of their networks to take charge of the complex, diversified livelihoods that meeting expenses in Jamaica's tourist areas entail. This has occurred in Negril, one of the most recent towns to join the list of gentrified tourist areas in Jamaica. In the past twenty-five years, Negril has changed from a small fishing village on Jamaica's west coast to a fifteen-mile stretch of bars, hotels, and gated beach and cliff resorts. While small and inexpensive guesthouses were still available for lower-income tourists only fifteen years ago, today nearly all the ocean-front property has been purchased and developed by capitalist interests. The cheapest rooms rent per night for about half the weekly salary of most Jamaican tourist workers. Like other tourist areas of Jamaica, along Negril's outskirts several businesses that cater to tourists have sprung up, among them wood carving shops, stores that produce or sell recreational drugs, guide and transportation services, prostitution, and smaller, less expensive restaurants and bars.

On this edge of Negril I encountered a young man I'll call Robert. Robert works at his mother's small restaurant, buys hallucinogenic mushrooms from farmers in the surrounding hills for sale to tourists, and cares for his children during the time that his "baby mother," Daphne, works at the high-priced resort, Sandals. Sandals resorts are gated, secure, completely private, and have their own beaches, bars, restaurants, and other entertainment. For those who can afford them, and few in Jamaican can, they are, in short, total institutions. Sandals and similar resorts, unlike the Waterloo, typically require that their chambermaids clean rooms more deeply than elsewhere in Jamaica and cater to guests as personal servants. A stay at Sandals can cost $700 to $1,200 or more per couple per night, which is around four to nine times the typical salary of J$6,000 (US$150) per week paid to chambermaids in the resorts. Unlike places like the Water-loo, resorts such as Sandals are less inclined to allow workers the flexibility most Jamaicans need to survive. Other members of their households and networks, then, like Robert, compensate for the discipline they experience on the job, subsidizing this discipline with their supportive roles.

Long breaks from work at the Waterloo Guest House and Robert's multiple livelihoods in Negril complement other practices that characterize work in Jamaica's tourist industry. Many hotels have dormitories for workers or allow them to stay in unoccupied rooms between seventeen-hour shifts. In others, as noted above, workers share jobs. Both practices, again, allow Jamaican tourist workers the opportunity to move among different economic activities or social obligations, maintaining the ties that support them during trying times. Multiple sources of income and the social obligations of diffuse Jamaican networks at once reflect the country's desperation and illustrate the resilience and ingenuity of so many who work in Jamaican tourism. In tourist Jamaica, too, these combinations of wage work with other tasks that generate income for households reduce consumption costs, or assist with survival in other ways, and also influence the ways that positions are assigned and tasks get accomplished in the hotels and resorts. Clerks, cooks, chambermaids, and others in Jamaica's hotels often bring their other economic activities and social obligations to work, offering services to hotel guests on the side, recruiting family and friends for sporadic employment on the hotel grounds such as repairing fences or building new units, or partnering with friends in other sectors of the tourist industry to generate demand for guiding services, rental cars, handicrafts, and so forth.

Once women leave Jamaica for the United States and are cut off from familiar, nearby social supports, their complex strategies for survival are replaced by a single contract that specifies wages, working conditions, and other aspects of work. In Myrtle Beach, South Carolina, the case with which I am most familiar, Jamaicans' employers expect them to devote the bulk of their waking hours to cleaning rooms and replenishing supplies of shampoo, towels, washcloths, shoe mitts, and shower caps. Given the high value Jamaicans attach to these jobs, Jamaican chambermaids are motivated to outperform their U.S.-citizen counterparts, leading their employers to prefer them to native South Carolinians.

Clearly, it isn't only a lack of workers that underlies employers' shifting to new and foreign sources for labor, but a lack of highly disciplined, reliable workers willing to submit to authority to the employer's satisfaction. Before Jamaicans entered the hotel industry in the late 1980s, chambermaids in South Carolina were primarily African American women, as in the blue crab industry. Typically, those cleaning rooms in Myrtle Beach, the first South Carolina location to receive H-2 workers, came from inland communities between Myrtle Beach and Florence (about sixty miles inland) or from closer, coastal neighborhoods of North Myrtle Beach or Little River. These latter areas are smaller, less elaborately developed stretches of the

South Carolina coast with strips of lower-cost motels and apartments that college kids might rent for spring break.

South Carolina's coast has developed in ways similar to coastal regions up and down the eastern seaboard, with one way of life gradually displacing and replacing another over time. This has been true since colonial times. Europeans settling South Carolina's coast in the sixteenth, seventeenth, and eighteenth centuries took advantage of Charleston's natural features for port facilities and its wet, fresh-water tidal flats to establish indigo and rice plantations. This region, today known as the South Carolina low country, was covered with swampy maritime forests and crossed by several large, slow-moving rivers that made the soil as rich and productive as similar soils in south Florida's sugar-growing region.

Unfortunately for early settlers, so much standing water provided breeding grounds for mosquitoes and other disease-carrying pests. South Carolina's coastal lowlands came to be considered unhealthy, harboring debilitating mists known as miasmas and plagued by malaria and yellow fever. Early in South Carolina's colonial history, white planters moved to higher ground and imported slaves from rice-producing areas of Africa to work their fields. Charleston gained prominence as the region's principal slave market, a distinction that the city, in typical American fashion, today celebrates by having converted the former slave market into a market where tourists can buy baskets, jams, breads, paintings, shell handicrafts, and other wares that are often produced by the descendants of people once bought and sold there.

Gradually, of course, the white families trickled back, but only after importing so many slaves to work their plantations that, at the time of the American Revolution, South Carolina was second only to Virginia in the number of slaves per capita (Ellis 2000). Following massive slave relocations during the mid-eighteenth century, in which many thousands of slaves from Virginia were moved to plantations further south and west to fuel expanding cotton production, South Carolina became one of the most African American states in the South. In 1900 nearly 60 percent of the state's population was African American, although that percentage dropped by around half in the twentieth century, in part because of an influx of white retirees from the Northeast and Midwest and the so-called selling of the South (Kovacik and Winberry 1987; Cobb 1982).

The South Carolina low country became a major cotton-producing area during the late eighteenth and nineteenth centuries, its famous sea island cotton dominating the coastal economy until the Civil War. African Americans typically outnumbered whites throughout the low country, with its inland forests and swamps and adjacent salt flats, a factor that encouraged the retention of Gullah and Geechee cultural attributes and accounts for their contemporary importance as a source of ethnic identity and cultural heritage among inhabitants of the area. Folklorist William Bascom, conducting fieldwork on Gullah and Geechee beliefs about childbirth in the early 1940s, attributed their persistence to the overwhelming number of African Americans relative to whites along much of the coast. "North of Sapeloe on Harris Neck," he wrote, "which is all but an island, there were between fifty and sixty Negro families in 1939 to about five white families, only two of which remained throughout the year. On Hilton Head there were 1,377 Negroes in 1930 to 97 whites, and by 1939 the latter figure had dropped to 40" (1991, 28). Other South Carolina sea islands had similar ratios of African Americans to whites.

The same skewed demography that encouraged pride in African roots allowed the economic marginalization of low country South Carolina after the decline of cotton and the slow growth of truck farming along the coast. Until the development of the tourist industry beyond Charleston, South Carolina's sea islands and many other parts of the coast were primarily a source of summer vegetable production, supplying markets with fresh produce between the earlier Florida and Georgia harvests and the later harvests along the North Carolina coastal plain and Virginia and Maryland's eastern shores. Low country families supplemented this seasonal farming with subsistence and commercial fishing, hunting, trapping, and handicrafts, and eventually became known for producing especially fine, expensive baskets from local grasses and reeds. Today they sell these baskets in the markets of Charleston and from seasonal booths along coastal Highway 17.

The growth of a mixed economy of farming, fishing, casual wage labor, and other activities tied to the swampy, low country landscape allowed many African American families engaged in multiple livelihoods, moving among settings where not only the work but also the conditions of work, supervision, and the social dimensions of jobs changed frequently. African American women experienced a variety of labor relations through the year, including working by and for themselves, with friends and family, as part of farm labor crews, and as members of household staffs for wealthier white families. When these women moved into the tourist industry, supplying the bulk of the chambermaid labor to Myrtle Beach hotels, they generally continued to engage in other kinds of work as well. Those who significantly scaled back their mix of economic alternatives did so, primarily, with the help of the state. One African American woman, MR, recalling her occupational history, said:

MR: Well, I did have housework, babysitting. Kind of like doing housework—keeping house, working to schools when they had big dinners, helped clean up them, and helped fix the food. That was when I was in my *young* days. . . . I have worked in tobacco, picked cotton, chopped, and did potatoes too. All of that stuff. Lilly [MR's sister] is about eight years older than I am. But we worked together in tobacco, chopped cotton, picked cotton, did all of that stuff. But I can't go way back and tell you what my mother did, but I do know she did cooking for white people, because I've heard her say that. But we worked in tobacco, from sunrise to sunset in tobacco, and I hated it. I hated that field. If I ever got out of there, if I didn't do nothing but smoke it, that would be enough for me. . . .
INTERVIEWER: What are some of the main reasons you switched jobs? Could you get more money at another one?
MR: No, no, no. What you mean? Wait just a minute. I guess it's been a good while ago, back in them days, that's the first time this employment came out. You'd hear talk of people working, and doing it in the summer, when your work ended, you'd draw this unemployment. You've heard of that, haven't you? Well, that's what we do now when a place closes up. We draw this unemployment during the wintertime. That's what this is all about.

Unemployment insurance enabled MR to cut back on the number of wage-paying jobs she took during the year, supplementing unemployment payments with other forms of assistance such as food stamps and energy assistance and still able to fish, garden, make handicrafts, or piece together other sources of income. Significantly, too, she used these forms of state support to leave a job—tobacco—that she vehemently hated and that, throughout much of the South, was long associated first with slavery and then with sharecropping, debt peonage, tenant farming, and the persistence of rural poverty and power disparities (Buck 2001; Daniel 1972; Griffith 2004). Tobacco was also important in the life histories of many families who eventually supplied chambermaids to Myrtle Beach; today it is one of the principal crops using H-2 workers.

A highly labor-intensive crop, tobacco requires significant hand and stoop labor during much of the year, from caring for the young plants to processing the harvested leaves. Workers transplant the seedlings, which are grown from seed in greenhouses early in the year, into fields in the spring, and harvest the plants as they mature through the summer. Before the introduction of new drying technologies, tobacco leaves were strung on long sticks and the sticks hung in tobacco barns to dry, a task made particularly unpleasant by dripping tobacco juice. The labor-intensive nature of tobacco is one reason why tobacco farmers today are among the principal beneficiaries of H-2 and undocumented immigrant workers.

The South Carolina low country, primarily the area surrounding Myrtle Beach known as the Pee Dee counties, is the principal tobacco-growing region in the state and hence the region hardest hit by the development of alternative economic opportunities for tobacco workers like MR. Myrtle Beach's Horry County was one of the largest tobacco-producing counties in the state. Begun in the late 1880s, South Carolina tobacco began to assume economic importance early in the twentieth century; by 1920 it was among the state's major cash crops. Until the 1960s tobacco production was primarily a small-farm enterprise, owing primarily to the allotment system put in place under the New Deal and strengthened by the Kerr-Smith Act of 1934. Briefly, this system limited the amount of tobacco individual farmers could produce by tying specific production quotas to specific plots of land. Even when farmers leased allotments from other farmers and landowners, they had to grow tobacco on the farm to which the allotment was tied. "Because of its limited acreages, labor-intensive character, and dispersed fields," write Kovacik and Winberry, "tobacco production long was dominated by small farmers" (1987, 165).

In the 1960s regulations relaxed to allow more flexible land-use policies for tobacco production. Allotments were no longer tied to specific plots of land and farmers could lease an allotment and grow that allotment's quota on their own land, consolidating their holdings. At the same time, South Carolina's land grant university, Clemson, developed a mechanical harvester and promoted a new method of drying tobacco leaves. These changes, combined with the expansion of unemployment insurance and state support during Lyndon Johnson's War on Poverty, altered employment patterns and labor relations in the low country, displacing some African American families from rural farm employment, forcing others to work in alternate cropping regimes, and encouraging others to enter long- and short-term farm labor migrant circuits or leave agricultural labor altogether (Hahamovich 1997; Griffith 1993).

As in other parts of the South, Myrtle Beach tourist development was taking off around the time that these changes in agriculture were taking place. Like the African Americans described in Chapter 2, displaced from the crab-picking industry, African Americans in South Carolina's low country experienced similar labor market changes in agriculture and sought work in the growing coastal tourist industry. African American women were recruited particularly as chambermaids.

The employment of black women as chambermaids in Myrtle Beach and other resort areas evolved out of their work as domestic servants in the homes of wealthy white South Carolinians. One woman I interviewed, a sharecropper's daughter, reported that African Americans learned about the habits of whites in the South by working in their homes. She added that this allowed African Americans to understand white culture more deeply than whites could ever understand African American culture, an observation particularly true throughout the Gullah and Geechee areas of South Carolina's low country. Domestics typically either lived in the houses where they worked or commuted to work each day from poorer African American neighborhoods, and their living conditions usually reflected their status relative to the families whose children they raised, houses they cleaned, or laundry they washed.

Divisions among African Americans working in white households have been common since the days of the antebellum plantation, workers' spaces being more or less circumscribed on the basis of how trusted they were or how long they had worked for the household. Some domestic workers, for example, could only approach the kitchen without actually entering the house, while others were confined to the kitchen or the ground floor and still others had the run of the house. The most trusted workers may have supplied fish or special services to the house or moved between the plantation lands and city markets to buy provisions for the household, spreading news that connected slave families and, occasionally, spurred slave insurrections (Cecelski 2001).

While divisions within the African American workforce have a rich history, divisions between African American and immigrant workers are far more recent in South Carolina and the South in general. Recently, the South has been called a new destination for immigrants from Latin America and the Caribbean, and there has been a proliferation of studies focusing on new immigrants moving into the carpet industry, construction, poultry processing, meatpacking, and other primarily rural industries (Goździak and Martin 2005; Zúñiga and Hernández-León 2005; Fink 2003). The designation "new" is not entirely accurate. Immigrant workers from Mexico, the Caribbean, and Central America have been arriving in a number of southern locations, particularly Florida, since at least the 1940s and 1950s, after the mechanization of cotton and sugar beets, and for the past thirty to forty years have been diffusing into more and more agricultural production areas across the region (Griffith et al. 1995; Griffith 1993). What is new has been the growth of *settled* populations of new immigrants and their dispersion into many more segments of the southern economy.

Carolina employers have been major beneficiaries of this process. Both North and South Carolina have seen their immigrant populations grow from the 1990 to the 2000 census, in some areas by as much as 600 to 700 percent, and the census misses many of the undocumented and those not home when the count is done. In Monks Corners, South Carolina, for example, one of the largest plant nurseries on the East Coast currently employs a mixed African American and Mixtec labor force; most of the Mixtecs are young women who speak only Mixtec and who are supervised by bilingual Mixtec-Spanish-speaking men from their villages in Oaxaca, Mexico. Similarly, in southeastern North Carolina, the region's turkey-, pork-, and chicken-processing plants have benefited substantially from the influx of Mexican and Central American workers (Stull and Broadway 2003; Griffith 1993).

This immigration comes at a time of increasing coastal gentrification and the problems and employment opportunities that gentrification has generated. Ironically, as more and more new immigrants move into coastal regions, rather than swelling the labor force to a point where no employers have trouble finding workers, they often contribute to the rapid expansion of certain sectors but not others, absorbing labor more rapidly into these sectors. While the construction industry, for example, has been a major employer of new immigrants along the coast, many employers in the hotel industry have consistently come up short in their search for workers for some positions. Hotels usually have little difficulty recruiting bartenders, desk clerks, and some restaurant wait staff, but recruiting chambermaids and other cleaning staff has been problematic over the past decade. According to the personnel director of the first hotel in Myrtle Beach to import Jamaican H-2b workers, "We explored housing, transportation, and even worked with some of the local daycare centers to give our workers 20 percent off, but even so, most of our cleaning staff can't afford to live in Myrtle Beach. We have to get workers from as far as two hundred miles away, and not many workers want to ride on a bus for four hours for six dollars an hour." Another hotel manager said, "This summer, actually, a lot of different companies have a big problem with keeping people and even getting people to walk in the door. We haven't had the same influx that we normally have. I don't know if it's—there's speculation that there's not much housing."

Wages? Transportation? Housing? Whenever I hear employers speculate like this I wonder whether they ever consider what labor historians observing H-2 programs suggest: that labor supply problems in regions such as the Carolina coast and other resort areas does not mean there are simply no workers but that hiring has become impossible *under current conditions.* The use of H-2B workers in hotels and resorts is somewhat distinct from their use in other industries that use guestworkers. I mentioned earlier that resort sites are not unpleasant, nor are they as isolated as some of the other industries that rely on H-2s. They are, on the contrary, locations that attract tourists for their charm, beauty, or unique natural environmental features: the mountains of Virginia and West Virginia, the vast watery landscape of Lake Michigan, the white beaches and golf havens of Myrtle Beach. They emit no noxious odors or industrial soot. They are places with high real estate values and correspondingly high costs of living, occupied seasonally by large numbers of people who expect to pay exorbitant prices for food, housing, and transportation. On vacation, these people expect to have their luggage carried, their passage through lobbies and up elevators smoothed, and their rooms cleaned; when they play golf they expect to have caddies; and when they take their meals at restaurants they expect the waiters, bartenders, and cocktail waitresses to be responsive and warm, and to meet complaints and jokes alike with a smile. These expectations are not without a solid foundation: in addition to expecting such service, they fully expect to pay for it. Over and above their direct expenses, they tip their bellhops, caddies, chambermaids, bartenders, waiters, and cocktail waitresses, or they allow gratuities for these services to be included in their bills.

This means that labor conditions are uneven and some jobs more desirable than others. A bartender or waiter in an expensive restaurant can make good money—much of it tax free, in cash—while a chambermaid or janitor often doesn't earn enough to pay for the high food, housing, and transportation costs characteristic of resort areas. Two economic forces thus create the conditions for the use of foreign workers: desirable low-skill service jobs (e.g., bartender), and undesirable, low-paying, low-skill service jobs (e.g., chambermaid) characterized by a high turnover of domestic workers who either move into the more desirable jobs or move out of the resort areas altogether.

Again, it isn't just that there aren't enough U.S. citizens willing to work. Hotel personnel managers themselves acknowledge that they have no trouble with staffing certain jobs. It's that their labor supply problems are unevenly distributed because of the inequality in wages, tips, working conditions, access to affordable housing, transportation, child care, and other factors. Unlike the staff of Jamaica's Waterloo Guest House, these employers fail to adapt their scheduling and staffing needs to those of workers in ways that are tolerable to a domestic workforce. Instead, they rely on the state.

Power imbalances, grounded in the state and class or caste relations, have always been at the core of low-wage labor markets (Griffith 1987, 1993). This was the case in the mid-1980s when a luxurious hotel on Michigan's Mackinac Island brought in its first Jamaican waiters with the help of the West Indies Central Labour Organisation (WICLO). A few years later several resorts on the island, as well as others in Michigan, Virginia, and South Carolina, joined the program, requesting Jamaican workers as waiters and chambermaids. The workers who came to these hotels not only helped solve the problem of obtaining seasonal labor, their British and Jamaican nationality enriched the ambiance of these resorts in ways that their employers considered classy and exotic. Karen Richman has noted that some Marriott Hotels routinely have their staff wear nametags with not only their names but also their places of origin, lending their establishments an international flair. Jamaicans brought a similar cachet, and most, as noted earlier, were hired from resort areas in Jamaica, arriving with experience and Jamaican employer recommendations behind them.

Recall Victoria Barrow, the widow with five children mentioned in Chapter 3. She was living and working in Montego Bay, Jamaica, when she first migrated to Kingston Plantation, in Myrtle Beach, South Carolina, to work as a chambermaid under the H-2B program. She had been a chambermaid in Montego Bay, working for one of the upscale resorts east of town, when she received assurances from her boss and a friend in the Ministry of Labour that she would receive good recommendations and a good chance at getting a visa if she applied for the program. Victoria saw this opportunity, with its higher wages, as her ticket to a more secure lifestyle, despite its obvious drawback of living abroad, separated from her family.

Victoria entered the program at age forty-two. Her oldest child, Paula, was twenty-five. Though Paula managed her own household in downtown Montego Bay, about two miles from her mother, she was able to care for her siblings with the help of her seventeen-year-old sister, Anne, and Victoria's sister, the children's aunt, Catherine. The other children were a daughter, Vivian, age four, and two sons, Michael and Robert, ages nineteen and fifteen. Leaving her family for eight or nine months every year, between March and December, was understandably difficult, but the high pay was just too important to pass up. Little Vivian, especially, hated to see her mother go.

Working in Myrtle Beach didn't make the separation any easier. Though a popular tourist destination, during the height of the tourist season Victoria's workload was grueling and her living situation far from desirable. Like most of the Jamaican chambermaids in the program, she lived in North Myrtle Beach, in one of the run-down motels in an African American neighborhood, sharing a room with two other chambermaids. Across the street was a nameless bar where youths milled around or cruised by in loud cars late into the night, and at the end of the street, across Ocean Boulevard, kids sold drugs in and around several abandoned beachfront motels. On one, someone had spray-painted "Keep Out" beneath a drawing of a knife and a machine gun.

A Kingston Plantation bus picked the workers up every morning and dropped them off every night. They had no car of their own. To shop they walked to a nearby Dollar General store or pooled their money for a taxi to Wal-Mart, something they always did at the end of the season, just before returning home. Victoria's days were difficult. A short woman, just five-feet-four, with a sweet round face to match her disposition, she didn't strike me at first glance as a woman who could lift couches to vacuum or zip from room to room as guests passed through the hallways, smiling and stepping aside, so adept at expressing humility and subservience that you would have thought she'd taken classes under British colonial rule. She was browner than she was black, a point she made the first day we spoke, referring to her sister-in-law. I told her I had spent several months in Christiana and Black River, Jamaica, in 1982 and 1983, and she asked me if I knew a woman named Sister Liz in Black River. "She's brown brown," Victoria said. "Like me."

Sister Liz was, in fact, our mutual acquaintance; she ran a rum shop about two miles from where I lived in Black River, on the road to Pedro's Cross, and when Victoria described her as "brown brown" she meant to place Sister Liz, along with herself, in a color structure far more sensitive to shades than U.S. white people's, with subtle class implications. She may have been cleaning rooms in a hotel in Myrtle Beach, hauling dirty towels to the laundry and wiping porcelain, but in Jamaica she was a step above. Even in the United States she considered herself superior to many of the African American South Carolinians she encountered on the street and at work, more than once calling them "bad people." Other Jamaicans I knew expressed similar sentiments, faulting African Americans for not taking advantage of the enormous opportunities they had in the United States and adding that African Americans disdained Jamaicans for their hard work.

And in fact Victoria's time in Myrtle Beach, which allowed her to maintain her social level, required that she work very hard. I noted in Chapter 3 that on a typical day Victoria cleaned between a dozen and sixteen rooms, most of them requiring the additional work associated with guests checking out. In addition, part of Victoria's workload came from the African American chambermaids at the hotel, who, she said, "leave as soon as their bus arrives, even if they're not through with their rooms. Then the Jamaicans have to finish them up." What Victoria didn't mention—perhaps she didn't know—was that most of the African Americans lived between Myrtle Beach and Florence, as far as an hour's bus ride into the low country. If they missed their bus, the only alternatives would be to call and ask a relative to make a two-hour round trip on their behalf or hire a taxi, whose cost was prohibitive.

The consequence was that Victoria, taking on additional work, cleaned hard. Some of the guests would stay for a week at a time and leave her $1, $5, or no tip at all, but most spent just a night or two. The short-term occupancy wasn't surprising. Single rooms at the Kingston Plantation cost between $185 and $385 per night—three to seven times what Victoria earned in an average day—and condominiums or rental houses rented for much more. The resort catered to two- and four-day conventions. These cornerstones of capitalist commerce, with their panels and exhibits, increased Victoria's and the other chambermaids' workload by structuring the schedules of hundreds of conference participants, encouraging the two- and three-night stays that increased the frequency of guest turnover while generating the additional tasks associated with lectures, lunches, meetings, and exhibits.

While waiting to talk with Victoria or one of the other Jamaican chambermaids through the spring, summer, and fall months from 1998 to 2001, I often wandered from booth to booth in the Plantation's large convention ballroom, collecting note cards and key chains and browsing through the latest in dental technology, recreational boating, real estate development, pharmaceuticals. Victoria and her fellow maids heard parts of lectures on creative financing, or statistics on the survival rates of heart patients, while wheeling coffee and pastries into the backs of meeting rooms or clearing away one set of beverages for another, half-melted ice sloshing about in pans. Whether or not such lectures enriched their experiences in the United States or merely distracted them is a question only they can answer, but I'm pretty sure Victoria was too tired after only a few weeks in Myrtle Beach to bother listening to lectures on root canal technology or protease inhibitors.

Victoria's experience is mirrored among H-2 workers throughout the hotel industry. As part of the mid-1990s study mentioned earlier, we interviewed eighty-nine workers and twenty-two employers in this industry, attempting to profile immigrants' experiences and understand employers' attitudes and treatment of employees generally, immigrants and natives alike. Central to these experiences and attitudes is the fact that the hotel and resort industry is an extremely competitive sector of the economy. Proprietors not only compete with other proprietors in their own areas, but areas compete with one another throughout the United States and even with other areas of the world, including those regions, like Jamaica, that supply the U.S. industry with some of its workers. It is also an area of the economy in a nearly constant state of flux from year to year and from season to season, characterized by high levels of franchising, population movement, business openings and closings, and seasonal shifts in commercial activity.

While Mexican workers are most common in other industries that use H-2B workers, hotels and resorts tend to hire workers from Jamaica. At the Jamaican Ministry of Labour, Luis Torres and I had the opportunity to discuss the program with the country's permanent secretary of labour, whose comments shed some light on the stake the sending nations have in temporary alien labor programs:

> What is the role of the state in the employment and welfare of Jamaican workers overseas? According to Mr. Irons [the permanent secretary of labour], the program hinges on Jamaica's liaison organization (WICLO) in the employing countries. "We won't send workers to the States or Canada without liaison services." A small proportion of workers' "compulsory savings" supports the liaison service, allowing a representative of the Jamaican government to travel to the United States personally and view the conditions in which the workers live and work. He is of the opinion that the Jamaican workers in the United States who aren't in the alien labor program are less likely to receive protections than those who have access to the liaison service. (Griffith's field notes, January 11, 1994)

Workers we interviewed reported meeting with personnel of the WICLO office and feeling that they could call this office if they experienced any serious problems. One told how she had forwarded medical bills she had incurred while working in the United States to the office and had them taken care of. In Secretary Irons's view, the sugar program was the cornerstone of the entire program, operating to protect all Jamaican workers in the United States and Canada, and when it was terminated, Jamaica cut back the liaison service to halftime, undermining state protections for all workers. There are, however, problems with the liaison service that extend beyond mere numbers of liaison officers or offices. First, liaison officers are typically trained as diplomats, with limited experience at resolving human service dilemmas, labor disputes, or other worker problems requiring skills more in line with psychology, counseling, the legal profession, or social work. Coming from a diplomatic background and usually appointed to these highly sought posts thought political patronage and social connections, liaison officers tend to come from professional classes in Jamaica and hence share little beyond nationality with the workers they represent.

While some liaison officers can become skilled at handling disputes and addressing social service issues, their hands are tied in other ways. Particularly difficult for them is that they operate from a weak position vis-à-vis employers of temporary foreign workers and U.S. and Canadian government officials, a factor constraining how effectively they can advocate on behalf of workers. At a meeting of several liaison officers in Ontario, Canada, in 2003, I observed and listened to several women and men in these positions express frustration over their posts. Although the consular officials from Mexico and Jamaica were noticeably quiet throughout much of the meeting, one of the Canadian liaison officers from the eastern Caribbean said he was afraid that if he advocated too hard for workers from his country he would lose jobs to workers from Jamaica, Mexico, El Salvador, or perhaps even Laos, or any other country hungry to establish guestworker agreements with Canada and the United States. Similarly, the secretary of labor Luis and I interviewed in Kingston viewed Jamaica as a competitor with other Caribbean countries and with Mexico in terms of sending guestworkers to the United States and Canada. Just as African American workers from the South Carolina low country compete with Jamaicans carrying H-2 visas, Jamaicans understand—and their liaison officers remind them lest they forget—that they are competing with other West Indians, Mexicans, and nearly any other worker from any nation as impoverished as theirs. We must consider their experiences in the United States against this background.

Most H-2B workers in the hotel-resort industry are women who work as chambermaids; only men are certified to work as waiters. Some of the

Jamaican women serve food and drinks in the lounges, but this is outside the terms of their contract and therefore technically illegal. Like most H-2 workers, those we interviewed were young but not, in general, very young, ranging from their midtwenties to their midforties and, on average, in their midthirties. They were no younger than the U.S. citizens they worked with, and in this they differed from workers in the crab industry, where the data indicated that domestic workers were older and in fact aging out of the workforce. These ages suggest that Jamaicans entering the program are more likely to be seasoned employees than young people entering the workforce for the first time. At this age they are likely, too, to have some grown and some dependent children, and to be capable of leaving their homes for extended periods even if divorced or separated. In fact, some workers we interviewed supported more than six children, with most supporting two or three.

Hiring workers with dependent family members is in the interest of both sending and receiving states, and Jamaica has played a more active state role than Mexico in constituting its H-2 workforce. Given that Jamaica supplies the bulk of H-2 workers to hotels and resorts, many features of the H-2B program in the tourist industry are somewhat more formally structured and more closely monitored than in other industries that use guestworkers. Jamaicans routinely receive written contracts, though at the last minute, after they have arranged their lives around participating in the program. This last-minute compliance with the terms of the international agreement gives workers little opportunity to raise questions about contractual arrangements or even inform loved ones about such things as how frequently they can expect remittances or where they can write. Contracts guarantee virtually all workers hourly wages, and two-thirds a minimum amount of work, but no one reported being guaranteed minimum earnings for the season. All knew where they would be working and what they would be doing, but only a third knew in what kind of accommodations they would be living. Three-fourths reported that their employers had lived up to their expectations regarding wages, working conditions, living conditions, and other attributes of the program. Put another way, a quarter of the workers felt duped.

From informal interviews with workers in Jamaica we learned that the weeks prior to their coming to the United States can be a particularly frustrating and intimidating time. Workers await postcards telling them of interviews. They are then made to wait for long periods at various agencies in Kingston to receive medical examinations and the necessary papers.

Unlike women H-2 workers from Mexico, Jamaican women are given pregnancy tests and denied admittance if they test positive. Several of the Mexican women with H-2 visas whom I came to know arrived three to four months pregnant, fully intending to deliver their children on U.S. soil, a common practice among undocumented female immigrants in the United States that I discuss in more detail in Chapter 7.

Arriving in the Miami by airplane, most Jamaicans are then bused to their final destinations. Different employers handle their travel arrangements differently, however, and some workers are flown directly to their destination, while others take the bus from Miami. Travel time can vary from a few hours to as many as seventy; the average trip among those we interviewed took fifty-five hours—time for which very, very few workers are paid. Travel advances, deducted from later earnings, average around $20, or enough to cover minimal food expenses along the way.

Arriving, usually, in late spring, their season lasts either almost all year or only until the early fall months. The amount of work fluctuates over this period, daily and weekly schedules changing throughout the season as guest occupancy rates rise and fall with holidays, changes of season, conventions, and other factors. Perhaps because domestic and foreign workers are affected equally by these fluctuations, domestic workers are more likely to cycle through these jobs as they mix them with others and with the responsibilities of home. H-2 workers do work in jobs outside their contracts during slow periods, but their principal responsibility is to the employer who signs their contract: if they fail to satisfy the employer, they are subject to deportation.

Summer is the peak employment season for most resorts, of course, and in the summer months there is often no shortage of labor because of students seeking summer jobs. Still, many employers prefer guestworkers to students, who tend to seek resort work mainly because it sounds like a fun way to spend the summer and who are not particularly reliable workers. In some areas H-2B workers become a critical source of labor after Labor Day, the official end of the summer season, when guest occupancy rates become more irregular yet concentrated. Some resorts experience slow periods between Labor Day and Thanksgiving, for example, with sudden spikes during the three to four days of Thanksgiving. This has led to one of the most persistent complaints among H-2 workers: that they would sometimes sit around for weeks, waiting for work. Most domestic workers quit during these "down times" and are welcome to return during the spikes, but H-2B workers do not have this option.

Daily hours fluctuate, not unlike the month-to-month schedules. On days they are called to work the range is from a low of six hours to a high of twelve hours per day when occupancy rates are high. This range excludes those days when workers have nothing at all to do, which in some of the more exclusive and isolated locations can last two months. The average workday lasts around eight hours, but, for chambermaids at least, tends not to begin early. Guests are allowed to sleep at least until 9:00 or 9:30 before the chambermaids begin knocking on their doors. While some wait staff work a breakfast rush, others don't begin work until 2:00 in the afternoon. Split shifts—working the lunch hour and the dinner hour with some time off in between—are not uncommon for wait staff.

Sporadic and irregular employment, then, is the industry norm for H-2 workers. It is one of the aspects of these jobs that reduce their appeal to all but a captive workforce with few other options and little power to complain. Of the 42 percent of workers we interviewed who had had problems with supervision or other aspects of the job, only a little more than half had these problems satisfactorily resolved. Stated another way, about one in every five H-2 workers had problems with employment that were not addressed. It's likely, too, that this is an underestimate. H-2 workers tend to be particularly reluctant to voice their true opinions about work. Always afraid of not being called back at the end of the season, they typically hold their tongues, even during the long stretch between Labor Day and Thanksgiving when there is little to do.

Reflecting weeks of slow or reduced traffic through the resorts, one-third of those interviewed reported working fewer than five days per week; 42 percent, however, said they usually worked six days per week and another 4 percent said they worked seven days, although hours vary over the season. There were no significant differences between the domestic and foreign workers in terms of days worked per week, which averaged around four and a half for both groups. Commonly, of course, their days off were taken during the week—Mondays or Tuesdays—rather than on the weekends, because of the high demand for service on weekends.

Many hotels and resorts using temporary foreign workers are very large employers, corporations that manage sprawling estates and have from a hundred to three thousand workers, yet others are smaller operations that entered the H-2 program only after larger hotels in their areas led the way. Regardless of the size of the company, however, work groups are nearly always fairly small. In these groups, workers tend to be matched by cultural background, which makes working less of a culture shock than it might be otherwise. Average work groups number only five or six workers, and it is common for workers to help one another out. Chambermaids typically have quotas, being assigned a particular number of rooms to clean; though meeting their quota is usually not a problem, several chambermaids reported giving or receiving help when faced with a particularly messy set of rooms to clean. Working in teams of co-ethnics certainly facilitates this cooperation. At the same time, this form of ethnic segmentation within the labor force lends a material dimension to existing divisions between foreign and domestic workers, underlying misunderstandings of the kind Victoria voiced about African American chambermaids whose rooms she had to clean. Small-group solidarity is accomplished, that is, at the expense of class-based alliance.

While most of the chambermaids we interviewed were paid hourly wages and occasionally received tips, we learned of a number of different pay arrangements during our informal interviews with waiters. At one resort, for example, when guests are on an "American Plan" waiters are paid on a "per head" basis (e.g., $1.28 for each person at a table during breakfast and $3 for dinner). At this resort, guests are charged a service charge of 16 percent. For guests on the "European Plan," this service charge is divided among waiters (who receive from 54 to 66 percent), captains (20 percent), and headwaiters (10 percent), with 10 percent kept by the house. Guests don't know, however, that their waiter receives only a partial tip.

At another hotel a 19 percent service charge is added to all bills, and prominent "No Tipping" signs are displayed throughout the hotel. There, waiters receive no portion of the mandatory service charge; the house pockets it entirely. Schemes of this sort, which further enrich employers at the direct expense of workers, are among the principal reasons that worker advocates object to guestworker programs as currently configured. They also lend additional weight to my contention, developed in more detail in the concluding chapter, that guestworker programs, without adequate government oversight, evolve over time to approximate illegal systems of staffing onerous occupations, including slavery and debt peonage

At the core of many such schemes is worker housing. Unlike H-2A workers in agriculture, H-2B workers in hotels and resorts, like H-2B workers in seafood processing, pay for their own housing. Those we interviewed were evenly split as to whether they received housing as part of their job package. In South Carolina temporary housing was provided to H-2B workers until they were able to locate housing on their own. In one exceptional case, employers provided housing and two weeks' worth of groceries to the

H-2B workers without charge, and also lined up rental units for the workers to consider in their search. This allowed workers to live without borrowing or spending their own savings until they received their first paychecks, although this was clearly the exception to the rule.

Those who were provided housing as part of the job were not all foreign workers, but providing housing for domestic workers is clearly less common than it is for H-2B workers. We found that employers housed 83 percent of the H-2 hotel workers either temporarily or for the entire season, but only 15 percent of the domestic workers. Most workers who are provided housing share their quarters, if not their rooms, with other foreign and domestic workers. Housing options are variable and largely or entirely up to the employer's discretion. In a few cases, employer-provided housing had a surplus of living space, offering workers a choice of rooms, and workers tended to report that they were free to choose their own rooms rather than be assigned housing, as is the case in agriculture and most other industries using H-2 workers. The trade-off here is that the cost of housing was somewhat higher than what workers paid in other industries, ranging from $15.65 to $75 per week. Usually this cost is deducted from workers' pay and represents a significant proportion of earnings.

No standard employer-provided housing exists for hotel-resort workers, but housing styles include houses, dormitory-style units, apartments, and trailers or mobile homes. Houses and dorms are most common, but housing ranges from spacious, well-maintained tract houses shared by several workers to small basement rooms shared by four to five workers, with cinder-block walls, exposed overhead pipes, and torn linoleum floors. Some workers are provided kitchens, while others, forbidden to cook in their rooms, have to pay for food at the employer-provided cafeteria. Slightly more than half of those we interviewed in the mid-1990s lived on the grounds where they worked; those who did not live nearby, including those in housing they secured on their own, lived anywhere from one to fifty-eight miles away. Lengthy morning and evening bus rides, generally unpaid despite labor laws to the contrary, are common among domestic workers particularly, as in the case of the South Carolina low country women I interviewed in the early 2000s. Again, the longer distances reflect the fact that the cost of living in resort areas is often too high for low-wage workers. Nevertheless, most of the Jamaican women in Myrtle Beach were able to find housing north of the main drag, in old motels or apartments in neighborhoods that weren't highly desired by the affluent.

Guestworkers generally have been called a "captive" labor force, a designation that refers to the limited labor market mobility that derives from being contracted to work for a single employer. This does not mean they are enslaved, though there are clearly degrees of freedom. No workers we interviewed said that they weren't free to roam around the community, but through our own observations and interviews we found that there was often nowhere to roam. Workers were generally not allowed to be in parts of the resorts in which they were not authorized to work, a practice common in many companies. In some cases these resort areas are self-contained, either by geography (mountains, island, etc.) or by sociology (security guards, privatized roads, etc.). Often the communities are centered around the resort complex, and the only shopping or entertainment possible for workers is in nearby gift shops and convenience stores. Just over one-third of the hotel-resort workers we interviewed face this kind of situation.

Among the consequences of this isolation has been a lack of opportunity for many hotel workers to interact with co-ethnics or others off the job, a shortcoming exacerbated by visitor policies at the resorts. Most workers in employer-provided housing have restrictions on visitors; some employers allow only other hotel personnel to enter the housing, and some keep the workers' passports to deter them from straying too far from the grounds. In one case this was done with Jamaican, but not Mexican, H-2 workers, perhaps because Jamaicans tend to speak better English and are thus more susceptible to "jumping ship" (becoming undocumented immigrants) than Mexicans. In her study of Canadian guestworker programs, sociologist Kerry Preibisch found that one of the benefits local churches and others provided guestworkers was the provision of alternative social spaces, places beyond the reach of employers where workers can feel fully human rather than like mere workers. Not surprisingly, not all employers appreciate or tolerate this practice. She also found that employers discourage workers from having sexual liaisons with locals, to the point of firing workers who are caught in such relationships: "'Good' workers were those who limited their social activity, refraining from drinking or sexual relationships. Some growers thought that having a social life distracted them from their work and therefore discouraged and in some cases attempted to control the social lives of their workers. Growers who formerly hired from one source country claimed to have switched to another 'to break up all the partying that was going on'" (Preibisch 2003, 65).

Preibisch's finding is reminiscent of Flagler's preference for workers who shunned "junketing trips" to Miami and suggests that employers' fear of Jamaicans' having sexual relations with locals has been a factor in the shift, under way in Canada and the United States, from Jamaica and the Caribbean to Mexico as a source of laborers. Mexican men are considered less likely to form sexual relationships with locals, and some employers stated in their rules that having sex with a local was grounds for repatriation. Preibisch documents cases in which liaison officers were called in to help an employer control his workers' sexual behavior after the employer had received complaints from the community.

But Preibisch primarily studied male guestworkers, and it is unclear that there are similar restrictions on female guestworkers. Indeed, it has been my experience that sexual relations with locals among both Jamaican and Mexican women have not been discouraged as blatantly as Preibisch found to be the case in Canada, something discussed more fully in Chapter 7.

Unlike the crab processors, who frequently provide workers rides to shopping centers and other destinations, few of the hotel workers' employers provide transportation to nearby towns, beaches, or other locations. If public transportation is available, it is often unaffordable; we learned of cases in which public transportation cost an exorbitant $20 to $25 per trip. Such prices discourage workers from leaving the resort area or the area where they work. Although they have to pay for housing and transportation, many hotel workers receive free lunches and occasional other meals, though those who are charged for meals can have up to $8 per day deducted from their pay. We heard many complaints from workers whose only option was to eat in the worker cafeteria, where the quality of the food was poor or its cost too high. In one resort, employers provided a single microwave oven for more than twenty workers. This was kept in the lounge area, and women would line up to prepare their own meals there rather than eat in the cafeteria.

As part of our study in the mid-1990s, curious about how some employers could justify such behavior as overcharging for poor and crowded housing or pocketing workers' tips, we interviewed twenty-two resort employers operating establishments that usually hire between twenty-five and thirty permanent employees and around twenty temporary employees in the H-2 certified occupation. About 75 percent of these workers are women.

Nearly all of the firms operate throughout the year and rarely hire more H-2 workers than domestic workers, though the size of the labor force tends to change throughout the year. Most foreign workers arrive in May and work until almost the end of the year, although some H-2 workers, as noted earlier, work through December and even into January to help handle holiday traffic. Employers' ability to keep H-2 workers on site during long periods of relative idleness is particularly beneficial to them.

Despite alleged difficulties recruiting workers, hotel and resort employers use a fairly restricted set of channels to attract people; beyond newspapers and the state employment service, which the laws governing guestworker programs require, fewer than one in five we interviewed used radio, television, private employment services, or the particularly effective mechanism of employee referrals. It is significant that, thus far, labor contractors have not entered this field, although a few employers have turned to temp agencies. Labor contracting is common in most other H-2 industries, though in varied forms, and it usually constitutes a principal medium of exploitive payment schemes and kickbacks. Its absence reflects the restricted range of recruiting mechanisms in hotels and resorts, which derives in part from the common practice of trying to build up a stable labor force from past workers, with most employers requesting that domestic and H-2 workers return at the end of the season. These policies have not been successful in reducing labor turnover.

Despite the growing use of H-2B workers in various areas and occupations, only one state employment office—Michigan's Employment Security Commission—has initiated a comprehensive program to encourage U.S. workers to seek employment in the hospitality industry and at the same time eliminate the need for foreign workers as long as Michigan workers are available for work. Like other so-called "enhanced recruitment" efforts, the initiative has met with limited success to date, placing a few workers in resort jobs but holding little promise for the future. H-2B employers, however, remain doubtful about the quality of the domestic workforce that this kind of initiative will net. Several factors intrinsic to these jobs continue to make them undesirable to U.S. workers, including fluctuations in work from week to week and season to season, long bus rides, low rates of pay relative to the quality of the work, and the daily conspicuous consumption among tourists that many workers view as immoral.

In most hotels and resorts that use H-2 workers, workers are supervised not by owners but by personnel or "human services" or "human resources" directors, individuals who have adopted a corporate approach to management. In this sense, this industry contrasts with other H-2-dominated industries, such as crab processing, but may be similar to some of the agricultural firms that hire H-2s, in that many supervise workers through labor contractors. About two-thirds of the employers we interviewed said that workers were supervised at all times; the remainder simply spot-check workers' work. Supervision does not vary between domestic and H-2B workers, although some personnel managers we interviewed recognized cultural differences between Jamaican and U.S. workers that demanded they treat them slightly differently in terms of things like joking or sarcasm. This did not mean that H-2B workers were supervised more closely or driven with any more intensity than domestic workers, but they were less likely to be supervised by individuals of the same cultural background.

In most firms workers are paid by the hour, usually at or near minimum wage, although a few pay workers by the "piece," as in the case, noted earlier, of waiters receiving a certain amount per diner rather than an hourly wage. A wider range of pay scales among domestic workers probably reflects seniority. Some H-2B workers build up seniority if they return to the same work location year after year, but at a much less consistent rate than domestic workers, and many H-2B workers complained that despite continued work for the same organization, they failed to build up seniority. In addition, only a handful of employers said they normally paid overtime, which reflects the fluctuating character of occupancy rates. In line with Victoria's complaints about having to clean rooms that African American chambermaids couldn't get to before their buses arrived, H-2B workers do, on average, work longer hours than domestic workers—which may reduce how much employers pay in overtime, as H-2B workers are less likely to complain if not paid overtime. In the hotel and resort industry, tipping is common, as are other opportunities to earn additional income (e.g., babysitting), but the payment of benefits, such as health insurance or into pension programs, is not common.

That Jamaicans moving from the resort areas of Jamaica to resort areas of the United States experience more highly structured occupational settings is understandable in light of the gradual way they have been integrated into the industry. In South Carolina, instead of fully replacing African American chambermaids, Jamaicans supplement a larger, predominantly domestic labor force. In only a few companies do they dominate even that portion of the workforce that cleans rooms and waits tables. The social, economic, and other dimensions of the jobs they perform have developed under management systems that are used to domestic workers and have factored H-2B workers into the workforce without significant differential treatment. Some of this may be explained by the fact that these are corporate rather than family-owned operations, where paternal relations are less likely to develop.

The role of the Jamaican government may also explain the undifferentiated treatment of H-2B as compared to domestic workers, as it advocates as actively as it can for the workers from its homeland.

Jamaicans fill in gaps and stay on through slow seasons as African American workers leave their shifts early in the day or in the season, their buses waiting or alternative winter employment calling them home. Meanwhile, separated from the diverse, complex multiple livelihoods of their homeland, Jamaicans spend hours and days idly, without earning, waiting for the last few days of work before the season ends. It is, by all accounts, a frustrating time, one that encourages them to seek alternative work in their communities when they can, or to devise ways to reduce their living costs. It is these idle and expensive times, when they still need to pay rent and sometimes buy meals but are earning little or nothing, that push Jamaican women into behavior they might otherwise eschew, seeking alternative work outside their contracts or arranging their living situations in ways that begin to resemble the fluid social relations of Jamaica.

Sex plays no small part in this. Although I learned of no cases where Jamaican women turned to prostitution under H-2 contracts, their behavior toward a male anthropologist like me and toward the young white and black men of the run-down neighborhoods where they lived was quite obviously designed to elicit favors, rides, cash, meals, and other goods and services through sex. I remember one young woman in particular, whom I'll call Paula, who agreed to let me buy her dinner while I asked about her family, her life, her work. She was young, slender, and beautiful in the pleasing and graceful way of Caribbean women, with skin so dark it was nearly purple, prominent facial bones, and a regal mien. I was twenty years her senior, at that time nearing fifty, and, like most white American men, overweight, my face the opposite of Paula's, succumbing to the force of gravity and pale. What could she have possibly seen in me? In fact, the place I normally stayed in North Myrtle Beach was in view of her apartment, and I'd observed her and her fellow chambermaids step from their buses in the evening, the summer sun still high, their uniforms already half-unbuttoned. I'd seen them flirt with the bartenders and lifeguards who crowded into the sagging houses around them, men their own age or younger, emerging onto their tattered wooden balcony in long, colorful T-shirts, fragrant with the French-milled fancy soaps from the resort. I'd seen how Paula behaved with men she truly desired.

Yet over dinner, seated across the table at the Boulevard Café, a bikers' bar in the neighborhood, Paula became quiet about halfway into our interview and lowered her eyes and whispered, "I'm a little nervous to say this, but I was thinking that you and I could get a little place together."

I wasn't, I suppose, as shocked as I should have been. "I don't think my wife would like that," I said.

"It would just be while you were here," she said. "I could take care of it while you were away."

I smiled and shook my head. I tried to get the subject back.

"Please," she begged, beginning to sound like those desperate marketing women from her home in Jamaica.

PART III

MEXICAN EXPERIENCES, 1988–2003

SIX

WHEN OWLS DIE, *ELLOS NOS HIERIERON*

There were one hundred men living in a horse barn, cold water all through winter.
They were all sick. Some of the men had pistols to control the workers, but one day they started
shooting at barn owls because, they said, wherever there is an owl around it means a Mexican
will die. It seems to me that wherever there's a Mexican around, it means an owl will die.

—OREGON BERRY GROWER

Sandy nos hirió [Sandy hurt us].

—Mexican crab worker, after her employer told them she wasn't going to
pay them overtime because she'd already given them so much

People who write about guestworker programs are often invited to present research findings to audiences representing various backgrounds—mostly colleagues and students, of course, but guestworker programs also interest nongovernmental associations (NGOs), labor unions, government representatives, and employers and other businesspeople with vested interests in keeping guestworker programs alive. Inevitably, how you present information on temporary foreign worker programs depends, in part, on the nature of your audience. At an academic conference you might emphasize the structural dimensions of the program—the inherent unequal power relations between workers from poor, desperate nations and employers whose businesses enjoy the protections of one of the most powerful countries in the world. Before a group of people from NGOs, you might want to emphasize the humanitarian needs of guestworkers—the importance of community groups and faith-based organizations that can create sanctuaries where guestworkers can enjoy their leisure time, worship, or talk freely without fear of deportation. For an audience of government representatives you might focus on the ways that existing practices have strayed from their original political intent, the vigilance or lack of vigilance of local authorities in enforcing labor law, or the role of housing inspections in the health and welfare of workers.

In each case you could probably expect relatively cordial responses from your audience. The academics might object to a point here and there, draw comparisons from their own research, or ask for clarification. NGO people might ask about your level of activism and advocacy for workers' rights, and they might conclude that, though your heart is in the right place, you don't quite measure up. And the government reps, though not quite apologetic, might defend their lack of attention to violations of housing and labor law on the grounds that they have suffered budget cuts or manpower shortages.

Speaking to a group of guestworkers' employers, however, requires a certain delicacy that you rarely need with other audiences. Employers, quite frankly, hold the bulk of the power. They are apt to vehemently dislike any suggestion that the program isn't running smoothly, let alone that it might be inherently inhumane, and they always account for cases of abuse with the theory of the bad apple. They always point to individuals, to specific farms, dodging questions that address the structure, the system, and the unequal power relations that underlie temporary foreign worker programs. And they always, always demand to see the numbers. They want to see the bottom line.

Many ethnographers shy away from quantitative exposition on the premise that it detracts from a more humanistic narrative flow, reducing complex human phenomena to equations, numbering and measuring humans in the same spirit as those who view them—or aspects of them—as commodities, and at times freezing dynamic processes into static formulations. This is strange to me, given that the multifaceted field of mathematics constitutes one of humankind's most eloquent inventions, its shapes of geometry and symbols of equations as lovely as the mists and effects of waterfalls, and given that the danger of reducing people to numbers can be minimized by giving equal emphasis to prose accounts. Though I admit I am among those who believe that graphs and charts often detract from prose, I still feel toward numbers about the same way that Saul Bellow's Charlie Citrine feels toward money. "It's no use trying to conceal it," he says in *Humboldt's Gift*. "It's there and it's base." So too with numbers: they're there and they are definitely, throughout government and industry, throughout much of the world, base.

Whenever you collect information from a large number of individuals, numbers can also be of great assistance: frequencies, means, relationships, ranking, and so forth all help us manage large amounts of data. The information in this chapter weaves around and through numbers from 823 structured interviews with 734 H-2 workers in the United States and Mexico. Most of these individuals were interviewed in one country or the other, but seventy-nine were interviewed in both, first in the United States and later in Mexico. We asked them about their general experiences with work, migration, family, living abroad, and community, and also about more specific aspects of the H-2 program: recruitment patterns, payment systems, housing, weekly and seasonal earnings, attitudes about working with H-2 visas in the United States, and so forth. In addition, several more detailed follow-up interviews with workers were conducted throughout the duration of the research period, and interviews with employers, recruiters, and neighbors and family members of H-2 workers have been useful in filling in some of the background and fleshing out important points raised by workers.

SAMPLING CONSIDERATIONS

The sensitive political nature of the H-2 program, the varied ways in which U.S. and Mexican labor recruiters and relations with growers influence the program, and the roles of producer associations prevented us from following a true random sampling methodology in the field. Each industry, each country, and each field location presented unique challenges to random sampling. Despite this difficulty, research directors and field workers made every attempt to sample a range of workers, including a number of different-sized firms and a number of individuals within firms in their samples. Most frequently we used a modified cluster-sampling approach, or area-probability sampling, selecting more firms than workers within firms. This sampling strategy was based in part on prior knowledge regarding recruiting and network ties among workers who work together in the program. Although associations organize recruitment for several firms that hire H-2 workers, we knew from previous research that workers at the same firm are often tied to one another by village of residence in Mexico, kinship, or in other ways.

At the same time, we did focus on some firms and regions more than others in order to understand many of the ways in which workers interact with one another in the United States and abroad, and how this may influence their home communities. Most of the detailed information presented here comes from more in-depth work with several workers from the same firm, whom we interviewed in the United States and Mexico. In many cases, the Mexican interviews were open-ended, allowing workers to speak freely about their experiences as H-2 workers in the United States. We also took the opportunity while in Mexico to interview members of workers' families and communities about the program's indirect influences on them and their communities.

Structured interviewing began in the summer of 1998 in the U.S. locations and continued through the fall of 2000. Most of 1999 was spent in several locations in Mexico. Slightly fewer than one-third of the interviews were done in the United States, the remainder in Mexico. I was able to continue interviewing Mexican immigrant workers, though in a less structured format, into 2003 with the aid of funds from the National Science Foundation and the U.S. Department of Agriculture's Fund for Rural America Program. Table 6.1 shows the distributions of the sample we interviewed with a structured survey form by industry, U.S. state, and Mexican state.

HOUSEHOLD AND FAMILY

Of all the individuals of Mexican origin we interviewed, unlike those from Jamaica, only around one in ten were women, and nearly all of those in the crab-picking industry. This is significant for two reasons. First, the number and proportion of women in the guestworker labor force have been rising and are likely to continue rising along with increased female participation in migrant streams generally; second, the central importance of women to the reproduction of labor contradicts the tendency of most female guestworkers to participate in these programs during their most productive childbearing years. As has been found in previous studies and among Jamaicans we interviewed (Wood and McCoy 1985; Griffith 1983b; Griffith, Heppel, and Torres 1994), the overwhelming majority of H-2 workers in our sample were in the early years of family formation, generally young if not quite youthful— thirty-three years old on average, most of them ranging in age from twenty-four to forty-two—and highly productive, raising children and living in households of around three to seven people that they established themselves (as opposed to living with their parents or in extended households). Nearly three-fourths were married and had been for an average of ten to eleven years, with only 2 to 3 percent widowed, separated, or divorced.

Thus they were not, by and large, very young workers entering the labor force for the first time but vigorous individuals with some years of work

Table 6.1 Distribution of Interviews by Type of Work, U.S. State, and Mexican State

Variable	Frequency	Percentage
Type of Work:		
Tobacco	471	57.2
Crab Processing	125	15.2
Vegetables	84	10.2
Shrimping	79	9.6
Other	64	7.8
U.S. State of Employment:		
North Carolina	414	50.3
Virginia	185	22.5
Texas	78	9.5
Georgia	56	6.8
New York	42	5.1
Tennessee	14	1.7
Other (MI, AR, KY, MD, LA, OK, MS, WA)*	33	4.1
Mexican State of Origin:		
Hidalgo	91	12.9
Morelos	78	11.0
Zacatecas	75	10.6
Tamulipas	67	9.5
Tlaxcala	64	9.0
San Luis Potosi	59	8.4
Nayarit	55	7.8
Sinaloa	35	5.0
Michoacan	28	4.0
Durango	27	3.8
Guerrero	26	3.7
Aguas Calientes	13	1.8
Tabasco	13	1.8
Guanajuato	11	1.6
Veracruz	11	1.6
Coahoila	11	1.6
Sonora	10	1.4
Nueva Leon	9	1.3
Other	51	6.9

* Includes some from Canada.

experience under their belts and bound to their homeland by children and spouses. It is important to keep in mind that Mexicans, like Jamaicans, participate in guestworker programs during critical years of family formation and thus alter ratios of consumers to workers in their households.

Despite the prominence of workers living in households of procreation, the H-2 workforce does include many workers who live with their parents or in extended households. Single workers, around a quarter of the H-2s we interviewed, tended to cluster in families of orientation/birth or extended families, while most married workers lived in nuclear families of their own creation. One in ten single workers headed his or her own household, and our qualitative work in Mexico suggests that those who lived with parents or in extended households contributed significantly to household funds.

In the small Sinaloa town of La Noria, for example, we interviewed a young married woman who lived with her husband, also an H-2 worker, in an extended household that included her uncle. As she prepared to enter the H-2 workforce as a crab picker, her uncle threatened that if she chose to go to the United States to work, she would not be welcome to return to the household. Her work and travel would have been an affront to patriarchal control (Pessar 1999). She went despite her uncle's warning, in part to be close to her husband, who was working in North Carolina tobacco at the time. When she returned, her uncle, seeing how much money she had earned at the crab plant, readily welcomed her back into the family and even encouraged her to migrate again.

Even those who reported living in nuclear families maintained intricate and complex ties with other households in their communities. The fluid nature of relations among dwellings, where family members and friends come and go among several households with ease—sleeping in some, eating in others, visiting in still others—supports the use of a more inclusive definition of household than merely a house or even an enclosed compound. While individual houses are important loci of significant social units in Mexico, as workers themselves make clear by investing substantial foreign earnings in house construction, family and community relations influence expenditures and channel remittances as well.

When asked about work performed by other members of the household, most of the married men stated that their wives did not work outside the home. Again, we know from in-depth interviews and from observations in Mexico that many women who call themselves *amas de casa* (housewives) actually perform a variety of tasks that generate income for the household, whether in the form of food, cash, or other goods and services. The data suggest that the households of H-2 workers are not idle or completely dependent on the H-2 worker's income. When we asked survey respondents about the jobs of those with whom they lived, they gave twenty-seven occupations for the first relative they mentioned alone, among them agricultural laborer (the most common), seamstress, construction worker, butcher, factory worker, teacher, driver, nurse, fisherman, electrician, street vendor, and craftsperson. This partial list shows that these workers come from households that include professionals and independent businesspeople as well as people doing the kind of work that H-2 workers perform in the United States.

Despite the fact that the H-2 program places migration within the reach of poorer households and thus should present opportunities to families without a history of migration, most of the workers we interviewed weren't the first in their families to migrate. While fewer than 5 percent had mothers who had migrated to the United States, one-quarter had migrant fathers and more than two-thirds had other family members who had migrated to the United States. The evident wealth of experience with migration to the United States within this population may account for the fact that aid from family members, in various forms, facilitates H-2 work. Nearly two-thirds reported that they received help from family to facilitate their migration, whether in the form of taking care of the house or family, giving or lending money for travel expenses, or caring for one's business, land, or domestic animals. These forms of support mirror those I found in Jamaica and point to ways that family members in Mexico subsidize the H-2 labor force, absorbing some of the costs of reproducing the labor supply. Because they migrate during their most productive years, moreover, after learning workplace discipline in Mexico, the Mexican state and Mexican employers, too, invest in H-2 workforces before they travel north. Even those who migrate to work in jobs requiring little skill leave Mexico with some state support behind them.

One of the interesting features of H-class visas is that they are issued to people to perform tasks at the extremes of the labor market—both individuals of exceptional talent or skill (famous rock stars, heart surgeons, computer programmers) and workers who perform menial tasks. But H-2A and H-2B workers, though they come to the United States to do jobs requiring few skills, jobs that Americans supposedly refuse, do not come entirely without skills. Again, Mexican employers, schools, and various state institutions have invested in them. More than a third of those interviewed reported having some marketable skills, usually in one or another branch of the construction industry. Nearly 40 percent of those who reported having skills listed *albañil* (bricklaying, masonry), while others reported experience as electricians, plumbers, and painters. Another 16 percent claimed to have agricultural skills, including cattle ranching, blacksmithing, and working with agricultural machinery. Others claimed to have skills in soldiering, auto mechanics, secretarial work, domestic service, accounting, driving/chauffering, baking, and working in commerce or trade.

Although a few of the skills listed required training in advanced degree programs (e.g., accounting), advanced schooling is uncommon among H-2 workers. Between six and nine years of schooling is common, with a mean of 7.28 years (s.d. = 3.10). Only 17 to 20 percent have more than nine years of schooling, and half have six years or less. Only 10 percent have completed twelve years of schooling, and 3 percent have more. Despite low average years of schooling, every year constitutes an important investment in human resources in a state as poor as Mexico—one whose benefits U.S. employers reap.

Lower levels of education relative to U.S. citizens are not surprising. In general, work is more important than school for most H-2 workers, and the relations between education and work are by no means as clear and direct as they are in the United States and Canada. Again and again in Mexico we heard stories that underscored the high value of working in the United States as opposed to pursuing an education in Mexico. Among the more telling was a story we heard in Hidalgo, where families with migrating individuals reported that schoolteachers would arrive at their doors at meal times to discuss the educational progress of their children, counting on Mexican hospitality for a meal. It was widely known that teachers, who earn less than migrants to the United States, needed to supplement their incomes by such means. Stories like this are part of a wider crisis in Mexican education and perhaps underlie the alarmingly high dropout rates among Latino youths in the United States. Principals and schoolteachers in Mexico lamented the loss of children to migration, reporting that people from their villages were migrating at younger and younger ages and that the migrant stream now represented a wider demographic slice of their towns, with more women, youths, and even elderly migrating. Similarly, principals and teachers in the United States commonly lamented that Latino youths were dropping out of high school, sometimes encouraged by their parents, to take jobs in meatpacking and other low-skill industries. As Paul Willis found among working-class youth in England (1977), many Mexican teenagers seem to be rejecting education as a path to upward mobility. Certainly part of this rejection results from the limited opportunities that face educated people in Mexico. In particular, many Mexicans see occupations requiring years of schooling as the province of the upper classes. The lure of higher wages, coupled with family pressures to join the wage labor force and contribute to household incomes, prompts many Mexican youths to join the migrant stream.

Most H-2 workers have worked in more than one job. The average reported was nearly three, but the number of jobs that these workers reported ranged from one to nine, and around 15 percent reported having had three or more jobs. Half of the H-2 workers, however, have more than nine years of work experience, and a quarter have around twenty years. Again, these figures represent a substantial bonus to U.S. employers, who need not bother to train workers in basic workplace protocol (e.g., coming to work on time, submitting to supervision).

As with informants' responses about their skills, most of their past work experience was earned, most commonly, in agriculture, and second-most commonly in construction. Some workers trained for specific H-2 tasks in the United States through their Mexican work experience. Many of the crab pickers, for example, worked in crab-picking plants in Mexico before coming to the United States, many of the tobacco workers migrated from the tobacco-growing areas of Mexico, and around half of the shrimpers reported shrimping as one of their top three previous occupations. In North Carolina we interviewed a crab-plant owner who preferred H-2 workers with experience working in Mexican crab factories. He encouraged such workers to apply through a bilingual woman who had become his principal supervisor in the United States and his principal recruiter in Mexico. The plant owner claimed that even if his supervisor wanted to recruit her own relatives, she would force them to work in one of the Mexican plants before coming to North Carolina. Evidently this practice is not uncommon; 41 percent of crab pickers listed crab picking as their occupation in Mexico.

The practice of working in similar jobs in Mexico before becoming an H-2 worker is particularly relevant to the development of workplace discipline. In the case of crab pickers, for example, workers interviewed about the conditions of work in the Mexican crab plants routinely answered, "Son mas estrictos" (they are stricter). They went on to describe hygiene practices that far surpassed those of U.S. crab plants, practices that have gone into effect since the passage of NAFTA as a means, in part, of placating U.S. food producers. Specifically, stricter standards of hygiene in Mexican plants to some extent offset the labor cost advantages that Mexican producers have over U.S. producers. At the same time, Mexican employers train food workers more highly than U.S. employers do; such highly trained workers bring not only their skills but also higher thresholds for strict workplace rules and procedures, making disciplining H-2 workers—or at least acclimating them to strict workplace standards—somewhat easier than disciplining native U.S. workers. Clearly, this provides an additional incentive to U.S. employers for shifting from native to H-2 workers.

While Mexican workers bring a wide array of skills with them, proficiency in English is usually not among them. In terms of language skills, relatively few of those interviewed spoke any English at all, with fully half reporting that they spoke no English and another 28 percent reporting that they spoke a little. Only two individuals claimed to speak English well. The lack of proficiency may be in part due to the relatively few years most workers have spent in the United States, combined with the isolation they often experience while working on farms, on shrimp boats, in pine forests, in crab plants, and so forth. In many cases the labor camps of H-2 workers neither require nor encourage extensive interaction with English speakers, and a good portion of the workers are relatively new to the United States. In many areas other Latinos live nearby or working beside them, sometimes as their supervisors. Nearly one-quarter have had less than one year of experience working in the United States, although the average number of years was slightly more than four. This number is slightly higher than that found in previous studies of H-2 workers, which indicates that few workers lasted more than three or four seasons in U.S. agriculture (Wood and McCoy 1985; Griffith 1983b).

Mexicans are able to move around many parts of the United States with little or no knowledge of English, given the growth of Latino communities and elaboration of Latino networks—including artificial networks developed by *coyotes* and *raiteros*—throughout the United States over the past few decades. As noted earlier, this growth has received a good deal of scholarly attention in recent years, particularly in the so-called new destinations. These include parts of the rural Midwest and South, where H-2 workers have been recruited in large numbers. Slightly more than half (51 percent) of those interviewed reported that they worked in areas where other Mexicans were living year-round, and most reported that they frequented places, usually weekly, where other Mexicans gathered. Of those who lived in such areas, three-fourths reported that they interacted with these individuals on a regular basis, visiting the same stores, bars, churches, soccer fields, and other locations. Around two-thirds had known these individuals for only six months, so most were not from their home villages.

Acquaintances such as these serve as the basis for a wealth of labor market, shopping, and other information useful to H-2 workers in the event that they regularize their work status or slip into the undocumented labor force. While the latter alternative is not a highly desirable one to most of the workers interviewed, the former is. If the opportunity to interact with non-H-2 Mexicans presented itself, most of the people we interviewed took advantage of it, and thus were able to move around in a Spanish-speaking world on and off the job, contributing to what several observers have called the Latinization of rural America (Heppel and Amendola 1992; Griffith et al. 1995).

The process of Latinization makes it possible, in many areas, for Mexican foremen who live in the United States year-round to supervise the H-2 labor force. This happens frequently in agriculture; many farms we visited hired Mexican or Mexican American foremen, with some language skills and with work authorization (usually through the SAW program) or citizenship, who acted as liaisons between H-2 workers and growers.

Unlike undocumented workers, SAW-authorized foremen and H-2 workers may find some affinity in their shared legal status, although SAW-authorized workers enjoy considerably more freedom and labor market mobility than H-2 workers. Still, it is clear from interviews with H-2 workers and with others in the Mexican villages from which H-2 workers are recruited that workers see many more advantages than disadvantages in having an H-2 contract. A primary advantage is the security it provides, and this was commonly given as a reason for participating in the program in the first place. Under H-2 contracts workers at least know where they will be working, what they will be doing, and approximately how much money they will make.

Family members of H-2 workers also value the stability and predictability the work provides. For wives and mothers of unauthorized workers, the uncertainty of their loved ones' experiences can be harrowing. This has been especially so since border security around cities like El Paso and San Diego has been increased, forcing undocumented immigrants to deal with labor smugglers or make treacherous high desert crossings. Border death rates have been rising as a result, and the occasional horror story of a crossing gone tragically wrong raises anxiety to unbearable levels. In October 2003, for example, after eleven badly decomposed corpses were discovered in a grain car in Dennison, Iowa, Mexicans I interviewed in nearby Marshalltown echoed newspaper accounts of bereaved family members in their own stories about crossing the border. Flora Ibarra's story of her brother's crossing is typical:

First, he walked all night with a friend, so much that he wore holes through the soles of his shoes, and then he was put into a car trunk with eight other people. They rode in that trunk four hours; he was lucky in one sense that he was on top, though he had an impression from the trunk lid on his face for days afterward and he was stuck in a fetal position, unable to move, for hours afterward. When they let them out the person at the bottom was nearly dead.

They were let out at a safe house where they were allowed to call the person who was going to wire the money, given one sandwich and a drink, and told that that was all the food they would get until they got the money. The person who was supposed to wire them money didn't come through. They couldn't get in touch with him and figured he had given up on them. The guys at the house said that unless someone came to pick them up, they would allow them to die of thirst or hunger.

Then he called her other brother, who was living in Los Angeles at the time. The brother needed to come up with $1,800 for each of them, $3,600, in a matter of hours. This was late in the afternoon, after the banks had closed, and he could only get $300 from his ATM. He called around to several friends and had them each get $300 from their ATMs until he got the $3,600. This took two and a half hours. He then had to drive from Los Angeles to a small Arizona town where he met the *coyote*'s assistant, who just said, "Give me the money." The brother refused, and they arranged an exchange very similar to the exchanges you see on TV of spies across bridges. The brother with the money stood at one end of the street while the other brother and the friend stood with the *coyotes;* gradually they moved toward one another until they could touch and physically exchange the cash for the pair. Then they backed away from one another. The *coyotes* had guns. The brother from L.A. had kept his car running and they leapt in and drove off.

Similarly, just outside New Bern, North Carolina, I encountered six men at a farm who told of evading police year after year before finally appealing to their employer, a tobacco farmer they had come to know well, to bring them in as H-2s. In many cases, families of undocumented workers don't know whether the immigrants made it across the border, where they are working in the United States, or when they can expect them to return. While many unauthorized immigrants to the United States telephone and send messages home, such contact is often unpredictable, thus increasing the worries of those at home.

More than half the H-2 workers we interviewed had neither worked in the United States without papers nor claimed that they would do so. One-third, however, said they would consider returning to the United States without papers if their contracts were not renewed, presumably because they'd now learned enough about the United States to negotiate its social, cultural, and economic landscapes as illegal immigrants.

Another reason that many H-2 workers do not seriously consider working illegally in the United States is that they worry about having to hide from authorities and take jobs that pay less than minimum wage. This does not reflect the experiences of most illegal immigrants in the United States, however, particularly in large parts of the U.S. South and Midwest. Many non-H-2 Mexicans we spoke with, in both Mexico and the United States, told border-crossing stories that suggested they saw the border as more of a nuisance than a true threat to working in the United States (Massey et al. 1987). This is in line with Josiah Heyman's (1999) contention that crossing the border is a social process involving multiple "cat-and-mouse" encounters with the border patrol. Lee Maril's (2005) recent ethnography of the border patrol supports this view. Of the H-2 workers in our sample who had experienced working in the United States outside the H-2 program, 80 percent reported that they had no problems working illegally. In some cases H-2 workers who had previously entered the United States illegally had performed work similar or identical to that which they performed as H-2 workers; their becoming H-2 workers simply regularized their status. We encountered several workers who, after establishing good working relations with their employers, appealed to them to enter the H-2 program.

From historical studies of the Bracero Program and other Mexican-U.S. migration studies (Galarza 1964; Calavita 1992; Massey et al. 1987; Portes and Bach 1985), we know that this program was instrumental in creating network connections between U.S. and Mexican locations that eventually eclipsed the program and made it less necessary to workers and growers. Recent declines in H-2 workers in North Carolina, down by around 20 percent in the past two years, may suggest that the growing sophistication of the underground networks is meeting employers' labor needs now as well. A process like this may account for the discrepancy between the percentage of workers who said they would not enter the United States without papers and the percentage who said they would consider it if their contracts were not renewed. It may also be a reflection of the fact that around two-thirds of the H-2 workforce have relatives working in the same or similar jobs or regions of the United States—relatives whom they might be able to rely on for temporary housing and network connections to employers. With the current program in place, however, it is clear that workers who hold H-2 visas prefer to maintain that status rather than join the large number of unauthorized Mexican workers in the United States.

Among the relatives that workers list who have migrated to the United States, those most commonly listed first are lateral kin: brothers, cousins, uncles, sisters, and nephews. Far less common are lineal kin: parents, sons, or daughters. The presence of lateral kin in the United States perhaps should not be surprising, as it reflects the fact that U.S. migration selects for workers who are most productive, of working age, and similarly positioned in terms of network ties, entertaining similar ideas about methods of improving their life chances. The types of lateral kin reported also show a gender bias among migrating relatives, with far more men than women reported, as well as a bias of those related by blood over those related through marriage. Although twenty-two jobs were listed among those worked by relatives—including work in construction, restaurants and hotels, and other occupations—most of these individuals worked either in agriculture or, more generally, simply as "laborers." These responses indicate that most of the migrating relatives land in jobs similar to those of the H-2 workers themselves.

Compared to their undocumented relatives, H-2 workers benefit from their contracts in terms of their work and housing guarantees and reductions in such costs as crossing the border or negotiating with *coyotes* and labor contractors for transportation to work or access to specific jobs. This latter process typically obligates workers to their employers or labor contractors for a few weeks or months. Entering the H-2 program, in other words, involves a different set of constraints and benefits than entering the United States without documents. In addressing these constraints and benefits, I consider, whenever possible, how working as an H-2 worker is similar to or different from working in the United States as an undocumented worker.

RECRUITMENT, CONTRACTING, AND TRAVEL TO THE UNITED STATES

International recruiting systems, not surprisingly, have assumed a number of different forms. One of the largest H-2 contractors, Del-Al Associates, has a three-tiered structure: (1) offices in the United States that receive the grower associations' requests for workers; (2) contractors in Mexico who oversee designated regions; and (3) local contractors (*enganchadores* or, literally, "hookers") who recruit directly in several Mexican communities. If a worker from a community outside the assigned area goes to the wrong *enganchador*, he will be referred to the correct one.

Local recruiters receive, via fax, the number of workers they need to recruit, along with a blacklist of workers who have for one reason or another earned the ill will of a recruiter or grower in the United States. Blacklisting is common in guestworker programs, serving as a common tool of labor control by threatening workers with lack of future access to the program. During fieldwork in Mexico, research associates learned of a list that excluded nine workers from a group of ninety-eight that had been contracted the previous year. The *enganchador* said these workers were barred from participating in the program for three years because they had violated their contracts in North Carolina. Interviews with six of these workers revealed that they had left work in agriculture to work in construction in Raleigh, where the pay was considerably higher. Workers can also be blacklisted for causing problems for the farmer or supervisor or overstaying the contract. The same contractor informed us that a particularly abusive farmer in North Carolina, whom workers called *el diablo* (the devil), received a new crew every year because workers were not willing to return to his farm. The *enganchador* said, "I tell them that if they ride out the first year with *el diablo*, I'll send them to another employer the next."

Contracting for H-2 workers in other industries—shrimping, crab picking, and hotel resort workers—is handled somewhat differently. In shrimping the employers contact directly a law firm that obtains workers' visas from the Matamoros consulate, charging workers between $350 and $750 for this service. Mexican chambermaids are contracted directly. Someone from the personnel office at the hotel contacts a woman in Mexico City who sets up interviews for specific workers at the consular office in Mexico City. After this interview the requested women return on their own to obtain visas.

Several studies have documented the importance of network ties—primarily those between kin and friends—in the job search (Griffith 1993; CAW 1992a; Massey et al. 1987; Griffith et al. 1995; Heppel and Amendola 1992). For jobs in industries that are seasonal and unpredictable, the credibility of labor market information is particularly important, as workers sometimes need to travel long distances before finding out about the specific attributes of work. Thus, in most low-wage seasonal industries, most people find work via information received through networks. In H-2 industries, however, because contracting in Mexico is so integral a part of the entire labor process, we find that contractors themselves often play key roles in spreading information about jobs, competing in importance with relatives and friends. Specifically, although 38 percent learned about H-2 jobs through friends and 18.9 percent through family members, fully one-third of those we interviewed learned about these jobs directly from contractors.

Most of those who reported learning of H-2 work through a contractor actually may have learned of the job through a network connection. Of the third of workers who learned about the job through a contractor, three-fourths of them knew the contractor through family members or friends, so less than 20 percent of the total H-2 workforce learned of jobs through sources other than family or friends. Slightly more than one-quarter of the workers (27 percent) reported that they had to work with their contractor in Mexico before coming to the United States, and only 19.2 percent reported that the contractor knew their U.S. boss. More than half (53.8 percent) said that their contractor worked for an association (most for the North Carolina or Virginia Growers Association, or their Mexican partner, Del Alamo), while 18.6 percent said they weren't sure who their contractor's employer was; 14.4 percent said they worked for another contractor (such as someone in the Del Alamo network), and 13.3 percent said that their contractor worked directly for their U.S. employer. This diversity of responses reflects the fact that, as for most of the H-2 as well as the non-H2 labor force, labor contracting between the United States and Mexico is a layered process, with several intermediaries between U.S. employers and potential Mexican workers.

Research conducted in Hidalgo found that more and more informal contractors have been emerging on the village level in Mexico, and that recruitment for border crossings and work in the United States may gradually be approaching the H-2 model, with several intermediaries tied into a general infrastructure of familiarity (Heppel 2000). The Dennison, Iowa, tragedy revealed that people from the victims' communities knew exactly who had put those eleven doomed people in that grain car, and in many cases labor smugglers are longtime village residents who happened to have experience crossing the border. Others are strangers with varying degrees of honesty and integrity, ranging from those who guarantee their work to those who simply ask for money up front with no intention of providing a service.

I discuss recruitment in crab picking in more detail in the following chapter but point out here that both more and less formalized recruitment systems operate in the H-2 workforce. Labor contractors, whether they operate as part of a formal network or not, provide a range of services, including arranging documents, matching workers and employers, and helping workers orient themselves to the United States, and only around a quarter of those we interviewed said that labor contractors did not help them at all. Those who said that labor contractors provided them with no services fell into no particular group: about one-third were shrimpers, one-third, crab workers, and one-third, tobacco workers, representing the three prevailing recruitment systems. The nature of recruitment and relations with contractors is such that workers are often confused about how and when they received their contracts, the information contained in them, how they acquired their visas, and other paperwork associated with the program. Some of this confusion may be due to functional illiteracy or distaste for legal documents, but with at least three recruitment systems operating in the H-2 program, the potential for losing track of promises in the shuffle of papers is high. In line with the typical reticence among H-2 workers in the United States to answer questions they think might reflect badly on their employers or labor contractors, our questions about having to pay for access to the program received mixed responses. Many refused to answer and those who did were split over whether or not they had to pay.

In Mexico, however, workers were more frank. In-depth interviews at workers' homes revealed that workers recruited for agriculture, contracted through the growers' association in the United States and a private contracting firm in Mexico, paid a total of $126 in fees to enter the program, including $35 for an interview that never took place; crab workers, recruited through less formally constituted labor contractors, paid $100 apiece.

These findings are not surprising, given the history of labor contracting in agriculture and other low-wage industries. Several works have shown how labor contractors and subcontractors in general often charge workers for accessing and maintaining employment (Hahamovich 1997; Heppel and Amendola 1992; Griffith 1993; Griffith et al. 1995; Vandeman 1988; Zlolniski 1994, 2005). Similar practices in contracting within the H-2 program, though not surprising, are more troubling than among undocumented and other more vulnerable workers, specifically because the legal status of H-2 is assumed to provide protection against these practices. Clearly, among Florida sugar workers these practices proliferated, and there is evidence that the potential for such practices to creep into H-2 recruiting is high, particularly with the growth of formal labor-recruiting companies in Mexico and the United States.

Wages and working conditions are at the core of H-2 workers' experiences once they enter the United States. Most workers are paid by the hour and just under one-quarter by the piece. With the exception of a handful of workers, mostly shrimpers, who are paid by percentage of production or other means, piece rates and hourly wages account for most of our sample. Rates of pay, however, tend not to increase much from year to year or with seniority, except with changes in the minimum wage or Adverse Effect Wage Rate. Workers who have worked for the same firms for many years complain about the lack of pay increases, yet employers view this as one of the benefits of the program. This is an example of how the H-2 system insulates a firm from free-market mechanisms. Table 6.2 shows average earnings of all H-2 workers in our sample and those workers who do not work in shrimping, as the earnings of shrimpers inflate weekly earnings figures.

These figures confirm wide variation within the H-2 program in terms of earnings, underscoring one of the factors that make H-2 jobs undesirable to U.S. workers: their unpredictability. Wide disparities between H-2 worker incomes result primarily from environmental and management problems that are beyond the control of workers and often beyond the control of employers. Many H-2 jobs depend on natural resources, such as marine life, or are influenced by the weather, and even jobs like those in hotels, as we saw in the previous chapter, are influenced by such factors as guest occupancy rates. Variations in hours worked and availability of work may explain why slightly more than one-third of the workers we interviewed hoped to earn more than they had earned during the current season. Half reported that their earnings were about what they expected, however, and around 15 percent said that they had earned more than they anticipated.

For many workers, taking these jobs precludes working in Mexico and thus these figures constitute the bulk (though usually not all) of their annual income. In support of those who complain that their wages have

Table 6.2   Average H-2 Worker Earnings (in U.S. dollars)

Variable	Minimum	Maximum	Mean	s.d.
Weekly (all) earnings	100	2,550	394.08	318.33
Weekly (without shrimpers)	100	425	265.53	68.60
Seasonal (all) earnings	1,000	12,000	5,075.42	2785.45
Seasonal (without shrimpers)	1,000	9,000	3,779.07	1623.26
Average hourly pay rate	5.00	9.50	6.21	.3577

not increased even after years of service to the same firm, the average seasonal earnings are not much higher than those I collected, or Wood and McCoy collected (1985), more than twenty years ago. Those studies found average annual earnings of between $3,100 and $4,000, suggesting that average earnings of H-2 workers have indeed stagnated. In blue crab, although piece rates rose from 1985 to 1990 by 20 to 36 percent (depending on the quality of the meat), when plants were suffering from severe labor shortages, the rates have not changed since the H-2 program began in earnest (Griffith 1993; Griffith, Heppel, and Torres 1994).

Despite this stagnation in wages, these earnings continue to be high when compared to earnings in Mexico. In many Mexican villages, the houses of those who have worked in the United States—as legal residents, contract workers, or unauthorized workers—tend to be more substantial and contain more amenities than those of their neighbors who don't have access to U.S.-earned income. This wage differential is often used by U.S. employers as a justification for keeping wages low for Mexican workers, despite the fact that the jobs are in the United States and thus should be subject to U.S., not Mexican, standards.

Two-thirds of the workers interviewed said that the type of pay did not vary through the season; if they were paid by the piece (or hour) or weekly at the beginning, then they were paid by the piece (or hour) or weekly through the end of their contract. Nearly 90 percent were paid weekly, with only 2.6 percent paid biweekly and fewer than 1 percent paid monthly or at the end of the season, although the shrimpers were paid per trip at sea. A minority, around 15 percent, received overtime pay, but only around three times over the course of the season. Similarly low numbers (around 11 percent) received bonuses. Deductions from paychecks, by contrast, amounted to nearly 40 percent of their pay, including not only taxes but also technically illegal deductions for transportation, food, equipment, and, for H-2B workers, housing.

Some H-2B workers did complain to us about paying into the Social Security fund, fearing that they would never have access to that money and that they were paying into general funds from which they would never benefit. Canadian workers interviewed by Verduzco and Lozano (2003), Basok (2002), and Preibisch (2003) made similar complaints. Perhaps in compensation, some of these H-2B workers take advantage of free clinics and other government services when they can. In one case, for example, a woman I will call Maria Ibarra, who arrived in the United States pregnant, had her child in a U.S. hospital, primarily because having the child on U.S.

soil facilitated bringing the child with her on subsequent trips. Maria added that her boss had chastised her for this, saying that they were taking advantage of Medicaid and thus contributing to the general burden that welfare recipients, to the boss's thinking, place on society. She thus felt that having any more children on U.S. soil, even though she was of childbearing age and desired more children, might jeopardize her chance to continue working in the program.

Gaining access to local health systems is one way guestworkers interact with their host communities, though obviously some employers discourage this or allow workers to see health providers only under tight constraints. During our research in 2004, we interviewed health providers who reported that H-2 workers presented with illnesses with their employers or supervisors by their sides; in some cases these supervisors accompanied workers into examination rooms. This practice, though not necessarily ubiquitous, is consistent with controlling and surveillance practices that usually begin with worker housing.

Housing for H-2 workers, whether they pay (in the case of H-2B workers) or receive housing free (H-2A workers), is highly variable, as are the services employers and supervisors provide to ease access to shopping, medical care, entertainment, and other services. Even for workers in the same firm, housing may vary from huge dormitory-style housing in isolated warehouses to small single-family homes or trailers in residential neighborhoods. In Belhaven, North Carolina, several of the women inhabit what appears to be an old tobacco warehouse surrounded by a chain-link fence, and in Aurora they live in an abandoned daycare center that was once a hunting lodge. Few H-2 workers live with children, most live with members of the same sex, and many room with people they have never met. On the farms, H-2A workers generally live either in trailers or in run-down farmhouses neighboring the properties of their employers. Few of these are new, although some operations, primarily the larger firms and those taking advantage of government funding sources, have built new dwellings to house workers. Apple growers along the southern shore of Lake Erie in upstate New York have built extremely fine dwellings with government funds, but in general most housing differs little from much of the housing we encountered among farm workers across the country, even though more rigorous rules supposedly apply to employer-provided housing for H-2A workers. The primary difference is in its guaranteed availability, something of primary concern among low-wage workers in general and farm workers in particular (Griffith et al. 1995; Hahamovich 1997).

If H-2B worker housing tends to be somewhat newer, it is because housing seasonal workers is a newer practice in H-2B industries. Many crab-plant owners have built concrete-block dwellings or new houses, while others rent houses in small towns across the mid-Atlantic region for the season. In general they charge between $17 and $25 per worker per week for housing, although some charge more and add charges for telephones, laundry machines, soda machines, and so forth. Given the isolation and condition of some of this housing, these rates can be high, with run-down houses in poor neighborhoods—houses that might otherwise rent for $1,000 to $1,500 per month—sometimes fetching as much as $450 to $500 per week. Crab workers interviewed in the springs of 1999 and 2000, before the season began, when there were few crabs to pick, complained about plant owners charging them rent when there was little or no work in the plants, arguing that they should not have to pay rent, or should pay reduced rent, when work was slow. Yet most plant owners argue that they need to recover either their housing-construction expenses or rent.

Interactions between H-2 workers and U.S. citizens tend to be confined to simple exchanges of goods and services, although some H-2 workers, seeking work outside their designated jobs during slow or idle times, do venture into communities to find other work. Their contracted employers may or may not know about or approve of this behavior, but some assist them in their job search and others screen their potential employers. In one of the small eastern North Carolina towns where several dozen Mexican women pick crabs every year, the owners of the crab plant allow the women to clean their neighbors' houses during idle times, but on the condition that they first approve the neighbors. If the owners don't like the neighbors or have had problems with them, they refuse to let the Mexican women clean their homes.

When workers do perform these other jobs, they meet new bosses and expand their knowledge of the labor market and the region in which they live and work. With rural industrialization and Latinization, as noted earlier, H-2 workers also have had more opportunities to interact with other Latino and foreign-born individuals while working in the United States.

As with my work in Jamaica in the 1980s, in my more recent work among Mexicans I was interested in how the families used the money they earned here. The approximately $4,000 seasonal earnings of Mexican H-2 workers are used in the United States and abroad in a variety of ways, including for the costs of migration. A minority of workers (between 14 and 20 percent) reported using a portion of their earnings to cover some costs associated with participating in the H-2 program. I reported earlier about a North Carolina tobacco farmer who deducted transportation and grower association fees from workers' pay. Evidently this practice is not restricted to North Carolina tobacco workers, as employers in several H-2 industries deduct for things ranging from the interview to the visa, food, transportation, fees to contractors and recruiters, and *mordidos* (bribes) at the border. Average costs per worker came to around $540, or more than 13 percent of their seasonal earnings. If we add on the costs that Western Union and other money transfer agencies charge to wire remittances, at least 15 percent of H-2 workers' U.S. earnings never reach their homes.

The process of transferring costs from employers, recruiters, contractors, and associations onto the backs of workers is highly uneven, making this one area in which more state oversight is clearly needed. These practices again drive home the point that, in any guestworker program, the potential for cheating workers exists and seems gradually to creep into relations between workers and employers.

Most workers send home considerable amounts of money, as well as carry home earnings at the end of the season. On average, workers send home nearly $2,000 ($1,985.96, s.d. = $1944.82) during the season, and carry home around the same amount ($2,051.66, s.d. = $1517.89). Slightly fewer than one in ten reported having problems carrying money home, and the uses to which workers put earnings are in line with those reported in other studies of income earned abroad. They include, in descending order, household expenses, house construction, debt payment, a target purchase (e.g., a head of livestock), savings, schooling, and miscellaneous other purchases—in short, nearly the same categories of expenditures I found in Jamaica.

Remittances have long been a primary way for immigrants to dispose of their earnings. H-2 workers are no different from other immigrants in this regard; fully 93.2 percent reported remitting money to Mexico regularly. Most (63.4 percent) remit at least every month, and slightly more than one-third remit more frequently. Remitting earnings has become easier over the years, in that now nearly all small Mexican *tiendas* (stores) provide remittance services—another dimension of the Latinization of rural America. About half of the workers use bank transfers to wire money home, with other common mechanisms being Western Union or other wire services (around 30 percent) or mail (around 15 percent). On average, respondents paid just over 23 percent of the amount to send that money home, although one-third reported spending 10 percent or less. Some said that they waited until they had a substantial amount to send, because some wire services charged flat fees.

Recipients of this money tend to be women, a finding consistent with the Jamaican research (Chapter 3). Three-fourths reported sending money to wives, and another 15 percent to their mothers. Others, including fathers, siblings, and other relatives, were listed with far less frequency. These remittances were used primarily to meet household expenses (71.3 percent), and less frequently for savings (8.9 percent) or education (5.8 percent).

People participating in the H-2 program tend to be reluctant to admit that their participation causes personal problems for them or their families, with only 10 to 20 percent of workers reporting problems that stemmed from their absence. Most listed problems in responding to the illness of a family member, economic problems, or problems with children, and equal proportions said that the problems tended to be solved by either a parent or another relative. Spouses and children were not often listed as among the problem solvers, which may indicate that their behavior is perceived as part of the problem instead of part of the solution. With regard to children, our anecdotal evidence from Mexico suggests that a parent's absence, and especially a father's absence, has resulted in a general deterioration of intergenerational authority; workers from rural Mexico again and again told stories of children not attending school, fighting, and otherwise causing problems because of absent or only sporadically present fathers. Mothers, in these cases, become the primary disciplinarians in the household, a role with which many women in the Mexican countryside seem uncomfortable, especially as their children enter their early teens.

ATTITUDES TOWARD THE PROGRAM AND SUGGESTIONS FOR IMPROVEMENT

H-2 workers may not be very forthcoming about describing problems with the program, but they were on the whole willing to respond to suggestions that have been made for its improvement. Several changes in the program have been suggested by close observers of H-2 as well as by the workers themselves. Specifically, we asked workers whether each of the following suggestions was a very good idea, a good idea, or a bad idea, and we summarize our findings in Table 6.3:

· Being able to return home to visit your family for a short while during the season.
· Being able to work over a longer period of time—as much as three years—in different types of jobs.

- Being able to work for different employers, in the same area and doing the same job.
- Having part of your pay (one-quarter to one-third) withheld and given to you upon your return to Mexico at the end of the season.
- Being able to live in the United States permanently after several years of working with an H-2 visa.
- Bringing your spouse and small children here while you are working.

Responses to these questions varied considerably by gender, women being more likely than men to believe that seeing family and children and regularizing their status were very good or good ideas. Women also seem more content than men with the idea of remaining with a single employer. By contrast, nearly twice as many men as women reported that they considered permanent residence a bad idea. Table 6.4 shows responses by gender.

When we asked which of these were the most important to them, the rankings were as follows, from most to least important:

Total Sample	Women	Men
Permanent residence	Seeing family	Permanent residence
Seeing family	Permanent Residence	Seeing family
Working different jobs	Seeing children	Working different jobs
Seeing children	Forced savings	Seeing children
Forced Savings	Working different jobs	Forced savings
Having different bosses	Having different bosses	Having different bosses

We also asked two related questions about the role of the Mexican government in H-2 programs: first, whether they would prefer the government to act as labor recruiter/intermediary (instead of the current formal and informal private systems in place), and second, whether they would like to have Mexican government offices in the United States where they could

Table 6.3   Attitudes Toward Suggested Changes in Program (percent)

Suggestion	Very Good Idea	Good Idea	Bad Idea
Return home during contract	36.9	44.9	18.2
Different jobs/longer period	28.7	45.2	26.1
Different bosses/same job and area	15.3	53.6	30.3
Forced savings	23.8	39.3	36.9
Lead to permanent residence	30.7	31.3	38.0
Bring spouse/children	19.9	33.4	49.6

Table 6.4 Attitudes Toward Suggested Changes by Gender (percent)

Suggestion	Very good (women)	Very good (men)	Good (women)	Good (men)	Bad (women)	Bad (men)
*Return to MX during contract	56.5	34.9	25.8	46.8	17.7	18.3
Different jobs/longer period	21	29.4	48.4	44.9	30.6	25.6
*Diff. Bosses/same job and area	16.7	16.1	30	55.8	53.3	28.1
Forced savings	32.3	22.9	37.1	39.6	30.6	37.5
*Lead to perm. Residence	50.8	28.8	27.9	31.6	21.3	39.6
*Bring spouse and children	40	15.1	44	32.6	16	52.4

* Statistically significant (chi-square analysis).

protest working conditions or other problems. The majority of workers supported both propositions: 70.1 percent said that they would prefer that the Mexican government replace current labor contractors/recruiters, and nearly all (94.7 percent) agreed that a Mexican government office where they could bring their problems would be preferable to the current situation.

At the same time, we asked open-ended questions about specific benefits of the H-2 program. While nearly everyone listed higher relative earnings as their principal reason for participating in the program, many added comments such as "experience," and "getting to know regions of the United States." They were reminding us, perhaps, that they aren't merely workers, but thinking, experiencing, learning women and men.

SEVEN

BODIES ON HOLD:
GENDER AND H-2

A year before the season that Anna and her husband, Juan, were fired, Anna's cousin Marta arrived in North Carolina three weeks pregnant. Marta wasn't really Anna's cousin but Juan's nephew's wife, though Anna referred to her as *mi prima*. Over the previous decade, Anna and Juan had set themselves up as informal labor contractors for the thirty to forty H-2B workers at Miramar Crab Company, and Juan had recruited Marta and her husband, his nephew, Pedro, for two of these coveted jobs. Luckier than most, Pedro and Marta were one of only two Mexican couples (the other being Anna and Juan) who worked at Miramar; all of the other workers were single women, away from their spouses and families for seven to nine months a year.

Anna and Juan had worked at Miramar since the company first started using H-2B workers, more than twelve years earlier, Juan at first pulling traps on crabbing boats while Anna worked on the picking line and improved her English. The company's owner, who hired them, had since died, and the plant had been taken over by his daughter, Sandy, and her husband, Andy Small. For the four years before Marta arrived pregnant, Anna and Juan had been coming to North Carolina with their young son, Gustavo, who had been born in Arizona after an earlier crabbing season. They lived in a small trailer behind the main workers' dormitory and got along so well with Sandy and Andy that they eventually assumed the lucrative role of recruiting new workers to the plant. Marta's pregnancy wasn't apparent when she arrived, but as the crabbing season progressed from the short and slow spring days into the busy summer season and Marta's middle began to swell, Sandy seemed to hold Anna and Juan responsible for Marta's condition.

Sandy's opposition to the pregnancy was only marginally related to the question of Marta's productivity. The crabs would still get picked. Instead, she objected to Marta's plans to have the child at the hospital in New Bern, at U.S. taxpayer expense. Harping on this theme through the summer and into the fall, as Marta's due date approached, she warned Anna, who had arrived pregnant four years earlier herself, against repeating Marta's mistake. Describing Sandy's anger to me, Anna said, "But I'm getting older. I want to have a child now. She expects me to put my body on hold." Before seeing how angry Sandy became over Marta's pregnancy, Anna had been planning to have a second child on U.S. soil as soon as she could. Despite Sandy's anger and warnings, Anna arrived the following season two months pregnant.

Anna and Juan knew that their decision to have a second child while still working for the Smalls was risky. Yet the couple had been with Miramar for so many years that they believed that Sandy and Andy would eventually accept their decision. After all, Sandy and Andy had been to Mexico to visit them in their homes. They had seen the improvements in their homes and lives that they had made with the money they earned at Miramar. Anna's depictions of Sandy in Mexico sounded remarkably like the women that Patricia Pessar (1999) described in her work on gender and immigration: women who assume a patriarchal role toward immigrant men. She spoke of the improvements as though she had made them herself, patting herself on the back for providing Anna and Juan employment. Having seen how Anna and Juan had spent the money they earned at Miramar, Sandy knew how important these jobs were to the couple, and Anna and Juan thought that Sandy would eventually come to see how important it was for them to have a second child. They were wrong.

Anna and Juan's experience was unusual among H-2 workers because most H-2 workers work in the United States not as couples but as single workers, living away from their spouses and families during their stay. Nevertheless, their experience shows that links between reproduction and guestworker programs are often contradictory and complex. Far more men than women enter the United States as temporary foreign workers, yet two factors suggest that we must understand the differences between male and female experiences with these programs. First, as noted earlier, far more women than men participate indirectly in foreign worker programs, receiving remittances and keeping households together while husbands, boyfriends, fathers, and sons work abroad. Second, more and more women began entering guestworker programs when H-2 visas expanded to include tourism and seafood processing.

In order to make sense of women's participation in guestworker programs, in this chapter I compare the H-2 experience in crab-processing factories and tobacco farms. Two of the major beneficiaries of H-2 programs, blue crab and tobacco operations share a few defining characteristics yet differ in ways that shed light on how temporary worker programs influence gender relations, Mexican communities, U.S. neighborhoods, and U.S. industry. Tobacco farms and blue crab–processing factories, for example, tend to be family owned and operated, yet of most interest here is the qualitative difference in their respective labor forces: tobacco farms use exclusively male H-2 workers while crab plants use primarily female H-2 workers. Both suffer from social developments that are, for the most part, far beyond their control: tobacco from the shadow cast over smoking as a public health threat and crab processing from coastal gentrification and the problems created for commercial seafood production by developments oriented toward leisure and retirement. Both industries historically recruited their workers from nearby African American neighborhoods, using ties based on kinship and paternalism, but contemporary recruitment practices within the H-2 program differ rather radically. Most tobacco farmers use (sometimes reluctantly) a well-developed formal system of grower associations in the United States and labor contracting in Mexico. In most crab-processing firms, by contrast, H-2 workers, at times in partnership with crab-plant owners, have developed their own recruiting systems, which are both more informal and more based on family and village ties—more similar to the network ties of new immigrants—than those that bring tobacco workers into the mid-Atlantic region.

These similarities and differences allow for particularly fruitful comparisons in terms of several key components of temporary worker programs. The ways in which the program influences relations between productive and reproductive labor in sending regions become clearer through comparisons of male and female H-2 workers. The comparisons below also highlight the differences between formal and informal recruiting and the ways in which family firms in threatened industries rely on the program. They thus offer insights into attributes of the H-2 program, temporary worker programs generally, and immigration and labor market policies that continue to concern policy scribes, social scientists, and the general public.

Both tobacco and crabmeat manufacturing, highly labor-intensive and primarily summertime activities, with peak labor periods during the mid- to late summer and early fall, discourage a high degree of economic diversification. Few crabmeat manufacturers deal with other forms of seafood, except, occasionally, minor amounts that arrive at their crab plants as by-catch. Typically, during the slow winter months, crab-plant owners take extended vacations around their maintenance and repair schedules. It is not uncommon for them to visit Mexico during one of these vacations, and most can tell you how, where, and under what conditions the H-2 workers who work for them live at home.

Tobacco, too, consumes most of the family farm's attention during the spring and summer months. Devoting time to any crop or livestock that draws labor and other farm resources away from tobacco thus threatens the crop's central position and potentially undermines its value. Growers have mixed various vegetable crops into their tobacco regimes, and many have long tended livestock in confinement operations, but tobacco, like blue crab, organizes a family's seasonal schedules and annual peaks and valleys of labor demand through the year.

The central position of these commodities in family production regimes and work patterns influences directly the experiences and lives of H-2 workers who work with tobacco and blue crabs. All other activities are secondary to their work in these commodities. They are brought into the United States at the earliest possible time that their labor is required and kept there until the latest possible time their labor may be required. Most (85 percent) of the crab pickers arrive from mid- to late April and stay through November or December, while 85 percent of the tobacco workers arrive in several waves, from April to July, and leave between October and December.

In both industries, this results in considerable idle time, particularly at the beginning and end of the season. Blue crabs become active as early as March, yet blue crab catches may be sporadic and unpredictable through the late spring and early summer. During this time workers at some crab plants may have fewer than five hours of work per week. Weather and the rates at which tobacco leaves ripen may cause similar prolonged periods of idleness among tobacco workers.

During these idle times, H-2 workers typically seek work in other areas. Although this is illegal under the terms of their contracts, finding alternative employment is neither difficult to accomplish nor uncommon. Yet both crab and tobacco workers find other sources of income only under the long shadow of their work in tobacco and crab, though often with the blessing of their primary employer. During interviews with crab pickers at Miramar Crab, as I noted earlier, it came out that the plant owner allowed them to clean houses and work in other seafood firms as long as the owners of those houses or other firms met with the crab-plant owner's approval. Workers also sought and took work without their plant owner's knowledge or permission, although this varied by the amount of control and surveillance they experienced. Similarly, many tobacco workers worked in the blueberry and other harvests during slow times in the tobacco harvest, but readily returned to tobacco if needed. That tobacco growers provide their housing rent-free is no small inducement to complying with the tobacco grower's needs.

In crab, where workers rent their living spaces from their employers, a prevailing belief among workers is that the plant owners bring them into the United States early primarily to charge them rent. The more enlightened employers will suspend housing charges during weeks when there is little or no crab to pick, and housing emerged as a point of contention early in the use of H-2 workers in crab (Griffith, Heppel, and Torres 1994). At that time, after several high-profile lawsuits and the threat of Labor Department action over rents charged the workers, many plant owners, through their association, agreed to a uniform rental charge of $17.50 per worker per week. Six years later this had become less uniform and the amount of rent had increased, again testifying to the tendency for employers and contractors in H-2 programs to develop, if gradually, more and more means to create and extract value from H-2 workers.

The amounts that some owners charge H-2B workers for housing suggest that they are using housing as a secondary income source, as some crab workers suspect. In one instance, a small concrete dormitory in an isolated area of the North Carolina coast was generating $800 a month in rental income; in another, a large run-down house in a low-income neighborhood of a small community generated more than $2,000 a month. Under normal market conditions, these two properties would rent for around half of what H-2 workers were charged.

In their defense, owners claim that they need to charge the additional rent because they pay rent or make payments on the properties all year long (three to five months longer than they are occupied). Yet clear cases of rent extortion continue, especially in cases where housing has been arranged in trailers, warehouses, former daycare centers or meeting rooms, or other accommodations in isolated or undesirable locations. One of the most abusive crab-plant owners characterized the housing he had built for H-2 workers as "investment property," adding, "This is America. When you build housing in America you expect to make a profit." Workers at this family's plant became so angry over his attempts to charge them for cost-of-living services that they staged a work stoppage one day when he was in a neighboring state buying crab. He had replaced their private phone (whose bills they paid, but at lower rates) with a pay phone, and they waited until they knew he would be gone to stop work. Unfortunately for the workers, he was able to continue with these practices, after the stoppage, by firing them all and replacing them with a fresh crew recruited directly from Mexico.

RECRUITMENT AND LABOR MANAGEMENT

Recruitment in H-2 programs varies from highly formalized systems of contracting, with multiple organizational levels and field sites in the United States and Mexico, to less formal methods that replicate the more common kinship- and village-based network recruiting schemes among other immigrants (Massey et al. 1987; Griffith et al. 1995). Yet even in the most formal arrangements, close field observations and repeated interviews with workers often reveal that workers, intermediaries, and employers renegotiate recruitment systems and organizations in several ways. Generally, while associations and state agencies attempt to structure recruitment in predictable and standardized ways, relations in the Mexican sending regions among employers, recruiters, and workers have pushed recruitment toward network-based models.

I made similar observations in Jamaica in the early 1980s and again in the 1990s and early 2000s. Compared to Mexico, the Jamaican state plays a far more active role in the recruitment of H-2 workers, channeling access to the program through elected representatives (ministers of Parliament) and local Ministry of Labour offices rather than through private contractors. Jamaican officials also administer pregnancy tests to those who work as chambermaids and do other health screening before allowing workers to leave for the United States. That Mexican officials do not become so involved is clear in the occasional practice of Mexican H-2B crab pickers arriving in the mid-Atlantic pregnant, in order to have their children in the United States and ease the problems of carrying them back and forth across the border. Yet even with the increased scrutiny of the Jamaican government, Jamaicans manage to shape certain elements of recruitment to the needs of their networks and households, exchanging or selling their job cards or traveling on others' visas with others' names. Similarly, when Mexican women bring their children with them, their position vis-à-vis the state and their employers changes in ways that policymakers probably did not anticipate.

The practice of arriving pregnant or bringing one's U.S.-born children to U.S. workplaces points to one of the principal differences between tobacco workers and crab pickers, one highlighted in the differences between male and female attitudes toward the program discussed at the end of the last chapter. While a handful of crab pickers, most of whom are women, bring their children with them, the only children that tobacco workers travel with are sons who are old enough to be H-2 workers themselves. This does not necessarily mean that tobacco workers are less family-oriented than crab pickers, or that fewer of them are married, but it reflects the different ways that the two workforces have developed since coming to the United States. Our statistics suggest that, if anything, those in the tobacco program have reason to be more family-oriented than those working in crab plants: while the two groups are similar in terms of age distribution, the tobacco workers are more concentrated in households of procreation (households they have formed themselves through marriage) than crab pickers are (see Table 7.1).

These two findings—that proportionally more tobacco workers than crab pickers come from families of procreation, and that crab pickers bring their young children with them more often than tobacco workers do—reflect more than gender differences. Developments in recruiting in Mexico and the United States explain these behaviors at least as well as the gender preferences of the two industries. We have seen that the two industries historically used African American workers before shifting to Mexican H-2 workers—but the shift occurred in tobacco at least a decade earlier than it did in crab. By 1980 most field labor in tobacco was Latino (not necessarily

Table 7.1   Age and Household Type: Blue Crab Pickers and Tobacco Workers Compared

Age	Mean	Standard Deviation	Significance (t-test)
Crab workers	30.66	9.48	P=.320 (not significant)
Tobacco workers	31.61	8.32	

*Percent Living in	Family of Orientation	Family of Procreation	Extended Family
Crab workers	33.9	28.6	37.5
Tobacco workers	16.5	69.3	14.2

* Chi-square = 63.029; df = 2; p<.000 (significant).

H-2), yet the first Mexicans didn't enter the crab-picking labor force until 1988, and most plants employed primarily African Americans into the early 1990s. In addition, the first Mexicans to work in the crab industry carried H-2 visas, while the first Latino workers in tobacco were Mexican Americans and Mexicans who had worked on Florida farms and who radiated out of the Texas border region during the 1950s and 1960s.

RECRUITMENT IN TOBACCO

In tobacco, forces encouraging the transition from African American to Mexican labor began long before the 1980s. Developments in both the Latino settlement of the South and African American rural communities combined to favor the change in much of southern agriculture. Mexican American families moved into south Florida after the mechanization of the cotton and sugar beet harvests, during the early 1950s, seeking agricultural work in the East as the Bracero Program saturated the western United States with contract labor (Galarza 1964; Calavita 1992). Prior to this, farm labor in the southern and eastern United States had been dominated by African Americans, with a few exceptional pockets of contracted Puerto Ricans and Jamaicans (CAW 1992b; Griffith et al. 1995; Heppel and Amendola 1992). Heppel's (1983) study of Virginia's eastern shore, which linked Florida with Virginia production sites, describes both Latino and African American harvesting crews working side by side in both locations. Crews of African Americans still remain scattered throughout the farm labor force in the South and East, yet in most cases they have been replaced by Latinos.

The transition from African American to Latino labor occurred unevenly. In Chapter 2 I described how this transition occurred in the Finger Lakes region of New York, and how it depended on growers' perceiving a decline in the quality of African American crews migrating north from southern Georgia and Florida. The change from African American to Latino crews also involved a change in the legal status of workers, from citizen workers to foreign-born and, increasingly, unauthorized workers. In many instances, legal contract workers, either H-2 or contract workers from Puerto Rico, worked in the same harvests and the same regions as resident alien and unauthorized workers (Griffith et al. 1995, chapters 3 and 6; Heppel and Amendola 1991, part 2, case study 2). The apple harvests along the Appalachian mountain chain were dominated by unauthorized Mexican workers around Hendersonville, North Carolina, and by crews of H-2A Jamaican workers further north, in the Shenandoah Valley (Bump 2005). Nurseries and vegetable and mushroom farms in southern New Jersey used contract workers from Puerto Rico alongside Haitian refugees and workers from Mexico and Guatemala, the bulk of the latter unauthorized. Today, southeastern North Carolina employers hire immigrant workers covering a range of legal statuses, including Honduran refugees from Hurricane Mitch, undocumented Guatemalans and Mixtec speakers, H-2 workers, and workers legalized under IRCA's SAW provisions. Sporadic INS enforcement in agricultural labor markets through the 1970s and 1980s, along with successive waves of immigration reform, with heavy employer sanctions for employing unauthorized workers, led to increased interest in legal immigration from Mexico. Testimony before the Commission on Agricultural Workers, along with several studies sponsored by the Department of Labor's International Labor Affairs Bureau (Papademetriou et al. 1988; Griffith 1993), illustrate the extent of employer unease over diminished access to immigrant workers. One result of their concerns was the expansion of formal recruiting agencies in the United States and Mexico that specialized in H-2 workers (Griffith 1999, chapter 4).

These agencies organize much of the recruiting of H-2 tobacco and other agricultural workers today. They are similar to the Florida Fruit and Vegetable Association, which aided the sugar companies in Florida by maintaining blacklists and assisting in the recruitment of workers. Briefly, the main organizational apparatus that recruits and transports H-2 tobacco workers from Mexico to the United States consists of partnerships between grower associations in the United States and labor-contracting firms in Mexico. In tobacco, as noted earlier, the principal firms are the North Carolina Growers Association, the Virginia Growers Association, and Del-Al Associates, Inc., an organization on the Mexico-U.S. border that has a vast network of recruiters and assistants throughout Mexico. In the United States, the various associations—which use different names in different states—first market the H-2 program itself, working to interest growers in replacing unauthorized workers with H-2s, employing the particularly effective strategy of targeting areas, such as upstate New York, that have experienced INS raids in the past. Once they have a new grower on board, associations add that grower to clearance orders and draw up contracts, based on a blanket contract between that grower's firm and each of the workers who will eventually work on the farm. Growers may identify specific workers for H-2 contracts, as was the case with the grower who wanted to legalize workers who had worked for him for several seasons. Growers may also draw workers from a pool recruited in Mexico by Del-Al Associates. This option allows growers to increase their workforce during the season, as work begins to pick up during the harvest, but also allows them to replace workers if they perceive problems with them. On one of the farms we visited in North Carolina, a grower who drew workers from the general pool showed the degree to which relations with the association can become a tool of labor management under conditions of relatively poor labor relations. This grower complained of various kinds of trouble with different workers from one season to the next and replaced his H-2 workers with new workers every year. One season, half of his workers "walked off the field one day," and he never saw them again. He told us that his current workers had gradually been working more and more slowly. The day after our visit, he told us, a man from the association was coming by to help him find excuses to get rid of some of them. He said that his tobacco, slightly too green to pick, was entering an idle time and he didn't wish to pay the workers' light bill. In response to the threat of unionization, which was just beginning that season as the Farm Labor Organizing Committee began organizing against the Mt. Olive Pickle Company, this same grower said, "What do they want with a union? I pay them over five dollars per hour, pay their light bill, give them a place to live, and carry them to the grocery store whenever they want. If they wanted more money, they should have stayed in school."

Obviously, this particular grower used the association as a highly active labor intermediary, relying on it to solve labor relations issues more than most. Grower reliance on the association ranged from this extreme of actively recruiting and dismissing workers through the season to the one-time provision of H-2 visas to workers whom growers knew previously. Between these extremes are those growers who rely on the association sporadically through the season, as problems specific to individual workers or farms arise. One grower, for example, compared payments to the grower association to crop insurance, adding, "But this insurance pays off every year." What he meant was that the association and the H-2 program offered him predictability by stabilizing his workforce. First, the overriding stipulation of being an H-2 worker (that you can work for one and only one employer under the law) assures that the workers will usually remain on his farm during idle or slow work periods. Those of us who have studied the farm labor market know that idle periods on farms can lead to worker attrition, making the recruitment of new workers at harvest time a nightmare. This is therefore no minor insurance against crop loss. Second, if a worker has a problem with pay, working conditions, housing, or any other aspect of the program, the grower can refer to a legal document (drafted by the association and signed by the worker) that shows the worker the conditions to which he agreed.

Workers do not have the same option of presenting their employers with a signed legal document showing *their* part of the bargain. As always, the balance of power in the H-2 relationship clearly works against workers and for employers. The associations enforce this power disparity with help from their Mexican counterpart, Del-Al Associates. Del-Al's network extends from the consulates into the countryside. Its responsibilities include recruiting workers in Mexico through an elaborate multitiered system of *enganchadores* or *contratistas* (people who recruit and funnel workers into the system), assisting selected workers in getting passports, visas, and receiving and signing contracts, and arranging their passage via bus to the United States, usually from Monterrey or Hormigueros.

Each of these phases of mobilizing the H-2 workforce involves the participation of many individuals and several specific activities. *Enganchadores,* for example, not only market the program to workers, they interview and screen workers in villages. Others maintain connections with the U.S. and Mexican consulates, arranging for visas and other documents in tandem with requests from associations and employers in the United States. Transportation usually includes arranging at least three legs of the journey: from the home village to Monterrey, from Monterrey to the border at Laredo, and from the border to Vass, North Carolina, Danville, Virginia, or another destination in the United States. Del-Al Associates has at least six regions within Mexico divided among its *enganchadores,* each of which includes a number of cities in specific states. In one, for example, the *enganchador* and his or her assistants are responsible for Ciudad del Máiz, Matehuela, Taman, Tamazuchale, Las Palomas, Milpillas, San Luis Potosí, and Pino. Del-Al claims to recruit workers for several U.S. occupations, in addition to tobacco, including planting pine trees in the Carolinas, Louisiana, Kentucky, Michigan, Tennessee, and Georgia; picking blue crabs in the Carolinas and Maryland; picking peaches in Georgia; harvesting onions and landscaping in Georgia and Virginia; farm work in vegetables in the Carolinas, Mississippi, Georgia, Washington, and New York; detasseling corn in Indiana; working in Christmas trees in Georgia, the Carolinas, Michigan, Tennessee, and New York; harvesting apples in New York; shrimping in Virginia; greenhouse work in New York; and working in hotels in Michigan.

Del-Al Associates has clearly worked to cultivate ties with several U.S. industries, using its vast Mexican network to keep these labor markets supplied with workers as needed. In Mexico *enganchadores* typically arrange for workers to be interviewed in their hometowns and then select workers to form the labor pool. They arrange passage for workers whom growers specifically request, and, like the Florida Fruit and Vegetable Association, they admit to maintaining a blacklist. Workers' names are entered on this list if they have a problem with their employer, their supervisors, or the association, or if they have left without finishing their contracts or overstayed their visas in the past.

The separation between Mexican H-2 workers and their U.S. employers by Del-Al representatives makes it relatively easy for Del-Al to exercise some authority even over workers whom growers specifically request. Any worker who fails to submit to the terms of recruitment that Del-Al representatives have established can be blackballed and denied future work in the United States as an H-2 worker. Del-Al can merely tell the association that a requested worker either could not be found or did not wish to return, and can replace that worker with another more to its liking. This may be difficult in cases where workers' relations with their employers are such that they may call them directly by telephone, or where employers regularly visit workers in Mexico, but Del-Al nevertheless exercises substantial authority over the complexion of the H-2 workforce. In the process, Del-Al charges $261 per worker for its services (or between 5 and 10 percent of workers' earned income), keeping $126 of this expense for themselves and using the remainder for various processing fees associated with passports and visas. The association charges growers an additional $50 per worker, and some growers pass this expense on to their workers. Additional fees sometimes come from transportation costs that are passed along to workers, gifts and kickbacks to recruiters at the local level, and payments to custom agents on both sides of the border. This results, obviously, in substantial gross income for employees of Del-Al and the association. Even if these agencies only negotiate for half of the estimated 110,000 H-2 workers imported every year, this amounts to gross annual earnings in excess of $2 million.

From many growers' perspectives, it is neither necessary nor particularly desirable for growers to use the association or Del-Al. While some growers do rely on them for labor relations issues, most fill out their own clearance orders and recruit workers directly from Mexico, using network ties they have developed with unauthorized Mexican workers over the years. Many growers we interviewed expressed dismay at what they perceived as their being forced to use the association and Del-Al, particularly disliking the $50-per-worker fee, even if they passed it on to the workers. Although the association and Del-Al certainly provide some growers with services that they believe are worth the costs, the proportion of workers' pay that ends up in the hands of these organizations seems high in light of the few benefits they receive. Workers, as well as many growers, would prefer to circumvent these organizations in their handling of the H-2 program. Given the high proportional costs of these recruiting services to workers, is it any wonder that more than two-thirds of the workforce would like to see the Mexican government perform the function of labor intermediary?

RECRUITMENT IN CRAB PICKING

Unlike the tobacco growers who rely on grower associations, most crab processors have built their recruiting systems on networks of current H-2 workers. This network approach is nearly identical to the way crab-plant owners used to recruit African Americans, relying on maternal ties (Griffith 1987). Recruitment thus occurs far less formally in crab than in tobacco, contributing to different worker experiences at the plants and different impacts on home communities. The less formal nature of recruitment into crab processing is reflected in the proportion of crab workers versus tobacco workers who report receiving contracts and the generally vaguer terms of the contracts issued to crab workers. Compared to the 95 percent of tobacco workers who received contracts, only 57 percent of crab workers reported (or remembered) receiving a contract, and crab workers were less likely to report that the contracts included reliable information about the type of work they would be doing, the pay, and their housing and transportation arrangements. More than 90 percent of tobacco workers, by contrast, were clear about these and other terms of their employment.

Informal recruitment has not always dominated crab picking. Some of first crab processors to participate in the H-2 program set themselves up as labor intermediaries and began recruiting workers for other crab processors in the mid-Atlantic region. In *The Estuary's Gift* (1999, chapter 4 and 135–39), I chronicle the genesis of that effort and its eventual demise after a series of lawsuits and subsequent marketing changes and capital concentration in the industry forced several crab processors out of business.

After the failure of early attempts to contract H-2 workers through labor intermediaries, many plants began negotiating with Mexican workers already working in their plants to recruit new workers in their home villages in Mexico. Again, this practice replicated an earlier model of network recruiting among African American women, and for similar reasons; African American women not only recruited workers, they also trained, supervised, and disciplined them. At times this discipline carried over into the community at large, giving elder workers a general, if vague, authority over younger ones. Similar systems of recruitment, training, supervision, and discipline have emerged with the Mexican workers in many of the crab plants. The description that follows is a composite from several plants in eastern North Carolina and Maryland, drawn primarily from repeated interviews with crab-plant owners and H-2 workers.

Generally, the informal recruiting networks that have developed in crab processing began by capitalizing on the English-language skills of specific Mexican women who came to the plants as H-2 workers during the first years of the program. In the cases I know most intimately, these were individuals who had spent some time in the United States earlier in their lives, or who saw the value of learning English and worked to learn as much as possible during their first months in the program, setting themselves up as translators. During these first years, English skills were particularly helpful to plant owners because almost none spoke Spanish and only a few hired locals who did. The latter were primarily individuals who had taken or taught high school Spanish, and often even the teachers' skills were rudimentary. Thus it became common for Mexicans proficient in English to move into first informal and then formal supervisory positions relatively easily, placing them in privileged positions vis-à-vis owners of crab plants. Rewards for such positions were not only the choice work in the plants but better housing for themselves and their friends and relatives, and, eventually, kickbacks from workers they recruited.

The function of these individuals as labor recruiters and general intermediaries thus grew out of their roles as translators and supervisors. Spending their winters in Mexico, they marketed the program in small *ejidos* near their homes, working through networks of friends and kin. Again, in the cases I know most intimately, even the relatives and friends they brought into the plants had to submit to their authority. This authority, as with African American workers formerly, has come to permeate time spent at work as well as to influence workers' leisure time in the United States and how they spend their time in Mexico. One of these informal labor intermediaries, for example, would not allow her own son to return to the plant for one season because he had spent too much of his time drinking in local bars during his idle time the previous season. This same recruiter—the most powerful one I encountered, in charge of around three hundred workers—

made all pickers get work experience in Mexican crab-picking plants before entering the mid-Atlantic workforce. The benefit to her employer is obvious, yet she too benefited: productive workers pick more crab, and her recruits paid her a nickel for every pound they picked.

The regulation of workers' leisure time has a long history in the United States and elsewhere. Henry Ford's infamous practices of integrating his immigrant autoworkers into American culture have been replaced by more subtle methods of controlling workers outside the workplace. Rouse (1992) has written eloquently about the slow process by which immigrants from Aguililla, Mexico, were weaned from "unruly" behavior such as drinking, cockfighting, and gambling to the pastimes of "good" consumers: "The influences exerted by the INS and the police were not confined to constraints on people's use of space. In an indirect way, they also played an important part in encouraging Aguilillans to be good consumers. Given the fact that officers from both agencies paid most attention to people who looked out of place, there was a strong incentive for new arrivals to replace their cheap, Mexican clothes with a more expensive U.S. wardrobe and for settlers in

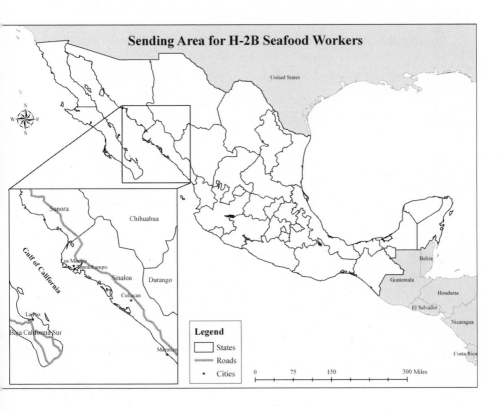

general to find themselves good-looking cars and to move from barrack-like apartment buildings and multi-family homes into owner-occupied, single-family dwellings" (Rouse 1992, 35).

Among Mexican crab pickers, the regulation of space is more direct and overt than the subtle mechanisms of control that Rouse describes, tied directly to their legal status in the United States and the power of recruiters to renew (or not renew) their contracts. Even so, the power of the recruiters in crab processing is not absolute, responding to village-level methods of social control such as those related in the introduction to this book, in the story of Amelia and Carlos José of La Noria. In villages and neighborhoods as small as La Noria, the work in the crab plants has become so deeply woven into the social fabric that the kind of authority Del-Al and the association enjoy in tobacco becomes far more difficult to enforce. Still, labor intermediaries in both tobacco and crab are in a position to take advantage of workers, reflecting the many problems that attend labor contracting, and recruitment remains an area of concern for both workers and worker advocates.

GENDER AND H-2 WORKERS

I began this chapter with a discussion of recruitment because it structures the general experience of H-2 workers in terms of their relations with other workers and with U.S. employers. Yet the underlying purpose of comparing crab and tobacco workers is to gain insight into the gendered dimensions of the H-2 program. That recruitment patterns differ between the two industries may be tied to historical developments, but it may be that occupations dominated by women are in fact more conducive to the intermingling of work and domestic life in the ways seen in the village of La Noria. Studies of industrial home work, much of which is performed by women, along with other studies of occupations dominated by women, invariably raise the issue of relations between home and work and the different ways that women and men negotiate the two (Gringeri 1995; Lamphere et al. 1994; Sutton 1992; Pessar 1999). Certainly these are not uniform across all groups of women and men but vary by class, ethnicity, and other factors. In this case, however, the men and women I am comparing come from similar ethnic, class, and national backgrounds and are entering occupations that were gendered prior to their arrival. Crab processing has always been dominated by women, and tobacco has been dominated by males since the shift from African American to Latino workers over the last two decades. Other work in H-2 has also disproportionately recruited either males or females, but rarely both. Chambermaids are nearly always women, while shrimpers and most other H-2 workers are nearly always men. Because these occupations are basically gendered, comparing tobacco and crab workers offers clues as to how the gendering of work has shaped the workforce and workers' experiences.

I noted earlier that tobacco and crab workers tend to be similar in terms of age, with an average age of around thirty, but that tobacco workers tend to be in households of their own creation more often than crab workers. Tobacco workers also are more likely to be married—more than twice as many tobacco workers than crab workers are married (81.4 vs. 35.7 percent). The higher incidence of single women working in the crab plants may be in part due to the program's influence over, and responsiveness to, gender relations in Mexico. On the one hand, married men may be averse to their wives' working in the United States for prolonged periods. On the other, in La Noria and other areas of Mexico where we visited families of H-2 workers, we observed that women who participated in the program had achieved status in their households that seemed to grate against traditional gender relations. Recall the young woman whose uncle warned her that if she went abroad to work she would not be welcomed back, only to be received with open arms when she returned with impressive sums of cash. Other women claimed that working in the plants had given them new authority in their households and in their wider extended families, and that many women who worked in the program were no longer willing to submit to traditional gender relations in Mexico.

Clearly, too, the absence of males from tobacco workers' villages has influenced not only gender relations but also relations between generations. We heard several stories of young people refusing to be disciplined by their mothers or grandparents while their fathers were absent. We found less clear evidence of women gaining prestige and power as a result of men's absence. Instead, male authority seems to fall to the older men in the absence of the younger. But it would be surprising not to see shifts in power relations when so many men are absent for long periods of time.

The program's influence on gender relations, then, appears to be related to how work has been gendered in the United States before workers arrive. Traditionally female occupations, selecting for women and possibly also for single workers, seem more apt to disrupt traditional gender relations than traditionally male occupations, while those that select for men and for married workers tend to disrupt traditional parent-child authority systems for the sake of preserving traditional gender relations.

Crab workers tended to receive less support than tobacco workers from parents and others in their decisions to migrate, perhaps because families may initially object to women traveling to the United States for work. Only 48 percent of crab workers reported receiving help, compared to two-thirds of tobacco workers. Nearly identical figures emerge when we compare migration aid by sex. This may also be linked to the fees that tobacco workers pay to Del-Al, of course—costs not borne by most crab workers. Workers in crab are somewhat more likely to come from families in which their mothers migrated before them, while tobacco workers seem more prone to follow in the footsteps of their fathers. A majority of both groups reported that other members of their families migrated, although slightly more tobacco workers reported this, 76 percent as opposed to 59 percent of crab workers. Yet these days it is probably safe to say that almost everyone in Mexico knows someone who has migrated to the United States to work.

EXPERIENCES IN THE UNITED STATES

Once in the United States, in the work settings and social contexts of the crab workers and the tobacco workers, we again find similarities and differences. In both industries the sizes of operations vary, yet crab workers tend to work under more factory-like production regimes and in larger workforces than the tobacco workers. Tobacco farms, constrained in their growth by an allotment system that has prevented capital concentration in the industry, tend to hire fewer than fifty workers, and usually fewer than ten, while some crab plants have as many as two or three hundred workers. These size differences are reflected in housing as well.

On the tobacco farms the accommodations we visited varied widely in quality, yet all were livable and some even quite pleasant. Phil Michaels, a young tobacco farmer who hires four H-2 workers each season, houses them in a small white house on a country intersection within walking distance of the nearest store. The house has curtains on the windows and wall hangings, along with ceiling fans and fancy light fixtures. Other dwellings were considerably sparer, with nothing on their walls but a calendar. The six H-2s who work for Perkins Small outside Cove City, having no kitchen table, have to eat standing up or from their laps. They are six men, a father and his five sons. The house has two rooms of living space—a kitchen and a living room—two bedrooms, and one bath. They have access to a Jeep, and the sparse furnishings include a television, two sofas, and beds crowded together in the bedroom. On another farm, five H-2 workers live in an old trailer with two bedrooms and a central area that doubles as a kitchen and a living room.

While most of the tobacco dwellings we visited were small farmhouses or trailers housing fewer than ten workers, most dwellings of the crab workers are dormitory-style and house between fifteen and fifty workers. Most plants do have some smaller, single-family dwellings that accommodate families of workers and women who travel with their children. Often these are reserved for workers with good relations with the plant owners (such as their key recruiting and supervisory personnel). While the smaller dwellings, usually trailers or small houses, tend to look clean and well maintained, with air conditioning, cable television, and other amenities, the dormitories vary considerably. Crab owners have also converted old rooming houses, schools, warehouses, lodges, daycare centers, and other abandoned buildings for dormitory use.

That women and men experience the H-2 program differently may result in the first place from the ways in which their occupations were gendered before they arrive, yet the differences do not end there. As the responses to the attitudinal questions and other observations suggest, women seem more interested than men in replicating the social settings of most Mexican immigrants who settle in the United States. This includes the desire to elaborate their networks to include children and other family members, social developments that often deepen their presence in local communities through dealings with daycare, schools, churches, and various other diversions. Men seem slightly less concerned about the program's tendency to separate, by great distances, people from their families, though they did rank highly the prospect of returning to Mexico to see their families during the season. Unlike women, many men maintained that they preferred to leave their families in Mexico while they worked in the United States.

CONCLUSION:
LASTING FIRSTS

I opened this book with the argument that local history can influence global processes, and I focused on the ways in which Henry Flagler's development of Florida in the late nineteenth and early twentieth centuries pioneered labor relations that were to shape much of the state's future development while forging links between Florida and towns throughout the Caribbean and Latin America. Anthropologists often try to make sense of local history and circumstances, of things that mean nothing to most people but a great deal to a few, and inevitably in such settings we encounter many more voices than we anticipate. The two local histories that introduce this concluding chapter draw out some of these linkages and illustrate much broader transformations taking place throughout the South. The first is the story of Stephen Long, an African American educator in Worcester County, Maryland, who was stabbed to death in 1921 by a white farmer on the streets of Pocomoke City for trying to see that orphans used as farm labor received the education they were promised in return. The second is the story of a Mayan farm worker shot to death in a tomato field outside Manning, South Carolina, in 1992 for disputing his pay with the labor contractor who helped him cross the border to work on farms in Florida, Georgia, and the Carolinas.

STEPHEN LONG

The idea of trading labor for education dates back to the early city-states, when Sumerians or Incas annexed villages for labor tribute and in return built schools to educate and indoctrinate village youth. In the New World, during the colonization of Mexico, Peru, and Brazil, an institution known as *encomienda* gave Iberians rights to the labor of huge populations of Native Americans on the promise of making Christians out of them. In the 1950s and 1960s it was common for large families to take in a nanny from an even larger, usually poorer family, a girl who would help with the wash, cooking, and childcare in exchange for room and board while she attended school. In Worcester County, Maryland, orphaned African American children were hired out to white farmers on the condition that the farmers allow and encourage them to attend school. If admirable in intent, this arrangement was unfortunately clouded by racism and by the difficulties of American agriculture in the 1920s.

The image of the farmer in the South during the early part of this century inspired figurines that you see in gift catalogs and holiday shops: gray-haired men in overalls and women in long skirts and scarves. Whether African American or white, they represent the sharecroppers and tenant farmers whose forever-impoverished class emerged as an alternative to hired labor after slavery. Bound to landlords by credit, in debt for land, seed, and other agricultural inputs, they remained tied to local communities and local customs of benevolence and cruelty. But the sharecropper existence could neither sustain large families nor hold every family member to the soil. During the five and a half decades between Emancipation and Stephen Long's assassination, the migration of southern men and families into cities and manufacturing centers, along with the ramblings of youth who either would not or could not accept the subservience of sharecropping, brought North and South—Arkie, Okie, hillbilly, African American, and white—together in ways never dreamed of in the antebellum South.

Those southern pioneers who moved into the new wilderness of meat-packing plants in Philadelphia and Chicago, steel mills in Ohio, coal mines in West Virginia, or auto manufacturing plants in Michigan, all renewed the fears of southern farmers about labor scarcity, especially during harvest time, when their perishable crops needed picking. On the Delmarva Peninsula, where Stephen Long lived, producing fresh fruits and vegetables has a long history because of the peninsula's blessed soil and its proximity to Washington, D.C., Baltimore, Philadelphia, and Norfolk. The wetlands and waterways surrounding and cutting into the peninsula add fresh blue crab meat, mullet, and sea bass to the cornucopia. To make it to the big urban markets, fresh fruits, vegetables, and fish require a sizable labor force.

After Emancipation, farmers throughout the South acquired the labor of their neighbors through various forms of coercion seated in family and community. Enforcing vagrancy laws, allowing debt peonage, and making the women and children of tenant farmers and sharecroppers work during the seasons of heavy labor demand were common methods used by plantations and smaller farms to harvest and prepare their crops for market. Before World War II, the labor of women and children was especially crucial. If they weren't employed directly in picking and packing, they provided key support tasks of child and elder care, household maintenance, and the gardening, fishing, hunting, and woodcutting that allowed a poor family to survive lean times.

Running farms and homes with the help of child labor was common enough during the 1920s that Maryland residents considered it fine, even virtuous, to use orphans in this way, especially when it helped meet the costs of their education. The orphans learned hard work as well as reading, writing, and arithmetic. For their part, farm families paid into the fund of the common good that turned young women and men into productive citizens.

Stephen Long was instrumental in orchestrating this arrangement. Professor Long's largesse involved painting houses and murals inside churches to raise money to pay for the schooling of poor children, designing curricula, raising funds for nine African American schools, recruiting teachers, and looking into the reasons why some children weren't attending school.

This last act of concern got him killed. On September 13, 1921, investigating the absence of two orphan boys, he learned that the farmer the orphanage referred to as the orphans' "white guardian" refused to let them leave the farm. Long pressured the orphanage to take the two boys from their guardian, after which the farmer got drunk, sought out Long, and, finding him on the streets of Pocomoke City, stabbed him to death in front of Long's daughter and several other witnesses.

It is said that two thousand people attended Long's funeral and a thousand attempted to enter the courtroom while his murderer was on trial. For the murder and the terror he produced in the heart of a little girl, the farmer was sentenced to three years in jail.

What I find most remarkable about this story is neither the absurdity of the sentence nor the accomplishments of Stephen Long, but the way Long is remembered, the form and content of the memory and the things made of stone, wood, and social cement that support it. Certainly Long's accomplishments were significant, exceptional, yet they do not overshadow so much as draw out the significance of all the African American teachers, parents, and role models who remain nameless.

At the Worcester County Library in Snow Hill, Maryland, I spoke with Saunders Marshall, a man who co-founded the Stephen Long Guild in 1980. Mr. Marshall is a thin man of medium height and a warm demeanor. His smile conveys kindness and a touch of weariness. He spent his career educating youth and is spending his retirement educating fellow Worcester County residents about their heritage. He has a deep, rich voice, a speaker's voice, yet he speaks softly, as though used to a quiet, well-behaved audience.

Saunders's remembering of Stephen Long is a small part of a larger memorial, a memorial swimming against a growing current of forgetfulness. Just how much are people willing to forget? To show me, Saunders told this anecdote: "I was at dinner and this guy was sitting next to me and he said, 'You know, I should remember you. We're the same age and probably were in the same class.' I said, 'No. I went to Worcester High. You went to Snow Hill. Remember, the schools were segregated? How could I have been in your class when in the forties we had the African American school and you had the white school? That went into the sixties.' I almost fell over. He didn't want to remember."

Willed forgetting. Saunders and his contemporaries in the area where Stephen Long was killed have seen the consequences of this loss of memory on the youth there. Several of us were sitting around discussing this one July evening, and a local African American businessman, around twenty years Saunders's junior, said, "I never knew anything about Stephen Long until the African American community named the Stephen Long Guild and then the Stephen Long Year. Then we found that after four or five years it began to come full circle. I guess you'd say, hidden history. Our teachers, our educators, really made quite a mark on us, many of us that are here now."

I was drawn to that notion of hidden history coming full circle, as though scraps of lives buried in lots where dismantled buildings once stood beckoned an archaeology of sorts, a retreat into the earth from which springs here a slave detention center, there an African American theater or hotel, here a community of free African American pioneers or a church named for all the hope a romanticized Liberia once held for men like Marcus Garvey. Yet in the minds of youths, the form and content of the struggle remains unclear: that same July evening another ex-educator, one of Saunders's colleagues, told about a day his daughter came home from school after a lesson on civil rights. "She said 'civil rights' just means you had the right to go and eat someplace. She didn't know you were persecuted for being African American, because they don't realize this. The people who write the books prepare a book that's for a community of educators, and if it's got too much of the kind of material that tells the truth about America's way and life and here, and things you should know something about—they don't want that book."

Reconstructing history is as porous a task as archaeology. That July evening, these men filled in the spaces between laundered lessons and iron shackles with what I considered a strange longing: they mourned the passing of a time when the schools were separate, the neighborhoods separate, the lunch counters, bus seats, bathrooms, even the drinking fountains separate. They longed for segregation, and they weren't alone. In Florida, in a neighborhood of old tourist motels that have become labor camps and crowded housing along a street called Broadway, a neighborhood where underage girls slip into strangers' cars, a solemn and wise African American man said to me, "Integration has some good things, but it has a lot of bad things. It destroyed the African American family. And the African American family was destroyed because the schools were taken out of the African American community, and school is an institution."

But neither this man nor Saunders Marshall, for all their longing and romanticism, would really wish to return to the times that killed Stephen Long and sentenced his murderer to an absurd term, to come full circle. The lengthy, continuing struggles that dismantled segregation and allowed, encouraged, an archaeology of African American history broke the ring of it, shattered the Grecian Urn, and disrupted Faulkner's fatalist sense that the Joe Christmases and Joanna Burdens will never locate a place for themselves in either South or North, among African Americans or whites, Mexicans or Frenchmen, with rural folk or the people of Memphis. Yet Faulkner's apprentice, Gabriel García Márquez, reminds us with Colonel Buendia's little gold fishes, or with Florentino Ariza's endless passages upriver and down, that the circle has become a spiral. The names have changed, but the innocents remain unprotected.

COMALAPAINOS

Until the 1960s, dark-skinned immigrants from the Caribbean bypassed the South for cities like New York and Chicago, moving into the same service and manufacturing jobs that southern African Americans took when they migrated north in the half-century following the Civil War. But African American struggles during the 1950s and 1960s began opening up the South to new immigrants from Latin America and the Caribbean: more and more barriers to residence and employment succumbed to a combination of civil rights struggles, increased federalism, and a growing class of young industrialists and financiers who needed workers who could read, write, cipher, operate machinery, and impede the growth of labor unions. Gradually, as African Americans left southern agriculture for southern industry, left the countryside for the city, left the South for the North, Caribbean and Latin American immigrants and refugees moved into harvesting and packing jobs. As early as 1955 crews of Mexican farm workers began moving into the farm towns of southern Florida, working in the winter vegetable harvests from November to February and then moving north through the fern, onion, tomato, and squash harvests as the crops matured along the eastern seaboard.

Green tomatoes emerged as the cornerstone crop of the migrant stream, the centerpiece of the cornucopia. The fruit itself has come a long way, from its Nahuatl origins in the Teotihuacan Valley to the thick-skinned, genetically altered firm tomato of today. It is picked green and then gassed to a pinkish color in packing sheds, an easily sliced fruit used to garnish hamburgers and club sandwiches in restaurants throughout the United States. Interesting parallels exist between the rise of green tomatoes and the fate of African Americans and immigrants and refugees from the Caribbean and Latin America. The 1950s and 1960s witnessed the founding and growth of several fast food sandwich chains, restaurant franchises that drew young African American workers out of hot fields and into hot kitchens and air-conditioned serving stations and dining rooms, creating, at the same time, a growing demand for fresh, handpicked tomatoes.

The rise of this firm green globe along with the growth of sandwich kingdoms encouraged a transition in the fields from predominantly African American workers to workers from Mexico, Central America, and the Caribbean. It was this transition and all its cultural and historical implications that laid the foundation for the murder of a Mayan farm worker from Chiapas outside of Manning, South Carolina, in the summer of 1992. Like the actual events surrounding the killing of Stephen Long, the place and time of the farm worker's murder are far less telling than the circumstances that put him in the path of three bullets, two to the body and a third to the head, after days and days of riding in a cramped van from Mexico.

Most of us know Chiapas at least as well as we once knew Jonestown, Guyana: for several days at the beginning of 1994, an armed uprising led by Subcommander Marcos threatened Mexican stability and, some believe, precipitated the crash of the Mexican peso and economy later that year.

Calling themselves Zapatistas, the peasants invoked the spirit of Pancho Villa's sidekick, Emiliano Zapata, whose acts of resistance in 1910 brought more than a quarter-century of the Díaz dictatorship to an end.

The southern Mexican state of Chiapas borders the northwest departments of Guatemala, where villages like Huehuetenango and Todos Santos witnessed the military's infamous scorched-earth policies of the late 1970s, policies that created several refugee camps in Chiapas and Yucatan. Chiapas is not, traditionally, what U.S. immigration specialists refer to as one of Mexico's sending regions—not, that is, like Michoacan or Oaxaca or Juarez, states that historically have relied heavily on migration to the United States for work. Instead, Chiapas is the Mexican heartland of the highland Mayan peasantry, dependent on that nutritionally rich balance of corn, beans, and squash that dates back to the great pre-Columbian Mayan empires that founded the cities of Tikal and Palenque. For many years the site of the Harvard Chiapas project, the people of Chiapas intrigued anthropologists with the depth of their imperial history and the intensity of their religious festivities and offices, their cargoes of civic responsibility to reinvigorate the community's identity.

The Zapatista rebellion, ostensibly a reaction to the North American Free Trade Agreement, gained much of its momentum two years earlier, during a period of heightened consciousness and indigenous protests against five hundred years of Western domination. In the summer of 1992, while many peoples of Mayan ancestry were celebrating their imperial heritage, two men took advantage of the increasing political violence in southern Mexico and northwestern Guatemala, recruiting refugees into grueling harvesting crews of Florida and the eastern United States.

Records compiled by two paralegals in Florida refer to these two men as MF and SG, perhaps because giving them full names would endow them with qualities too human. More than seventy years after Stephen Long's death and more than a decade after the founding of the Stephen Long Guild, the methods SG and MF used to recruit and keep labor in their crews were remarkably similar, in form if not in content, to the enslavement of orphans that precipitated Long's death. They were based on debt: the refugees became indebted to MF and SG for transportation expenses—$1,000 for the trip across the border and the forty-hour ride from Arizona to LaBelle, Florida—for food consumed prior to their first pay, and for those miscellaneous expenses incurred during the workweek. Until workers paid off these debts, they were bound to work in MF's and SG's crews, travel in their buses and vans, live in their labor camps.

The problem with this arrangement lies in the time it takes to work off one's debt as a farm worker. Harvest work is almost always sporadic, interrupted by unseasonable frosts, rain, or the slow and irregular maturing characteristics of crops. Farm workers often spend days traveling across country only to arrive at a farm where the harvest is still a week or two away. In these cases, farmers and crew bosses like MF and SG discourage members of their crews from seeking work on other farms or, God forbid, in rural industries like chicken processing. In the 1920s, under the best of conditions, the farmers who benefited from orphan labor also paid for their educational expenses and saw to it that they attended school. On green tomato farms today, the most conscientious farmers and crew bosses will find work for migrants on adjacent farms or in alternative tasks—farm maintenance, field preparation or cleaning, tending livestock—or, failing that, will seek out forms of assistance from government sources or private charities to cover food and clothing needs until they get back to work. At the other extreme are those farmers and crew bosses who handcuff crew members to their beds at gunpoint.

SG and MF fell at the latter end of the spectrum. Their crews were composed primarily of illegal immigrants—political refugees from Chiapas and Guatemala and Mexican economic immigrants. Crews of this sort are built up from a complex infrastructure of vulnerability. Ironically, in this case, having family increased rather than decreased this vulnerability, exposing instead of protecting, because the intricate soft webbing that love of family produces crisscrosses countries, regions, and political geographies. Distributed so thinly over the landscape, a father cannot answer a son's complaint with either comfort or power, or even hear a wife's appeals.

Before becoming farm labor contractors, SG and MF served in the Guatemalan military, where they learned, in large part from the CIA, the most effective methods of terror known to people whose business is subterfuge and killing. On top of the debts incurred through travel and advances toward room and board, SG and MF daily woke the crew at 4:30 A.M. by firing their handguns into the air, intimidated them through random public beatings and stories of murders and disappearances, and kept them in the fields from before dawn until after dusk to prevent them from buying and cooking their own food. They took photographs of everyone, they kept contact with each other and their field bosses with CB radios, they patrolled the fields' and labor camps' perimeters and stopped any worker trying to leave or any lawyer or priest or anthropologist trying to speak to any member of the crew. After the ancient Mayan saying, they claimed the trees had ears, threatening to kill the family of any worker who failed to pay his debt and to cut out the tongues of anyone who spoke against them.

The murder occurred on a Friday night. Friday was payday, and one of the Mayan workers SG had recruited in Comalapa, Chiapas, confronted him about his pay. SG shot him twice, either in the legs or in the side, then instructed one of this crew bosses to finish the job. The crew boss shot the Comalapaino in the head. All of this happened in front of several other workers, including ten other Comalapainos who were recruited into SG's crew with the murder victim.

Accounts of subsequent events are disjointed and hazy. SG told only one of the witnesses, a Chicano from Immokalee, Florida, that if he remained with the crew he would be dead in the morning. Evidently this was the only witness he forced to leave. The other witnesses fled two days later, only after SG and MF were distracted by the brief and inconclusive county sheriff's investigation that followed. The morning after the murder, SG and MF stayed behind in the labor camp, a first for them, presumably to dispose of the body and the gun. When the sheriff's men arrived, SG dared them to find either victim or weapon. Neither was ever found.

When I first read the paralegals' accounts of this case, I was deeply entrenched in studying the dynamics of the farm labor market. This case, except for the murder, wasn't much different, formally speaking, from others I elicited from Haitians, African Americans, and Mexicans who also worked for unscrupulous crew bosses in the fields. Debt, intimidation, authoritarian control over workers, pay disputes, even beatings and routine cruelties—all characterized conditions in camps in Pennsylvania tomatoes and mushrooms, Georgia and South Carolina peaches, Michigan cherries, central Florida ferns, Blue Ridge Mountain apples, and New Jersey ornamental shrubbery. I had become disturbingly complacent about suffering, the same way some Guatemalan writers adopt a neutral, fatalist tone when describing political violence that claimed members of their families and home villages. This flat style of writing and speech accompanies a reluctance among victims to assign blame or speculate on the causes of cruel acts, hampering those applying for political asylum by making no appreciable impression on American judges used to the shrill cries of the terrorized.

I had become so used to the cruelty that initially I passed over the different ways SG dealt with the witnesses. Why did he force only one to leave yet force all the others to stay? The one forced to leave was neither Mayan nor Mexican, neither political refugee nor illegal immigrant, but Chicano, a Mexican American who suffered from quite a different quality of vulnerability than the other witnesses. He wore a cloak of citizenship, a thin yet protective legal status that enabled him to work for SG and MF without incurring the initial burden of the thousand-dollar debt for the border crossing. Other documents said that SG and MF were deducting social security and taxes without paying into these safety net funds, charging him for food and wine at exorbitant rates and deducting it from his pay, but the man's legal status, his rights of citizenship, however meager, were enough of a threat to SG that he forced the man out of the camp.

If citizenship provides even a thin cloak, reducing one's vulnerability and altering its form and content, families, neighborhoods, and communities add layers to that protection that change the character of vulnerability once again, but with weaves and designs and colors that display one's allegiances, one's passions, in far more intricate detail than a flag or a military insignia. The vulnerability of refugees is the vulnerability of orphans: citizens without countries, people in exile, without the local stimuli of food and soil, are like individuals without families. Yet those enclosures that African cattle herders call kraals and Puerto Rican fishers call Villas Pesqueras and Americans call Greenvilles and Montgomerys are not only spaces that protect us, they are rich in local customs, local history, and they negotiate between daily struggles and lasting firsts. The Chicano farm worker who witnessed the murder of the Mayan—has he stitched together his Mexican and his American ancestry in the same uneven and patchy way that southerners—white southerners in particular—stitch together the two flags expressing their allegiance? Did he see his own struggle in the killing?

In his hometown of Immokalee, Florida, I once interviewed another Chicano who came to Florida with his parents and brothers and sisters in the 1950s to work in the tomato harvest. By the time I interviewed him, his parents were dead and most of his brothers and sisters gone. He lived with one brother in the home his parents built. He no longer worked in the fields. Somewhat despondently he told me that he clerked and butchered in a small grocery store in Immokalee, next to the big parking lot where farm workers clogged the doorways of buses, competing for work in the fields every morning. The store's owner had lent his parents money and extended them credit in the store when they were down on their luck, and he felt a certain loyalty to his boss that kept him working there. I asked him to tell me about his family, about their Mexican roots and why they left Mexico for Texas and Texas for Florida. He spoke of boardinghouses operated by aunts, of grandmothers caring for children, of migrating into the cotton fields of Mississippi from south Texas, and of switching to work in tomatoes and citrus when the cotton producers turned to machines. He painted images of huge baskets of steamy tortillas, feasts and celebrations, honors bestowed on saints, and of the more solemn occasions of burial and worship. At times he became quite animated or nostalgic, as the subject required. But when I asked about the move to Immokalee, his expression became pained, he seemed to have difficulty breathing, and he said, "The children of Spanish speakers from the Southwest came to Florida to build themselves up, but we didn't get anywhere. We didn't get anywhere."

Yet he enjoyed recalling his history. He enjoyed the remembering. It enlivened him, even drew him out of his otherwise morose mood. I would have talked to him longer but he was late for work. He had to get to his tedious job of collecting money for cigarettes and sodas and cutting meat. He told me quite frankly that he hated his job. It was where he ended up, an everyday struggle, after years and years of traveling with harvesting crews around the South. He told no stories of murder, recounted no horrors of those days, but instead described life in labor camps the way my daughter describes summer camp.

Would things have turned out differently for him if he had had horror stories to tell? Would the suffering and struggle that those stories contain have become a source first of outrage and later of organization and even later of pride, the way civil rights struggles and victories at once electrify and inspire African Americans, enforcing remembering? What enduring impact on remembering will the nameless Mayan's murder have on the daughters and sons of today's refugees? Suffering creates opportunities, but whether people like SG and MF or people like Saunders Marshall take advantage of those opportunities depends on whether those opportunities father the silences of censorship and forgetfulness or mother the act of remembering.

If history is written in struggle and experience in contradiction, as Marx said, what are the chances that the great-grandchildren of the ten surviving Comalapainos will mark the place where the Mayan fell with a Styrofoam cross adorned with plastic lilies or a stele carved in the imperial Mayan tradition? The ten Comalapainos—now, no doubt, dispersed throughout the transnational spaces of political refugees—never emerged as witnesses, never tempered their delirious fear and outrage with resolve. The murder is sure to haunt them, to infect their everyday struggles and corrupt whatever peace they might know, one day, when their children are grown and their parents dead and their brothers and sisters scattered across the earth. This is the lesson of lasting firsts. This is the sense of small and large moments influencing one another, of your first taste of a favorite food or your first sex coloring your lifetime diet and all the loves of your life, or the marches and fiestas, the deaths and trials and protests shoring up your identity during the course of an ordinary day. This is what Faulkner taught us when he created the characters who witnessed the paramilitary terrorist Percy Grimm kill and then castrate Joe Christmas, saying, "For a long moment he looked up at them with peaceful and unfathomable and unbearable eyes. Then his face, body, all, seemed to collapse, to fall in upon itself, and from out the slashed garments rush like the sparks rising from a rising rocket; upon that black blast the man seemed to rise soaring into their memories forever and ever. They are not to lose it, in whatever peaceful valleys, beside whatever placid and reassuring streams of old age, in the mirroring faces of whatever children they will contemplate old disasters and newer hopes. It will be there, musing, quiet, steadfast, not fading and not particularly threatful, but of itself alone serene, of itself alone triumphant" (1932, 407).

In a presentation at the 15th Annual East Coast Migrant Stream Forum, in October 2003, Laura Germino, one of the paralegals who brought the Comalapaino case to trial, showed the audience articles in the *New Yorker* and *National Geographic* about twenty-first-century slavery. The edition of *National Geographic* produced in the United States showed frolicking zebras on the cover, but the edition produced in England, Europe, and Spanish-speaking nations, dated September 2003, showed on its cover an enslaved young African-looking man peeking out between blinds. It bore the caption, in large print: "Hidden in Plain Sight: The world's 21 million slaves." Laura made the point that we were too squeamish in the United States to accept the international cover, though the magazine carried the same story. She added that the *New Yorker* story, published in April 2003, included one important paragraph to the effect that when Congress wanted to pass an antislavery bill, a senator from Utah struck a clause that extended the law to "anyone who profited from slavery," which essentially absolved corporations, growers, and the like, of liability for slavery. Obviously, the senator's objection to the clause did not stem from enduring humanitarian principles but from his desire to protect the economic interests of his powerful constituents.

Like many of the debates surrounding slavery, arguments for and against H-2 programs can both rest on humanitarian principles. Humanitarians arguing for the expansion of guestworker programs point out that the alternative to a regulated system with some government oversight is a system that encourages outright slavery and debt peonage of the kind SG and MF engaged in, resting on a vast underground network of trafficking, violence, kickbacks, cheating, and intimidation. Humanitarians who argue against the expansion of guestworker programs point to empirical work that exposes the program's tendency to approximate indentured servitude and evolve a variety of mechanisms to cheat workers, usually through payroll deductions.

I have tried to show that the tendency has been for the H-2 program—in various settings, from small farms to large plantations, in tiny rural seafood houses, and from family-operated to corporate-run businesses—to devolve into a system that approximates the exploitive, illegal, underground labor market it was (in part) designed to replace. Indeed, there is some evidence that without this downward trend in conditions within H-2 programs, legal guestworkers become less attractive to U.S. employers than undocumented immigrant workers. As noted earlier, over the past two years the H-2A program has declined by around 20 percent in North Carolina, which may be due to the growing sophistication and efficiency of underground networks to match employers with workers, networks that depend on linkages among new immigrant workers, labor smugglers, *raiteros* who transport workers from locations near the border to distant work sites in North Carolina and elsewhere, labor contractors, and employers of seasonal labor. The more sophisticated these networks become, however, the less likely they are to match immigrant workers with the kinds of jobs guestworkers currently hold. Instead, new immigrants have increasingly been diffusing into different sectors of the economy, particularly the construction and rural food-processing sectors, where jobs may be as difficult and dangerous as those H-2 workers currently hold but are more stable, often lasting year round, and may pay more.

We have yet to fully understand the occupational trajectories of new immigrants in the United States, how they combine multiple livelihoods, and the ways these livelihoods link them to their homelands and the families they leave behind. Mark Grey (1999) suggests that many new immigrants move among meatpacking jobs in an effort to relieve themselves of the muscular and other stresses associated with these jobs, as well as to approximate seasonal rounds that allow them to attend to responsibilities in different areas. In our study of Puerto Rican fishers (Griffith and Valdés Pizzini 2002), as well as Jorge Duany's (2002) work on the Puerto Rican nation on the move, the empirical evidence points to the movement among multiple livelihoods as a way of coping with material poverty as well as reaffirming one's cultural and occupational identity. Women seafood workers who arrive in the United States carrying both H-2 visas and unborn children are clearly forwarding their identities as mothers even as they jeopardize jobs that have become an integral component of their lives and the lives of their born and unborn children. Other women, who resist the patriarchy of elder male kinsmen to migrate and live and work beside their husbands, also assert a form of gender identity that reinforces even as it partially dismantles that patriarchy (Pessar 1999).

Particularly disturbing in cases like this, as in the program at large, are the changing relationships between productive and reproductive labor that are occurring within guestworker programs. On the one hand, increasing demands for women guestworkers alter gender relations in sending countries in ways that may seem encouraging to those of us who believe in expanding rights for women, giving women access to power via new earning capacity. On the other, that they also continue to care for and have children while they are guestworkers—or struggle with the choice of working instead of bearing children, putting their bodies on hold—suggests that this new freedom, power, and earning capacity may come at a high price: sacrificing motherhood or doubling their individual workload.

Similarly, Mexican and Jamaican men who either submit to the matriarchal authority of female employers in the United States or attempt to shift their status from undocumented to H-2 worker, consciously suppress aspects of their own gender identities in the interest of reducing their risks and increasing their employment stability. In the promise of this stability lie the seeds that threaten to transform well-intentioned contractual working relationships into relationships that approximate the highly exploitive underground labor processes that the contracts were designed to replace. From the promise of stability arise the highly structured working and living environments that begin to resemble total institutions. Central to them are methods of controlling of workers' space and time, usually through housing, forms of surveillance and enforcement, and pressure on workers to organize their cultural lives in particular ways.

Yet the German minister of labor—if it *was* the minister who said this—was right when he said that guestworker programs don't just import workers, they import people, and these people are indeed living, breathing, *thinking* people. They aren't mere cogs in a machine and they are not stupid. They see especially clearly when the expansion of control and surveillance leads to new methods that employers use to recoup portions of the wages they earn, such as bringing female crab pickers in early to charge them for housing, or raising their rents from year to year without increasing their pay. It is when they see how and how much they are being exploited that H-2 workers begin working off their contracts, taking odd jobs here and there during idle times, becoming undocumented altogether ("jumping ship"), or staying in the United States beyond their contracts. These practices are ubiquitous, and they represent the most basic form of resistance to the multileveled surveillance that attends guestworker programs, surveillance that expands initially from the two nation-states to include employers, supervisors, contractors, recruiters in their home communities, and other H-2 workers. At times even their family members join employers in this surveillance, as occurred in the case related above of the young man whose mother disapproved of his behavior and, as the plant's principal recruiter, made him sit out the program for two years before letting him return. The infamous blacklisting that occurs in H-2 programs underlies the effectiveness of this surveillance. Workers truly fear not being called back.

Yet working off the contract provides a hedge against the possibility of being cut from the program, allowing workers to learn about U.S. labor market opportunities and other aspects of life outside of the narrow confines of their contracted jobs and living spaces. Working off the contract exposes H-2 workers to more than simply other sectors of the economy, other employers, or other jobs. Through the increased communication taking place among Latino co-workers, H-2s working off contract learn about housing opportunities, healthcare systems, places where Latinos gather, new churches, and centers that address issues of social justice. By working off their contracts, H-2 workers become more deeply intertwined in networks of Latinos and working-class folks who are settling, more and more every day, in the rural United States. In light of this practice, it is no wonder that the Bracero Program in the West laid the groundwork for the development of mature social networks that eventually rendered the program obsolete: Braceros had learned how to find employment outside the narrow confines of their contracts, with and without the aid of labor contractors. With the decline in H-2A contracts in North Carolina just noted, we may be witnessing a similar occurrence, although it is occurring unevenly and with the assistance of a growing settled population of Spanish-speaking individuals in new destinations across the United States.

Sometimes employers assist H-2s in working outside their contracts, either helping them find work or not objecting when they do. This is against the law and the contract and undermines the authority of the state or its local surrogates, the labor-contracting firms or associations, yet employers will assist H-2s in their search for other work for both moral and financial reasons. Most employers of H-2 workers, like the workers themselves, despise idleness. Idleness, as distinct from rest, has direct costs for both workers and employers. Employers who pay for workers' housing complain during idle times that they have to continue paying the workers' utility bills and other housing expenses; workers who pay for their own housing complain that they have to continue paying rent and other expenses while not earning income. Employers and workers object to idleness for moral reasons, too: at the heart of their relationship is work. H-2s come to the United States to work; employers bring H-2s to the United States to work. Idleness squanders value, letting a valuable asset (ready and willing labor) go to waste. To prevent idleness, some farmers who hire H-2 workers will plant extra crops to keep workers busy during idle times, even if the sale of these crops earns just enough to pay workers and cover their housing and other expenses. Other farmers make arrangements with their neighbors to employ their workers during idle times, if possible.

Yet idleness is not always so abhorred. We saw earlier that seafood processors will bring in workers early in the season, when there are low volumes of crab and thus high levels of idle time, in part in order to charge workers for housing that has been sitting unoccupied through the winter. For agricultural workers, the growers' associations have also developed a mechanism to *create* idle time as a way of encouraging H-2s, toward the end of the season, to forfeit transportation expenses that they are supposed to receive *if they complete their contracts.* At the end of the tobacco season, the association will inform workers and their employers that they are going to need to move workers to sweet potato harvests, but not for a few weeks. At the end of the season, after living and working in the United States for up to eight or nine months, most workers miss their families desperately, and the thought of waiting around without work for the sweet potato harvest is, for many, too much to bear. Digging sweet potatoes is a dirty task—dirtier than tobacco—and the harvest is usually of short duration and does not pay well. Again, this results in a substantial loss to the worker and a substantial benefit to the association, which deducts a portion of the worker's transportation expenses from every check throughout the season.

It should not surprise us that most methods of returning a portion of labor's value to employers and employers' representatives, the growers associations, involve payroll deductions. Such practices date back to debt peonage, the company store, and what labor contractors call "working a line"— providing workers liquor, cigarettes, and other goods and services every evening, keeping a ledger of these transactions, and deducting their costs from workers' pay on payday. Janet Siskind's recent work on an eighteenth- and nineteenth-century New England merchant family, *Rum and Axes* (2002), makes the point that accounting practices like these acted as veils between merchants' comfortable and secure lives in New England and the slavery and brutality of West Indian sugar production that lay at the heart of their commercial transactions. H-2 programs have been the mechanism for payroll deduction schemes for many years. The 1991 congressional investigation into Florida sugar found that the 2 percent deducted for insurance was nothing less than a transfer of cash to West Indian insurance companies, with virtually no benefit to workers. The Jamaican investigation into the Ministry of Labour's use of workers' compulsory savings deductions to buy goods in Canada for resale in Jamaica was essentially an investigation into payroll deductions.

If payroll and other abuses are to end, of course, what is needed is a shift in the current balance of power. At the November 2003 conference in Ottawa, Canada, I mentioned earlier, sociologist Kerry Preibisch made the point that, in the Canadian guestworker program, growers had literally all the power. Until recently, this was true of U.S. employers as well, and it is still true of most employers of H-2B workers. In the late summer of 2004, however, after a prolonged struggle and boycott of the Mt. Olive Pickle Company, a farm workers' union calling itself the Farm Labor Organizing Committee (FLOC) signed a union contract with the North Carolina Growers Association, transferring at least some power from growers' to workers' hands. How much power FLOC will exercise on the workers' behalf will be seen in the seasons to come; many of my colleagues have expressed pessimism regarding the extent to which it will be able to respond to worker grievances, get rid of payroll deduction schemes, and prevent future abuse. Nevertheless, FLOC's approach to this transfer of power has been innovative in several ways.

First, FLOC has worked for more than a decade to organize cucumber workers along the "pickle corridor" stretching from Michigan to North Carolina. This organizing strategy strikes me as particularly innovative on a larger scale. In North Carolina many of these cucumber workers are H-2 workers, hired by the growers association, and are farmed out to cucumber farmers as needed. FLOC's targeting of cucumber workers, rather than all farm workers, is innovative for at least three reasons: it is based on organizing workers who are united by their production of a specific processed commodity rather than a specific grower, firm, or industry; it targets integrators, who contract with growers, rather than firms; and it is transnational, which allows or encourages linkages between productive and reproductive labor.

ORGANIZATION BY COMMODITY

What is innovative about targeting a processed commodity instead of an industry or a firm is that specific commodities, as Marx pointed out, embody specific social relations. Different firms producing the same commodity compete with one another, which encourages them to adopt similar production practices. If one firm producing that commodity becomes the target of union activism and signs a contract, it is in that firm's interest to see that other firms strike similar agreements so as to level the playing field. It forces a firm, through economic pressure, to support other unionization efforts.

In the case of pickles, too, brand recognition occurs at the level of the commodity, a business strategy that has become common throughout the food industry and other industries as well. Few consumers know that Peter Pan peanut butter, Butterball turkeys, Reddi-wip whipping cream, Hunt's catsup, Orville Redenbacher's popcorn, and Wesson canola oil are all owned by ConAgra Foods, Inc. Each of these products is advertised under a recognized brand name, a factor that makes them more vulnerable to boycotts and other forms of public scrutiny; this kind of public scrutiny enabled the unionization of farm workers working in Coca-Cola-owned Minute Maid orange groves and processing plants in Florida. Indeed, the lack of brand recognition in a commodity like cucumbers has made it more difficult to target them and similar products, like grapes and strawberries, for boycott than branded products like Vlasic or Mt. Olive.

Because class and cultural background influence the consumption of commodities, and specific forms of specific commodities, targeting commodities for boycott can benefit from the communication that accompanies cultural and class ties, ceremonies, rituals, and other public events (Mintz 1985; Roseberry 1995). During a boycott of table grapes, for example, an agricultural economist friend told me that he and his colleagues, served grapes at a banquet, passed around a bowl into which each person at the table ceremoniously placed the grapes from his or her plate. Such an event reinforces the importance of the boycott and enforces compliance through simple peer pressure.

TARGETING INTEGRATORS

The targeting of the integrator—in this case, the pickle processor—is innovative because, as noted earlier, subcontracting arrangements are becoming
more common throughout the economy, and integrators, as the designation
implies, integrate several different producers, and different kinds of producers, into one production process. Subcontracting relations, while bene-
fiting integrators, often make it difficult for contract workers to voice their
opinions about production processes because they risk having their contracts cancelled at the end of the current contract period. At the same time,
companies like the pickle companies targeted by FLOC, or like poultry and
hog companies, rest on a series of contracting arrangements, negotiating
individual contracts with cucumber growers who may be negotiating their
own contracts through growers' associations, farm labor–contracting firms,
or other kinds of temp agencies. In the summer of 1998 berry growers in
Oregon quite happily reported to me that temp agencies could absorb all
the risks associated with I-9 documentation, workman's compensation, and
other labor regulations, yet easily avoid any labor law enforcement because
many of these agencies operate from temporary offices, using portable computers and cellular phones. I noted earlier that, for several decades, building on the inherent mobility of seasonal farm labor, farm labor contractors
have relied on technologies of mobility such as CB radios and strings of
post office boxes. By contrast, integrators are usually highly visible and easy
to target with both legal and illegal tactics.

TRANSNATIONAL ORGANIZING

Finally, organizing workers transnationally is perhaps the most innovative of
FLOC's strategies, because it recognizes not merely the transnational experiences of workers but also the more subtle relations between reproductive
and productive labor that exist among workers who move between various
livelihoods, regions, and countries. Migration among several livelihoods,
some involving movement between countries, increases the tendency for
reproductive work, and other nonwage work, to be organized in ways that
accommodate the seasonal and daily schedules of wage laborers. As this may
create tensions among the scheduling demands of domestic enterprises such
as fishing and farming, it may also, in the process, raise the consciousness
of those involved in the domestic enterprises at least to the extent that they

view their own work as subsidizing labor siphoned off by capitalist industry. Making this connection redoubles their stake in workers' rights issues.

At the same time that workers move among multiple livelihoods, they often move into and out of different class and authority positions, becoming an employee of wage labor in one setting, a partner in another, an independent producer in another. Poultry farmers typically see themselves as exploited by poultry processing firms, yet they hire workers whom they exploit in turn. In his long-term work on Belize agriculture, Mark Moberg argues that many of the labor relations of local growers can be traced to structural constraints imposed on them from merchant houses in core states. We can expect these contradictions to create tensions in households and production settings, as individuals use practices in their own enterprises that they object to having applied to themselves. As experience benefits from contradiction, forcing individuals and family members to justify inconsistencies in their behaviors, viewing working and living conditions from different class perspectives provides the same kind of lessons we learn, as anthropologists, as we attempt to describe and explain other cultures.

The recognition that most farm workers in the United States come from Mexico seems simple enough, and the idea of organizing both sides of the border is an obvious logical extension. One of the problems that I foresee in FLOC's strategies is the difficulty it may face in responding to a substantial ethnic change in the farm labor force. One wonders, in fact, what might happen to FLOC if, say, Somalis, eastern Europeans, or even Mixtecs from Oaxaca, began making up an increasing proportion of farm labor markets.

Currently, however, instead of concentrating solely on farm workers in the United States, FLOC's transnational organizing efforts help blur the lines between sending and receiving communities. In the same way, many Mexican families resist being seen as mere contract workers by engaging in behavior that blurs the lines between productive and reproductive labor, between farm work and work in other occupations, and that allows them the choice of settling out of migrant streams or stabilizing their employment in the United States if they so desire. This development is reason for hope. While we are not likely to erase completely from the low-wage labor landscape abuses like those that led to the murder of Stephen Long or the Comalapainos—or the abuses of pay and comprehensive control that too often creep into guestworker programs—FLOC's success, however limited, is a step toward acknowledging that the balance of power in these programs will have to shift before we fully acknowledge that H-2 workers are not merely workers but people with parents, children, friends, fears, and, above all, basic human rights.

REFERENCES

Amin, Samir. 1974. *Accumulation on a World Scale.* Vol. 1. New York: Monthly Review Press.

Appadurai, Arjun. 1992. *Modernity at Large.* Minneapolis: University of Minnesota Press.

Bach, Robert, and Howard Brill. 1991. *The Impact of IRCA on the U.S. Labor Market and Economy.* Final Report to the U.S. Department of Labor. Binghamton: SUNY Institute for Research on Multiculturalism and International Labor.

Bach, Robert, and Lisa Schraml. 1982. "Migration, Crisis, and Theoretical Conflict." *International Migration Review* 16 (2): 320–41.

Basch, Linda, Nina Glick-Schiller, and Cristina Blanc-Szanton. 1994. *Nations Unbound: Transnational Projects, Postcolonial Predicaments, and Deterritorialized Nation-States.* Langhorns, Pa.: Gordon and Breach.

Bascom, William. 1991. "Gullah Folk Beliefs Concerning Childbirth." In *Sea Island Roots: African Presence in the Carolinas and Georgia,* ed. M. Twining and K. Baird, 27–36. Trenton, N.J.: Africa World Press.

Basok, Tanya. 2000. "Migration of Mexican Seasonal Farmworkers to Canada and Development: Obstacles to Productive Investment." *International Migration Review* 34 (1): 79–97.

———. 2002. *Tortillas and Tomatoes: Transmigrant Mexican Harvesters in Canada.* Montreal: McGill-Queen's University Press.

Belshaw, Cyril. 1976. *The Sorcerer's Apprentice.* New York: Pergammon Press.

Beneria, Lourdes, and Gita Sen. 1981. "Accumulation, Reproduction, and Women's Role in Economic Development: Boserup Revisited." *Signs* 7: 279–98.

———. 1982. "Class and Gender Inequities and Women's Role in Economic Development—Theoretical and Practical Implications." *Feminist Studies* 8: 157–76.

Benson, Janet. 1990. "Households, Migration, and Community Context." *Urban Anthropology* 19 (1–2): 9–30.

———. 1999. "Undocumented Immigrants and the Meatpacking Industry in the Midwest." In *Illegal Immigration in America: A Reference Handbook,* ed. D. Haines and K. Rosenblum, 172–93. Westport, Conn.: Greenwood Press.

Binford, Leigh. 2002. "Social and Economic Contradictions of Rural Migrant Contract Labor Between Tlaxcala, Mexico, and Canada." *Culture and Agriculture* 24 (2): 1–19.

Boserup, Ester. 1971. *Woman's Role in Economic Development.* London: George Allen & Unwin.

Brandes, Stanley. 1975. *Migration, Kinship, and Community: Tradition and Transition in a Spanish Village.* New York: Academic Press.

Buck, Pem Davidson. 2001. *Worked to the Bone: Race, Class, Power, & Privilege in Kentucky.* New York: Monthly Review Press.

Buitrago Ortiz, Carlos. 1973. *Esperanza.* Tucson: University of Arizona Press.

Bump, Micah. 2005. "From Temporary Picking to Permanent Plucking: Hispanic Newcomers, Integration, and Change in the Shenandoah Valley." In *Beyond the Gateway: Immigrants in a Changing America,* ed. Elżbieta Goździak and Susan F. Martin, 137–76. Lanham, Md.: Lexington Books.

Calavita, Kitty. 1992. *Inside the State: The Bracero Program, Immigration, and the INS.* New York: Routledge.

Carter, Kenneth. 1997. *Why Workers Won't Work: The Worker in a Developing Economy; A Case Study of Jamaica.* London: Macmillan.

Cecelski, David. 1994. *Along Freedom Road: Hyde County, North Carolina, and the Fate of Black Schools in the South.* Chapel Hill: University of North Carolina Press.

———. 2001. *The Waterman's Song: Slavery and Freedom in Maritime North Carolina.* Chapel Hill: University of North Carolina Press.

Chandler, Alex. 1986. *Henry Flagler: The Astonishing Life and Times of the Visionary Robber Baron Who Founded Florida.* New York: Macmillan.

Chaney, Elsa. 1979. *Supermadre: Women in Politics in Latin America.* Austin: University of Texas, Institute of Latin American Studies.

———. 1984. *Women of the World: Latin America and the Caribbean.* Washington, D.C.: U.S. Agency for International Development.

Chaney, Elsa, and Marianne Schmink. 1980. "Women and Modernization: Access to Tools." In *Sex and Class in Latin America,* ed. June Nash and H. Safa, 160–82. Brooklyn: J. F. Bergin Publishers.

Chayanov, A. V. 1966. *The Theory of Peasant Economy.* Ed. D. Throner, B. Kerblay, and R. Smith. Homewood, Ill.: American Economic Association.

Chibnik, Michael. 1978. "The Value of Subsistence Production." *Journal of Anthropological Research* 34 (4): 561–76.

Clarke, Edith. 1957. *My Mother Who Fathered Me.* London: George Allen & Unwin.

Cloud, Patricia, and David Galenson. 1987. "Chinese Immigration and Contract Labor in the Late Nineteenth Century." *Explorations in Economic History* 24: 22–42.

Cobb, James. 1982. *The Selling of the South.* Baton Rouge: Louisiana State University Press.

Cohen, Jeffrey. 1999. *Cooperation and Community: Economy and Society in Oaxaca.* Austin: University of Texas Press.

———. 2001. "Transnational Migration in Rural Oaxaca: Dependency, Development, and the Household." *American Anthropologist* 103 (4): 954–67.

Cohen, Yuedi. 1954. "A Selected Community in Jamaica." *Social and Economic Studies* 2 (4): 104–33.

Collins, Jane. 1984. "The Maintenance of Peasant Coffee Production in a Peruvian Valley." *American Ethnologist* 11: 413–38.

Collins, Jane, and Martha Giménez, eds. 1990. *Work Without Wages: Domestic Labor and Self-Employment Within Capitalism.* Albany: State University of New York Press.

Comitas, Lambros. 1974. "Occupational Multiplicity in Rural Jamaica." In *Work and Family Life,* ed. Lambros Comitas and D. Lowenthal, 21–43. Garden City, N.Y.: Anchor Books.

Commission on Agricultural Workers (CAW). 1992a. *Report of the Commission on Agricultural Workers.* Washington, D.C.: U.S. Government Printing Office.

———. 1992b. *Appendix I: Case Studies and Research Reports, 1989–1993.* Washington, D.C.: U.S. Government Printing Office.

———. 1992c. *Appendix II: Hearings and Workshops, 1989–1993.* Washington, D.C.: U.S. Government Printing Office.

Country Life Commission. 1909. *Report of the Country Life Commission.* Washington, D.C.: U.S. Government Printing Office.

Daniel, Peter. 1972. *In the Shadow of Slavery: Debt Peonage in the South.* Urbana: University of Illinois Press.

Deere, Carmen Diana. 1983. "The Allocation of Familial Labor and the Formation of Peasant Household Income in the Peruvian Sierra." In *Women and Poverty in the Third World,* ed. M. Buvinic, M. Lycette, and W. McGreevey, 104–29. Baltimore: Johns Hopkins University Press.

Deere, Carmen Diana, and Alain de Janvry. 1979. "A Conceptual Framework for the Empirical Analysis of Peasants." *American Journal of Agricultural Economics* 61: 601–11.

De Janvry, Alain. 1983. *The Agrarian Question and Reformism in Latin American.* Baltimore: Johns Hopkins University Press.

Dickinson, Emily. 1960. *The Complete Poems.* Ed. Thomas H. Johnson. Boston: Little, Brown.

Dinerman, Ina. 1978. "Patterns of Adaptation Among Households of U.S. Bound Migrants from Michoacan, Mexico." *International Migration Review* 12 (4): 485–501.

Duany, Jorge. 2002. *The Puerto Rican Nation on the Move.* Chapel Hill: University of North Carolina Press.

Durrenberger, E. Paul. 1979. "An Analysis of Shan Household Production Decisions." *Journal of Anthropological Research* 35 (4): 447–58.

Edwards, David. 1961. *An Economic Study of Small Farming in Jamaica.* Mona, Jamaica: Institute of Social and Economic Studies.

Ellis, Joseph. 2000. *Founding Brothers.* New York: Knopf.

Faulkner, William. 1932. *Light in August.* New York: Modern Library.

Fink, Leon. 2003. *The Maya of Morgantown.* Chapel Hill: University of North Carolina Press.

Fox, Nichols. 1997. *Spoiled: The Dangerous Truth About a Food Chain Gone Haywire.* New York: Basic Books.

Frank, Andre Gunder. 1966. "The Development of Underdevelopment." *Monthly Review* 18: 17–31.

Furtado, Celso. 1976. *Economic Development of Latin America.* 2d ed. Cambridge: Cambridge University Press.

Galarza, Ernesto. 1956. *Strangers in Our Fields.* Washington, D.C.: Joint U.S.-Mexico Trade Union Committee.

———. 1964. *Merchants of Labor: The Mexican Bracero Story, 1964.* Santa Barbara, Calif.: McNally & Loftin.

Germino, Laura. 2003. "Slavery in U.S. Agriculture." Paper presented at the fifteenth East Coast Migrant Forum, Terrytown, New York, October 15.

Gibson, Jane. 1990. "Shellcracker Haven." *Human Organization* 49 (2): 121–28.

Glick-Schiller, Nina. 1999. "Transmigrants and Nation-States: Something Old and Something New in the U.S. Immigrant Experience." In *The Handbook of International Migration: The American Experience,* ed. Charles Hirschman, Philip Kasinitz, and Josh DeWind, 94–119. New York: Russell Sage Foundation.

Gmelch, George. 1980. "Return Migration." *Annual Review of Anthropology* 9: 135–59.

Goldring, Luin. 1990. "Development and Migration: A Comparative Analysis of Two Mexican Migrant Circuits." Working Paper 37. Washington, D.C.: Commission for the Study of International Migration and Cooperative Development.

Goldschmidt, Arthur, and Harvey Blustain. 1980. *Local Organization and Participation in Integrated Rural Development in Rural Jamaica.* Ithaca: Cornell University Rural Development Committee no. 3.

Gonzalez, Nancy. 1969. *Black Carib Household Structure: A Study of Migration and Modernization.* Seattle: University of Washington Press.

———. 1970. "Toward a Definition of Matrifocality." In *Afro-American Anthropology,* ed. N. Whitten, 231–44. New York: Free Press.

Goździak, Elżbieta, and Susan F. Martin. 2005. *Beyond the Gateway: Immigrants in a Changing America.* Lanam, Md.: Lexington Books.

Grasmuck, Sherri. 1980. "Migration Within the Periphery: Haitian Labor in the Dominican Republic Sugar and Coffee Industries." *International Migration Review* 16 (2): 365–77.

Grasmuck, Sherri, and Patricia Pessar. 1996. *Between Two Islands: Dominican International Migration.* Berkeley and Los Angeles: University of California Press.

Grey, Mark. 1999. "Immigrants, Migration, and Worker Turnover at the Hog Pride Pork Packing Plant." *Human Organization* 58: 16–27.

Grey, Mark, and Anne Woodrick. 2002. "Unofficial Sister Cities: Meatpacking Labor Migration Between Villachuato, Mexico, and Marshalltown, Iowa." *Human Organization* 61 (4): 364–76.

Griffith, David. 1983a. "International Labor Migration and Rural Development: Patterns of Expenditure Among Jamaicans Working Seasonally in the United States." *Stanford Journal of International Law* 19 (2): 357–70.

———. 1983b. "The Promise of a Country: The Impact of Seasonal U.S. Migration on the Jamaican Peasantry." Ph.D. diss., University of Florida, Department of Anthropology.

———. 1985. "Women, Remittances, and Reproduction." *American Ethnologist* 12 (4): 676–90.

———. 1986a. "Peasants in Reserve: Temporary West Indian Labor in the U.S. Labor Market." *International Migration Review* 20 (4): 875–98.

———. 1986b. "Social Organizational Obstacles to Capital Accumulation Among Returning Migrants: The British West Indies Temporary Alien Labor Program." *Human Organization* 45 (1): 34–42.

———. 1987. "Nonmarket Labor Processes in an Advanced Capitalist Economy." *American Anthropologist* 89 (4): 838–52.

———. 1993. *Jones's Minimal: Low-Wage Labor in the United States.* Albany: State University of New York Press.

———. 1995. "Names of Death." *American Anthropologist* 97 (3): 453–56.

———. 1999. *The Estuary's Gift: An Atlantic Coast Cultural Biography.* University Park: Pennsylvania State University Press.

———. 2000. "Social Capital and Economic Apartheid Along the Coasts of the Americas." *Urban Anthropology* 29 (3): 255–84.

———. 2003. *The Canadian and U.S. Migrant Agricultural Worker Programs.* Ottawa: North-South Institute.

———. 2004. "People, Poultry, Pickles, Pork: Immigration into Southeast North Carolina." Report prepared for Aguirre International, Burlingame, California.

Griffith, David, Monica L. Heppel, and Luis Torres. 1994. *Labor Certification and Employment Practices in Selected Low Wage/Low Skill Occupations.* Report to the West Virginia Employment Service. Washington D.C.: Inter-American Institute on Migration and Labor.

———. 2001. *Guests of Rural America: Profiles of Temporary Worker Programs from U.S. and Mexican Perspectives.* Report to the Ford Foundation. Washington, D.C.: Inter-American Institute on Migration and Labor.

Griffith, David, Ed Kissam, Jeronimo Camposeco, Anna Garcia, Max Pfeffer, David Runsten, and Manuel Valdés Pizzini. 1995. *Working Poor: Farmworkers in the United States.* Philadelphia: Temple University Press.

Griffith, David, and Manuel Valdés Pizzini. 2002. *Fishers at Work, Workers at Sea: A Puerto Rican Journey Through Labor and Refuge.* Philadelphia: Temple University Press.

Griffith, David, Manuel Valdés Pizzini, and Jeffrey C. Johnson. 1992. "Injury, Therapy, and Trajectories of Proletarianization in Puerto Rico's Artisanal Fisheries." *American Ethnologist* 19 (1): 53–74.

Gringeri, Christina. 1995. *Getting By: Women Homeworkers and Rural Economic Development.* Lawrence: University Press of Kansas.

Hahamovich, Cindy. 1997. *The Fruits of Their Labor: Atlantic Coast Farmworkers and the Making of Migrant Poverty, 1870–1945.* Chapel Hill: University of North Carolina Press.

———. 2000. "Creating Perfect Immigrants." Paper presented at the Labor History Conference, Wayne State University, Detroit, Michigan, October 17.

———. 2001. "'In America Life Is Given Away': Jamaican Farmworkers and the Making of Agricultural Immigration Policy." In *The Countryside in the Age of the Modern State*, ed. C. McNicol Stock and R. Johnston, 134–60. Ithaca: Cornell University Press.

Hammond, Dorothy, and Alta Jablow. 1976. *Women in Cultures of the World.* Menlo Park, Calif.: Cummings.

Heppel, Monica L. 1983. *Harvesting the Crops of Others: Migrant Farm Labor on the Eastern Shore of Virginia.* Vols. 1–2. Ph.D. diss., American University, Department of Anthropology.

———. 2000. "Field Report on Conditions of Children in Agriculture." Washington, D.C.: U.S. Department of Labor.

Heppel, Monica L., and Sandra Amendola. 1992. *Immigration Reform and Perishable Crop Agriculture: Compliance or Circumvention?* Lanham, Md.: University Press of America.

Heppel, Monica L., Luis R. Torres, and Joanne Spano. 1993. "The 1992 Apple Harvest in West Virginia." Report prepared for the West Virginia Department of Employment Services. Washington, D.C.: Inter-American Institute on Migration and Labor.

Heyman, Josiah McC. 1998. *Finding a Moral Heart for U.S. Immigration Policy: An Anthropological Perspective.* American Ethnological Society Monograph Series 7. Arlington, Va.: American Anthropological Association.

———. 1999. "United States Surveillance over Mexican Lives at the Border: Snapshots of an Emerging Regime." *Human Organization* 58 (4): 430–38.

Hill, Donald. 1976. "The Impact of Migration on the Metropolitan and Folk Society of Carriacou, Grenada." Anthropological Papers of the American Museum of Natural History, vol. 54, part 2, 191–391. New York: American Museum of Natural History.

Ho, Christine. 1995. "Child Sharing in the Caribbean." *Human Organization* 54 (1): 32–45.

Human Rights Watch. 2003. *Unfair Advantage: Workers' Freedom of Association in the United States Under International Human Rights Standards.* New York: Human Rights Watch.

Hunter, Guy. 1969. *Modernizing Peasant Societies.* New York: Oxford University Press.

Immigration and Naturalization Service (INS). 1921, 1923. Annual Reports of the Commissioner General of Immigration. Washington, D.C.: U.S. Government Printing Office.

Jamaican Department of Statistics. 1982a. "The Labour Force." Kingston: Jamaican Department of Statistics.

———. 1982b. "Statistical Abstract." Kingston: Jamaican Department of Statistics.

Jamaican Ministry of Agriculture. 1979. Annual Report, Ministry of Agriculture, 1977 to 1978. Kingston: Agricultural Information Service.

Katzin, Margaret. 1971. "The Business of Higglering in Jamaica." In *Peoples and Cultures of the Caribbean,* ed. M. Horowitz, 340–81. Garden City, N.Y.: Museum of Natural History Press.

King, Russell, and Alan Strachen. 1980. "Effects of Return Migration on a Gozitan Village." *Human Organization* 39 (2): 175–79.

Kissam, Ed, David Griffith, Anna Garcia, and Nancy Mullenax. 2001. *Children No More: Conditions of Underaged Agricultural Workers in the United States.* Final Report to the Department of Labor. Washington, D.C.: U.S. Department of Labor.

Kolata, Gina. 1999. *Flu: The Story of the Great Influenza Pandemic of 1918 and the Search for the Virus That Caused It.* New York: Farrar, Straus and Giroux.

Kovacik, Paul, and William Winberry. 1987. *South Carolina: A Cultural Geography.* Columbia: University of South Carolina Press.

Krissman, Fred. 1999. "Cycles of Poverty in Rural California: The San Joaquin Valley Towns of McFarland and Farmersville." In *The Dynamics of Hired Farm Labour: Constraints and Community Responses,* ed. J. L. Findeis, A. M. Vandeman, J. M. Larson, and J. L. Runyan, 15–24. Oxford: CABI Publishing.

Kruijer, G. J. 1967. "A Sociological Report on the Christiana Area." Kingston: Jamaican Information Service.

Kurlansky, Mark. 1997. *Cod: The History of a Fish That Changed the World.* New York: Penguin.

Lamphere, Louise, Alex Stepick, and Guillermo Grenier. 1994. *Newcomers in the Workplace: Immigrants and the Restructuring of the U.S. Economy.* Philadelphia: Temple University Press.

Leal, Magdalena de Leon, and Carmen Diana Deere. 1979. "Rural Women and the Development of Capitalism in Colombian Agriculture." *Signs* 5: 60–77.

Lehman, Nicholas. 1985. *The Promised Land: African-American Migration to the North.* New York: Random House.

Levitt, Peggy. 1998. "Social Remittances: Migration-Driven, Local-Level forms of Cultural Diffusion." *International Migration Review* 32 (4): 926–48.

———. 2001. *The Transnational Villagers.* Berkeley and Los Angeles: University of California Press.

Long, Norman. 1977. *An Introduction to the Sociology of Rural Development.* London: Tavistock.

Long, Norman, and Paul Richardson. 1978. "Informal Sector, Petty Commodity Production, and the Social Relations of Small-Scale Enterprise." In *The New Economic Anthropology,* ed. J. Clammer, 34–52. New York: St. Martin's Press.

Lowenthal, David. 1972. *West Indian Societies.* London: Oxford University Press.

Magnarella, Paul. 1979. *The Peasant Venture.* Cambridge, Mass.: Schenkman Publishing.

Mahler, Sarah. 1995. *American Dreaming: Immigrant Life on the Margins.* Princeton: Princeton University Press.

Mahler, Sarah, and Patricia Pessar. 2001. "Gendered Geographies of Power: Analyzing Gender Across Transnational Spaces." *Identities: Global Studies in Culture and Power* 7 (4): 441–59.

Maril, Robert Lee. 2005. *Patrolling Chaos: The U.S. Border Patrol in Deep South Texas.* Lubbock: Texas Tech University Press.

Massey, Douglas, Rafael Alarcón, Jorge Durand, and Humberto González. 1987. *Return to Aztlán: The Social Process of International Migration from Western Mexico.* Berkeley and Los Angeles: University of California Press.

Mathews, Holly. 1985. "We Are Mayordomo." *American Ethnologist* 12: 285–301.

McCoy, Terry, and Charles Wood. 1982. "Caribbean Workers in the Florida Sugar Cane Industry." Occasional Paper No. 2 of the Caribbean Migration Program. Gainesville: University of Florida, Center for Latin American Studies.

Meillassoux, Claude. 1972. "From Reproduction to Production: A Marxist Approach to Economic Anthropology." *Economy and Society* 1: 93–105.

Menjívar, Cecilia. 2000. *Fragmented Ties: Salvadoran Immigrant Networks in America.* Berkeley and Los Angeles: University of California Press.

Mintz, Sidney. 1961. "Pratik: Personal Haitian Economic Relationships." *Proceedings of the Annual Spring Meeting of the American Ethnological Society.* Seattle: University of Washington Press.

———. 1971. "Men, Women, and Trade." *Comparative Studies in Society and History* 13: 247–69.

———. 1974. *Caribbean Transformation.* Chicago: Aldine.

———. 1985. *Sweetness and Power: The Place of Sugar in Modern History.* New York: Penguin.

Moser, Katy. 1994. "Crab Picking in North Carolina." Master's thesis, University of North Carolina, Chapel Hill, Department of Communications.

Mueller, Martha. 1977. "Women and Men, Power and Powerlessness in Lesotho." *Signs* 3: 154–66.

Nash, June, and Helen Safa, eds. 1980. *Sex and Class in Latin America: Women's Perspectives on Politics, Economics, and the Family in the Third World.* New York: J. F. Bergin.

National Agricultural Workers Survey (NAWS). 2000. *Findings from the National Agricultural Workers Survey (NAWS) 2000.* Washington, D.C.: U.S. Department of Labor.

National Public Radio. 1990. *Morning Edition.* December 24.

Nestle, Marion. 2002. *Food Politics: How the Food Industry Influences Nutrition and Health.* Berkeley and Los Angeles: University of California Press.

Ngai, Mae. 2004. *Impossible Subjects: Illegal Aliens and the Making of Modern America.* Princeton: Princeton University Press.

North Carolina Division of Marine Fisheries. 1995. "Blue Crab Landings, Processed Product, and Employment." Morehead City, N.C.: Division of Marine Fisheries.

Ong, Aiwa. 1989. *Spirits of Resistance and Capitalist Discipline: Women and Factory Production in Malaysia.* Berkeley and Los Angeles: University of California Press.

Organization for Economic Cooperation and Development (OECD). 1978. *Migration, Growth, and Development.* Paris: OECD Publications.

Ortiz, Sutti. 1999. *Harvesting Coffee, Bargaining Wages.* Ann Arbor: University of Michigan Press.

Osterman, Peter. 1988. *Employment Futures: Reorganization, Dislocation, and Public Policy.* Oxford: Oxford University Press.

Painter, Michael. 1984. "Changing Relations of Production and Rural Underdevelopment." *Journal of Anthropological Research* 40: 271–92.

Papademetriou, Demitrios G., Robert Bach, Kyle Johnson, Roger Kramer, Briant Lindsay Lowell, and Shirley Smith. 1988. *The Effects of Immigration on the U.S. Economy and Labor Market.* Washington, D.C.: U.S. Department of Labor, Bureau of International Labor Affairs.

Papademetriou, Demetrios G., and Monica L. Heppel. 1999. *Balancing Acts: Toward a Fair Bargain on Seasonal Agricultural Workers.* Washington, D.C.: Carnegie Endowment for International Peace.

Pearse, Andrew. 1975. *The Latin American Peasant.* London: Frank Cass.

Peck, Gunther. 1996. "Reinventing Free Labor: Immigrant Padrones and Contract Laborers in North America, 1885–1925." *Journal of American History* (December): 848–71.

Pelto, Pertti, and Gretel Pelto. 1978. *Anthropological Research: The Structure of Inquiry.* 2d ed. New York: Cambridge University Press.

Pessar, Patricia. 1980. "The Role of Households in International Migration and the Case of the U.S. Bound Migration from the Dominican Republic." *International Migration Review* 16 (2): 342–64.

———. 1999. "The Role of Gender, Households, and Social Networks in the Migration Process: A Review and Appraisal." In *The Handbook of International Migration: The American Experience,* ed. Charles Hirschman, Philip Kasinitz, and Josh DeWind, 53–70. New York: Russell Sage Foundation.

———. 2004. "Anthropology and the Engendering of Migration Studies." In *American Arrivals: Anthropology Engages the New Immigration,* ed. N. Foner, 75–98. Santa Fe: School of American Research Press.

Pixley, Richard. 1986. "Fired Farm Workers Return." *Daily Gleaner* (Kingston, Jamaica). November 24, 1A.

Portes, Alejandro, and Robert Bach. 1985. *Latin Journey.* Berkeley and Los Angeles: University of California Press.

Portes, Alejandro, and John Walton. 1979. *Labor, Class, and the International System.* New York: Academic Press.

Preibisch, Kerry. 2003. *Social Relations Practices Between Seasonal Agricultural Workers, Their Employers, and the Residents of Rural Ontario.* Report to the North-South Institute. Ottawa: University of Guelph.

Rasmussen, Wayne. 1951. *A History of the Emergency Farm Labor Supply Program: 1943–47.* Agricultural Monograph No. 13, September 1951. Washington, D.C.: USDA, Bureau of Agricultural Economics.

Reichert, Joshua. 1981. "The Migrant Syndrome: Seasonal U.S. Wage Labor and Rural Development in Central Mexico." *Human Organization* 40 (1): 56–66.

Reubens, Edwin. 1979. "Temporary Admission of Foreign Workers: Dimensions and Policies." Special Report No. 34 of the National Commission for Manpower Policy. Washington, D.C.: National Commission for Manpower Policy.

Rhodes, Robert. 1978. "Intra-European Return Migration and Rural Development: Lessons from the Spanish Case." *Human Organization* 37 (2): 95–106.

Richman, Karen. 1992. "*Lavalas* at Home/A *Lavalas* for Home: Inflections of Transnationalism in the Discourse of Haitian President Aristide." In *Towards a Transnational Perspective on Migration: Race, Class, Ethnicity, and Nation Reconsidered,* ed. Nina Glick-Schiller, Linda Basch, and Cristina Blanc-Szanton, 189–200. New York: New York Academy of Sciences.

———. 2005. *Migration and Vodou.* Gainesville: University Press of Florida.

Roberts, George, and Sonja Sinclair. 1978. *Women in Jamaica: Patterns of Reproduction and Family.* Millwood, N.Y.: KTO Press.

Rogers, Everett. 1971. *Modernizing Among Peasants.* New York: Holt, Rinehart and Winston.

Rogers, Jackie Krasas. 2000. *Temps: The Many Faces of the Changing Workplace.* Ithaca: Cornell University Press.

Rosaldo, Michelle Zimbalist. 1975. "Women, Culture, and Society: A Theoretical Overview." In *Women, Culture, and Society,* ed. M. Z. Rosaldo and Louise Lamphere, 17–42. Stanford: Stanford University Press.

Roseberry, William. 1976. "Rent, Differentiation, and the Development of Capitalism Among Peasants." *American Anthropologist* 78: 45–58.

———. 1983. "From Peasant Studies to Proletarian Studies." *Studies in Comparative Economic Development* 18: 69–89.

———. 1995. "The Rise of Yuppie Coffees and the Reimagination of Class in the United States." *American Anthropologist* 98 (4): 762–75.

Rouse, Roger. 1992. "Making Sense of Settlement." In *Towards a Transnational Perspective on Migration: Race, Class, Ethnicity, and Nation Reconsidered,* ed. Nina Glick-Schiller, Linda Basch, and Cristina Blanc-Szanton, 25–52. New York: New York Academy of Sciences.

Rubenstein, Hymie. 1983. "Remittances and Rural Underdevelopment in the English-Speaking Caribbean." *Human Organization* 42 (3): 295–306.

Russell, Roy. 2003. *Report to the North-South Institute on the Experience of Jamaicans in the Canadian Migrant Agricultural Workers Program.* Ottawa: North-South Institute.

Schell, Gregory. 1987. Letter from Gregory Schell, Florida Legal Aid Bureau, to H-2 Workers, June 2, 1987. On file at Belle Glade office of Florida Rural Legal Services.

Schlosser, Eric. 2002. *Fast Food Nation: The Dark Side of the All-American Meal.* New York: Farrar, Straus and Giroux.

Scott, James. 1979. *The Moral Economy of the Peasant.* New Haven: Yale University Press.

Scruggs, Otey M. 1960. "Evolution of the Mexican Farm Labor Agreement of 1942." *Agricultural History* 34 (3): 24–37.

Sibisi, Harriet. 1977. "How African Women Cope with Migrant Labor in South Africa." *Signs* 3: 167–77.

Sider, Gerald. 1987. *Culture and Class in Anthropology and History: A Newfoundland Illustration.* Cambridge: Cambridge University Press.

Siegel, Frederick F. 1987. *The Roots of Southern Distinctiveness: Tobacco and Society in Danville, Virginia, 1780–1865.* Charlottesville: University Press of Virginia.

Skaggs, Jimmy. 1985. *Prime Cut: Livestock Raising and Meatpacking in the United States.* College Station: Texas A&M University Press.

Smart, Alan, and Josephine Smart. 2005. "Introduction." In *Petty Capitalists and Globalization: Flexibility, Entrepreneurship, and Economic Development,* ed. Alan Smart and Josephine Smart, 1–22. Albany: State University of New York Press.

Smart, Josephine. 1997. "Borrowed Men on Borrowed Time: Globalization, Labour Migration, and Local Economies in Alberta." *Canadian Journal of Regional Science* 20 (1–2): 141–56.

Smith, Lee. 1999. *News of the Spirit.* New York: Ballantine Publishing.

Solien, Nancy Gonzalez. 1970. "Household and Family in the Caribbean." In *Peoples and Cultures of the Caribbean,* ed. M. Horowitz, 133–42. Garden City, N.Y.: Natural History Press.

Spengler, J. J., and G. Myers. 1977. "Migration and Socioeconomic Development: Today and Yesterday." In *Internal Migration: A Comparative Perspective,* ed. A. Brown and E. Neuberger, 11–35. New York: Academic Press

Stein, Stanley, and Barbara Stein. 1970. *The Colonial Heritage of Latin America.* New York: Oxford University Press.

Striffler, Steve. 2002. *In the Shadow of State and Capital: The United Fruit Company, Popular Struggle, and Agrarian Restructuring in Ecuador, 1900–1995.* Durham: Duke University Press.

Stull, Donald, and Michael Broadway. 2003. *Slaughterhouse Blues.* New York: Holt, Rinehart, and Wilson.

Stull, Donald, Michael Broadway, and David Griffith, eds. 1995. *Any Way They Cut It: Meat Packing and Small-Town America.* Lawrence: University Press of Kansas.

Siskind, Janet. 2002. *Rum and Axes: The Rise of a Connecticut Merchant Family, 1795–1850.* Ithaca: Cornell University Press.

Sutton, Constance. 1992. "Some Thoughts on Gendering and Internationalizing Our Thinking About Transnational Migrations." In *Towards a Transnational Perspective on Migration: Race, Class, Ethnicity, and Nation Reconsidered,* ed. Nina Glick-Schiller, Linda Basch, and Cristina Blanc-Szanton, 241–50. New York: New York Academy of Sciences.

Taylor, Allen. 2003. *American Colonies.* New York: Penguin Books.

Taylor, Mark. 1992. "Seiners and Tongers: North Carolina Fisheries in the Old and New South." *North Carolina Historical Review* 69 (1): 1–36.

Thiessen, Ilka. 2002. "'*Leb I Sol*' (Bread and Salt): The Changing Meanings of Work in the Changing Macedonia. *Anthropology of Work Review* 23 (1–2): 8–13.

Thu, Kendall, and E. Paul Durrenberger. 1998. *Pigs, Profits, and Rural Communities.* Albany: State University of New York Press.

U.S. Bureau of Labor Statistics. 2000. *Labor Statistics of the United States.* Washington, D.C.: U.S. Government Printing Office.

U.S. Congress. 1921. Senate. Committee on Immigration. *Hearings on Emergency Immigration Legislation, Part I.* 66th Cong., 3d sess.

———. 1978. Senate. Subcommittee on Immigration. *The British West Indies Temporary Alien Labor Program: 1943–1977.* 95th Cong., 2d sess. Washington, D.C.: U.S. Government Printing Office.

———. 1981. Senate. Judiciary Subcommittee. *A Summary of Hearings Held by the Senate Judiciary Subcommittee on Immigration and Refugee Policy, July–April, 1981.* 97th Cong., 2d sess. Washington, D.C.: U.S. Government Printing Office.

———. 1991. House. Committee on Education of Labor. *Report on the Use of Temporary Foreign Workers in the Florida Sugar Cane Industry.* 102d Cong., 1st sess., July. Serial no. 102-J. Washington, D.C.: U.S. Government Printing Office.

U.S. Department of Labor. 1993. "H-2 Workers by Industry and State." Washington, D.C.: U.S. Department of Labor.

Vandeman, Ann. 1988. *Labor Contracting in California.* Ph.D. diss., University of California at Davis, Department of Agricultural Economics.

Veblen, Thorstein. 1899. *The Theory of the Leisure Class.* New York: Macmillan.

Verduzco, Gustavo, and Maria Isabel Lozano. 2003. "A Study of the Program for Temporary Canadian Workers in Agriculture." Report to the North-South Institute, Ottawa, Canada.

Verma, Veena. 2003. "The Mexican and Caribbean Seasonal Agricultural Workers Program Institutional Framework: Labour Policies, Regulations, Farm Industry Level Employment Practices, and the Future of the Program Under Unionization." Report to the North-South Institute, Ottawa, Canada.

Vickers, David. 1994. *Farmers and Fishermen.* Chapel Hill: University of North Carolina Press.

Wagley, Charles. 1957. "Plantation America: A Culture Sphere." In *Caribbean Studies: A Symposium,* ed. V. Rubin, 3–13. Seattle: University of Washington Press.

Waldinger, Robert. 1986. *Through the Eye of the Needle: Immigrants and Enterprise in New York's Garment Trades.* New York: New York University Press.

Wallerstein, Immanuel. 1970. *The Modern World System.* New York: Academic Press.

Weston, Ann. 2000. "Concerns About Living and Working Conditions for Migrant Farmworkers in Canada." Paper presented at the Trilateral Conference on Agricultural Migrant Labour in North America, Los Angeles, California, November 3.

Wilkinson, Alec. 1989. *Big Sugar: Seasons in the Cane Fields of Florida.* New York: Knopf.

Willis, Paul. 1977. *Learning to Labour.* Hampshire, England: Gower Publishing.

Wolf, Eric. 1966. *Peasants.* Englewood Cliffs, N.J.: Prentice-Hall.

———. 1982. *Europe and the People Without History.* Berkeley and Los Angeles: University of California Press.

———. 1999. *Envisioning Power: Ideologies of Dominance and Crisis.* Berkeley and Los Angeles: University of California Press.

Wolf, Eric, and Edward Hansen. 1970. *The Human Condition in Latin America.* New York: Oxford University Press.

Wood, Charles 1981. "Structural Changes and Household Strategies: A Conceptual Framework for the Study of Rural Migration." *Human Organization* 40 (4): 338–43.

———. 1982. "Equilibrium and Historical-Structural Perspectives on Migration." *International Migration Review* 16 (2): 289–319.

Wood, Terry, and Charles McCoy. 1985. *Bittersweet Harvest.* Manuscript.

Zlolniski, Christian. 1994. "The Informal Economy in an Advanced Industrialized Society: Mexican Immigrant Labor in Silicon Valley." *Yale Law Journal* 103 (8): 2305–35.

———. 2005. *Janitors, Street Vendors, and Activists: The Lives of Mexican Immigrants in Silicon Valley.* Berkeley and Los Angeles: University of California Press.

Zuñiga, Victor, and Rubén Hernández-León, eds. 2005. *New Destinations: Mexican Immigration in the United States.* New York: Russell Sage Foundation.

INDEX